Ted Hughes in Persia, 1971

THE ART OF
TED HUGHES

KEITH SAGAR

Senior Staff Tutor in Literature
Extra-Mural Department, University of Manchester

CAMBRIDGE UNIVERSITY PRESS

CAMBRIDGE

LONDON · NEW YORK · MELBOURNE

Published by the Syndics of the Cambridge University Press
The Pitt Building, Trumpington Street, Cambridge CB2 1RP
Bentley House, 200 Euston Road, London NW1 2DB
32 East 57th Street, New York, NY 10022, USA
296 Beaconsfield Parade, Middle Park, Melbourne 3206, Australia

Library of Congress Catalogue Card Number: 74–31787

ISBN: 0 521 20714 2

First published 1975

Printed in Great Britain
by W & J Mackay Limited, Chatham

The author and publisher are grateful to the following for permission
to use copyright material: Faber and Faber Ltd for extensive quotation
from the works of Ted Hughes published by them – *The Hawk in the
Rain*, © Ted Hughes 1957, *Lupercal*, © Ted Hughes 1960, *Wodwo*, ©
Ted Hughes 1967, *Crow*, © Ted Hughes 1970, *Selected Poems*, © Ted
Hughes 1972; Victor Gollancz Ltd and Curtis Brown Ltd for the
Kingsley Amis poem 'Against Romanticism' from *A Case of Samples*;
Harper and Row Inc. for extensive quotation from the works of Ted
Hughes published by them – *The Hawk in the Rain*, © Ted Hughes
1956, 1957, *Lupercal*, © Ted Hughes 1960, *Wodwo*, © Ted Hughes
1959, 1960, 1961, 1962, 1963, 1964, 1965, 1966, 1967, *Crow*, © Ted
Hughes 1971, *Selected Poems*, © Ted Hughes 1972; William Heinemann
Ltd, Laurence Pollinger Ltd, the Estate of the late Mrs Frieda
Lawrence and the Viking Press for the D. H. Lawrence poem 'A
Living'; Olwyn Hughes for extensive quotation of the Ted Hughes
poems published by the Rainbow Press, 100 Chetwynd Road, London
NW5 – *Poems: Fainlight, Hughes, Sillitoe*, © Ted Hughes 1971, *Eat
Crow*, © Ted Hughes 1971, *Prometheus on His Crag*, © Ted Hughes
1973, and for those published by other private presses, and those not
yet collected in book form.

CONTENTS

ACKNOWLEDGEMENTS

I welcome this opportunity to acknowledge my debt to the following: Walter Stein, Mrs A. Schofield and Michael Black for detailed constructive criticism of the work in progress; Philip Hobsbaum for allowing me to draw on his vast knowledge of Cambridge poetry in the 1950s; Gerald Lacy for helping with much of the spadework on the bibliography, particularly the American side; Pat Hughes for help with the proofs and the indexes; and all the students with whom I have studied the work of Ted Hughes.

Manchester   K.M.S.
January 1975

INTRODUCTION

I began reading Ted Hughes in 1957 when my attention was drawn to *The Hawk in the Rain* by a couple of enthusiastic reviews I happened to see. My admiration grew with each succeeding book. After *Lupercal* I began to teach Hughes; after *Wodwo* to write about him; and after *Crow* to think of him as a major poet of the first rank, a worthy successor to the great English poets of the first half of the century, Yeats, Lawrence and Eliot. To have followed his development step by step over seventeen years has been one of the richest experiences literature has yet given me. Every step seems bigger than the last, and Hughes may yet have far to go.

Ted Hughes is no longer a promising young writer. He has published over 400 poems (several times more than Eliot's entire output). He is at the age at which Lawrence's career ended.

Ever since the appearance of *The Hawk in the Rain*, large claims have been made for Ted Hughes. Yet there is still no consensus about his importance, because there is no consensus about the nature, meaning and relative value of his poems. Since this is the first book on him, it must focus primarily on individual poems, all the important or representative ones, trying to take possession of them (or be possessed by them), asking what they are, what they mean, how they relate to each other, to the tradition, to the work of other contemporary and recent writers, to the experience of living in our time or in any time.

F. R. Leavis says of the business of the critic: 'He endeavours to see the poetry of the present as continuation and development; that is, as the decisive, the most significant, contemporary life of tradition' (*Revaluation*, 1–2). Hughes has a vital relationship with tradition. He draws heavily upon it; but he transforms what he draws. And he enters into a dialogue with it, both consciously and unconsciously. It is surely very significant that the set of names one finds oneself continually invoking in response to Hughes' earlier work – Hopkins, Yeats, Lawrence, Wilfred Owen, Dylan Thomas – should be gradually replaced, in reading his later work, by a quite different set – Blake, Kafka, Eliot, Beckett and Vasko Popa. In his latest work there seems to be a further move towards much older influences – folklore, mythology and religion, the Greeks, Shake-speare, Milton – or, it may well be, towards a territory wholly his own which happens to overlap the territory of all great writers who were preoccupied with the problem of man's relation to the powers of the non-human universe. In his very best recent work he seems to move even further back, to the roots and sources of the myths and legends in the depths of the human psyche.

The objectives I have set myself in this book and the standards by which I should like to be judged are finely set out by Eugene Ionesco in 'A Writer's Problems':

A criticism or an interpretation is good in so far as the interpreter approaches the work freshly, sincerely and objectively, in so far as he is prepared not necessarily to abandon his criteria, but to call them perpetually into question ...The critic who describes the work, to be precise, someone who follows the work following it step by step, throws light on it; this is, in fact, the only way to do so. This is the way to tell whether it is possible to move through the universe of the work; we see where it leads, whether it leads anywhere, whether it contains culs-de-sac or blind alleys, and whether it has a coherence transcending its incoherences and contradictions. To write, also, is to think while in motion; to write is to explore. The critic must repeat the itinerary of the poet. Often the poet has moved forward in a kind of darkness or twilight. The critic covers the same ground with a lamp in his hand and illuminates the path. (*Encounter*, September 1964)

There will be many contradictions or inconsistencies in my interpretations. Partly this will be due to the inadequacy of my own insight, but partly it will be due to the fact that Hughes is not very interested in consistency. He is not attempting to formulate a philosophy or any fixed attitudes towards life. In a British Council interview in 1963, Peter Orr asked Hughes: 'Is there a consistent "you" that emerges in all your poems – you as a poet, as Ted Hughes, with a certain attitude to life?' Hughes replied:

Not really, no. I tend to suspect that my poems are written by about three separate spirits or three separate characteristic states of mind, which are fairly different. They are obviously all written by the same person, but if they went under different names it's possible they'd deceive most people as being written by different people.

The poems are explorations, 'reconnaissances', bulletins from an internal internecine battleground.

All great writers are mapping unknown lands, that is, bringing more and more of the unknown into consciousness. These maps

2

are then available for later writers. But the great writer will eventually reach a point where the old maps will take him no further. He is on his own. The old maps may even become an encumbrance or begin to divert him from his true path – the path which leads to the centre. They must be jettisoned, with everything else.

His most difficult task is to remove the obstacles, the clichés of thought, feeling and expression to bring himself into a state of full awareness, openness, excitement, concentration. The rest is a gift, but a gift not so uncommon as the emphasis of our education and culture on language as rational discourse has led us to believe.

The gift is partly metaphor:

Metaphor, for the authentic poet, is not a figure of rhetoric but a representative image standing concretely before him in lieu of a concept . . . All one needs in order to be a poet is the ability to have a lively action going on before one continually, to live surrounded by a host of spirits (Nietzsche, *The Birth of Tragedy*).

I believe Hughes to be a great poet because he possesses the kind of imagination which issues in the purest poetry, charged poetry, visionary, revelatory poetry that sees into the life of things, that takes over where all other modes of apprehending reality falter. Words, though controlled up to a point, are allowed to retain a life of their own and express more than the poet consciously knows. His imagination, which draws on his unconscious, on the racial unconscious, on his sixth sense and perhaps innumerable further senses, speaks through him. He is, in a word, 'inspired', though the word is not now fashionable. He performs a function essential to the race, a function analogous to that performed in more 'primitive' cultures by the shaman, whose function is to make the dangerous journey, on behalf of his society, into the spirit world, which is to say, into his own unconscious:

In preparing his trance, the shaman drums, summons his spirit helpers, speaks a 'secret language' or the 'animal language', imitating the cries of beasts and especially the songs of birds. He ends by obtaining a 'second state' that provides the impetus for linguistic creation and the rhythms of lyric poetry. Poetic creation still remains an act of perfect spiritual freedom. Poetry remakes and prolongs language; every poetic language begins by being a secret language, that is, the creation of a personal universe, of a completely closed world. The purest poetic act seems to re-create language from an inner experience that, like the ecstasy or the religious inspiration of 'primitives', reveals the essence of things. It is from such linguistic creations,

3

made possible by pre-ecstatic 'inspiration', that the 'secret languages' of the mystics and the traditional allegorical languages crystallize. (M. Eliade, *Shamanism*, 510–11)

The 'secret language' is partly metaphor; it is also 'the animal language' in the sense that words can communicate as sheer sound beneath their meanings. They can, as Lawrence put it, 'sound upon the plasm direct'. It is the language of another being within us buried much deeper than the repressed self psycho-analysis seeks to let speak:

And in fact this other rarely speaks or stirs at all, in the sort of lives we now lead. We have so totally lost touch, that we hardly realise he is absent. All we know is that somehow or other the great, precious thing is missing. And the real distress of our world begins there. The luminous spirit (maybe he is a crowd of spirits), that takes account of everything and gives everything its meaning, is missing. Not missing, just incommunicado. But here and there, it may be, we hear it.

It is human, of course, but it is also everything else that lives. When we hear it, we understand what a strange thing is living in this Universe, and somewhere at the core of us – strange, beautiful, pathetic, terrible. Some animals and birds express this being pure and without effort, and then you hear the whole desolate, final actuality of existence in a voice, a tone. There we really do recognise a spirit, a truth under all the truths. Far beyond human words. And the startling quality of this 'truth' is that it is terrible. It is for some reason harrowing, as well as being this utterly beautiful thing. Once when his spirits were dictating poetic material to Yeats, an owl cried outside the house, and the spirits paused. After a while one said: 'We like that sort of sound.' And that is it: 'that sort of sound' makes the spirits listen. It opens our deepest and innermost ghost to sudden attention. It is a spirit, and it speaks to spirit. ('Orghast: Talking Without Words', *Vogue*, December 1971)

From the beginning Hughes is searching for a way of reconciling human vision with the energies, powers, presences, of the non-human cosmos. At first his main concern is to identify these energies and describe them, not only in human terms but in their own, that is in Nature's terms. And the discrepancy between these two descriptions gives the most powerful of his early poems, for example the hawk and jaguar poems, their characteristic tension. Hughes is also concerned to discover whether negotiations are possible between man and Nature, that is between man and his Creator, and, if so, why they have so completely collapsed in our time and what the consequences of this collapse have been and may yet be. The destructiveness of Nature is so clearly seen and deeply felt that it seems in many of the poems in *Wodwo* and

Crow that negotiation is impossible, but in some there are hopes and intimations and in most a determination to go on trying. After the descent into destruction he goes forward a step, and a step, and a step. And, slowly, something begins to come clear. The faces of things are transformed and inner meanings revealed. The imagination begins to yield its secrets, and with this renewed vision, neither negotiation nor, indeed, reconciliation seems quite beyond the scope of man.

I am advancing no dogmas about what poetry should be. But it is surely necessary to have in every generation at least one poet who is at the limit, concentrating extraordinary intellectual psychic and linguistic resources on the effort to get clear of all contingencies and explore that territory which only the poetic imagination, in one form or another, can reach. And those who are exclusively concerned with the contingencies and with the civilized human world, and who deny the need for the larger awareness won by the visionaries, have no foundation more substantial than a heap of begged questions.

Man is always, all the time and for ever, on the brink of the unknown. The minute you realize this, you prick your ears in alarm. And the minute any man steps alone, with his whole naked self, emotional and mental, into the everlasting hinterland of consciousness, you hate him and you wonder over him. Why can't he stay cosily playing word games around the camp fire.

(D. H. Lawrence)

BEGINNINGS

Edward James Hughes was born on 17 August 1930, in Mytholm-royd, deep in a sodden valley of the Yorkshire Pennines, near the Brontë country.

From the beginning, as he recalls in 'Poetry in the Making', he was fascinated by animals, first collecting toy lead animals until they went right round the fender, then drawing them and modelling them in plasticine, then acting as retriever when his older brother (who was later for a short time a gamekeeper) went shooting magpies, owls, rabbits, weasels, rats and curlews; and finally, and best, capturing them by writing poems about them.

Ted was the youngest of three children. His father, William Hughes, a carpenter, was one of the seventeen men from his entire regiment who returned from the Dardanelles. The boy's imagination was filled with images of Flanders in the First World War (vividly recalled in 'Out') which closely matched those implanted there by his own experience of the bone-strewn moors and the farms which fringed them.

The valley seemed always dark, under the shadow of a huge, almost vertical, looming cliff to the north, a mere corridor between the cotton towns of south Lancashire and the woollen towns of the West Riding, a shadow trap imposing on the growing boy the need to escape, upwards, onto the high moors, exposed and bleak. Hughes' spirit responded to that of the moors 'the peculiar sad desolate spirit that cries in telegraph wires on moor roads, in the dry and so similar voices of grouse and sheep, and the moist voices of curlews'.

Everything in West Yorkshire is slightly unpleasant. Nothing ever quite escapes into happiness. The people are not detached enough from the stone, as if they were only half-born from the earth, and the graves are too near the surface. A disaster seems to hang around in the air there for a long time. I can never escape the impression that the whole region is in mourning for the first world war. The moors don't escape this, but they give the sensation purely. And finally, in spite of it, the mood of moorland is exultant, and this is what I remember of it.

From there the return home was a descent into the pit, and after each visit I must have returned less and less of myself to the valley. This was where the division of body and soul, for me, began.   ('The Rock')

6

This shut-in, in-bred, industrial community of the Calder Valley has bred strong values – dignity and decency, cleanliness and honesty, hard work and thrift, good neighbourliness, solidarity. This shaped Hughes, and he has much to be grateful for. But the opposite side of the coin is stifling respectability, a self-righteous and self-denying puritanism, and an aggressive self-congratulatory materialism and philistinism. Against the realities of work and muck and brass, all intellectual or artistic activity is traditionally scorned as effeminate and wasteful. For a child to use an unfamiliar word in the playground is to risk being mocked for having 'swallowed a dictionary'.

Yet the familiar words were a rich inheritance. The West Riding dialect has remained Hughes' staple poetic speech, concrete, emphatic, terse, yet powerfully, economically, eloquent. It is a speech in which a spade is called a spade; facts are looked in the face, especially the unpleasant facts; and a saving humour is never far from reach to ward off all self-indulgence, evasion or pretentiousness. The regional anthem of the West Riding is a comic song in dialect about a man who catches his death of cold on Ilkley Moor, is buried, eaten by worms, which are eaten by ducks, which are eaten by his mates. The song ends with the grisly pun:

> That's wheer we gets us oan back.

When Hughes was seven, the family moved to Mexborough, in South Yorkshire, where his parents kept a newsagent's and tobacconist's shop until they returned to the Calder Valley in 1952. In Mexborough, like Lawrence before him in a similar area, Hughes was obliged to lead a double life, one with the town boys, sons of miners and railwaymen, the other in his bolt-hole – a nearby farm or a private estate with woods and a lake.

At fifteen he was writing poems, in galloping Kiplingesque rhythms, most of them about Zulus or the Wild West. One of his heroes, Carson McReared the terrible killer, the man with a hide like an armadillo, was 'shot to hell' in the Grand Canyon after shooting 1,200 men,

> And knee deep in blood, where he had to paddle
> Stood Diamond Ace, with an empty saddle.

A succession of perceptive English teachers at Mexborough Grammar School (culminating in John Fisher, who was able to

do a great deal for him) fostered his interest in poetry. Before he
left school, he had matured to the point where he could write
these lovely lines:

> O lady, consider when I shall have lost you
> The moon's full hands, scattering waste,
> The sea's hands, dark from the world's breast,
> The world's decay where the wind's hands have passed,
> And my head, worn out with love, at rest
> In my hands, and my hands full of dust,
> O my lady.

('Song')

In 1948 Hughes won an Open Exhibition to Cambridge, but
before taking it up he did two years of National Service as a
ground wireless mechanic in the RAF on an isolated three-man
radio station in east Yorkshire where he had 'nothing to do but
read and reread Shakespeare and watch the grass grow'.

Hughes went up to Pembroke College, Cambridge, in 1951.

His supervisor was M. J. C. Hodgart (an expert, of course, on
the ballads) whom he found very sympathetic. He rarely attended
lectures, though he occasionally went to hear F. R. Leavis whom
he found fascinating to watch and listen to and highly entertaining.

In his fine study of Hughes and shamanism (*Boston University
Journal*, XXII, 3), David Porter quotes a remarkable story recorded
by W. S. Merwin:

At Cambridge he set out to study English Literature. Hated it. Groaned having to write those essays. Felt he was dying of it in some essential place.
Sweated late at night over the paper on Dr. Johnson et al. – things he didn't
want to read. One night, very late, very tired, he went to sleep. Saw the door
open and someone like himself come in with a fox's head. The visitor went
over to his desk, where an unfinished essay was lying, and put his paw on the
papers, leaving a bloody mark; then he came over to the bed, looked down at
Ted and said, 'You're killing us,' and went out the door. (Carroll, *The Poem
in its Skin*, 149–50)

As for the wider life of Cambridge, Hughes belonged to no
societies. 'Luckily' (he says) the Amateur Dramatic Club rejected
him as an actor. But he saw plenty of good theatre, for Cambridge
at that time was almost an embryonic Royal Shakespeare Company, with Peter Hall and John Barton running things, and actors
of the calibre of Peter Woodthorpe. Hughes had thrown the discus

for his school, but the only sport he practised at Cambridge was archery.

In his third year Hughes changed from English to Archaeology and Anthropology. His grounding in these disciplines has proved of immense and growing value in his creative work. His imagination is at home in the world of myth and folklore. Cambridge also gave him time to read a great deal.

Hughes graduated in June 1954, the same month in which his first poem appeared in a Cambridge periodical, 'The Little Boys and the Seasons' in *Granta* under the pseudonym Daniel Hearing. It is a pleasing poem, but too much under the influence of Dylan Thomas for the true Hughes to show through. During the next two years Hughes worked briefly as a rose-gardener, night-watchman in a steel works, zoo attendant, schoolteacher, and reader for J. Arthur Rank. Most of the time he lived in London or Cambridge, kept up his friendships there, and published a handful of poems in the Cambridge poetry magazines. In the early and middle fifties Cambridge was rich in budding poets, but the two Hughes poems published in the November 1954 number of *Chequer*, 'The Jaguar' and 'The Casualty', attracted an unusual amount of attention. The jaguar,

> hurrying enraged
> Through prison darkness after the drills of his eyes...

was the first of Hughes' beasts to be captured in all its vivid otherness in a poem. The last two stanzas were originally quite different from the version in *The Hawk in the Rain*. At the end it is the crowd of spectators who stare out through bars at the greater reality,

> But what holds them from corner to corner swinging,
> Swivelling the ball of his heel on the polished spot,
> Jerking his head up in surprise at the bars
> Has not hesitated in the millions of years,
> And like life-prisoners they through bars stare out.

The central impulse of 'The Casualty' is also to lay open the reader to a wider, deeper reality than he is normally aware of. The witnesses

> ...stand, helpless as ghosts: In a scene
> Melting in the August noon, the burned man
> Bulks closer greater flesh and blood than their own...

9

Early in 1956 Hughes and some of his friends decided to launch a poetry magazine of their own, the 'St Botolph's Review'. The first and only issue contained four poems by Ted Hughes, 'Fallgrief's Girl-friends' and three untitled poems which in *The Hawk in the Rain* became 'Law in the Country of Cats', 'Soliloquy of a Misanthrope' and 'Secretary'. Of these four poems three are about women. The Misanthrope looks forward to death when he will see 'every attitude showing its bone'. But he will 'thank God thrice heartily'

> To be lying beside women who grimace
> Under the commitments of their flesh,
> And not out of spite or vanity.

Fallgrief is this same Misanthrope who, seeking to

> break out of the dream
> Where admiration's giddy mannequins
> Lead every sense to motley;

and to

> stand naked
> Awake in the pitch dark where the animal runs,

determines to choose 'a muck of a woman' to match 'this muck of man in this Muck of existence', but finds, by chance, 'a woman with such wit and looks He can brag of her in every company'. Whether he thus falls into or out of grief is not clear.

At the party held to inaugurate the 'St Botolph's Review', on 25 February 1956, Hughes met Sylvia Plath and within four months he had married her.

Sylvia Plath was a Bostonian, two years younger than Hughes, at Newnham on a Fulbright. She had had an illustrious academic career, both at school and college. Her first published work appeared in 1950 in *Seventeen* and the *Christian Science Monitor*. In 1953 some of her poems were accepted by *Mademoiselle* and by *Harper's*. But between acceptance and publication had come her '6 month crash' – breakdown, attempted suicide, hospitalization – the experience she later recorded in her novel *The Bell Jar*. By 1956, however, her recovery seemed complete. She married Hughes not only because of their mutual attraction and shared commitment to poetry, but also because 'he was very simply the only man I've ever met whom I could never boss...'

His was the stronger, surer poetic voice, and the immediate

effect was of ventriloquism. Her 'Spinster', one of the first poems she wrote after their meeting, is a variation on his 'Secretary' and echoes the vocabulary of 'Fallgrief's Girl-friends':

> But here – a burgeoning
> Unruly enough to pitch her five queenly wits
> Into vulgar motley –
> A treason not to be borne. Let idiots
> Reel giddy in bedlam spring:
> She withdrew neatly.

And another poem of that period, 'Strumpet Song', ends with a passage of pure Hughes, the wrenched syntax, the savage consonants, the pounding monosyllables:

> Walks there not some such one man
> As can spare breath
> To patch with brand of love this rank grimace
> Which out from black tarn, ditch and cup
> Into my most chaste own eyes
> Looks up.

Later Sylvia seized on 'View of a Pig', 'The Green Wolf', 'Out' and several other poems in *Wodwo*. Hughes introduced her to the work of John Crowe Ransome, whom he and his friends admired unreservedly at that time, and for a while she adopted a few of his mannerisms. But Sylvia was, on the whole, resistant to influences, and the most important effect Hughes had on her was to increase her concentration on poetry and to supply her with a fully worked out belief in the poetic mythology of Robert Graves' *The White Goddess*.

Sylvia was able to act as a guide to American poetry for Hughes, and he could hardly have had a better one. Apart from Ransome he knew little of it at that time. Also she helped him to get his poems published, sending out beautifully typed manuscripts in a very efficient American way.

That summer of 1956, much of it spent in the Spanish fishing village of Benidorm, they began their remarkable creative partnership. Each had poems accepted by the *Nation*, *Poetry* and the *Atlantic*. Her scholarship was extended for a further year. They took a flat neighbouring Grantchester Meadows. He taught English and drama at a nearby secondary school. They would get up at five in the morning to do their own writing. By the time she graduated and they left for the United States in the spring of 1957, *The Hawk in the Rain* was finished.

THE HAWK IN THE RAIN

All the time I am struggling in the dark – very deep in the dark – and cut off from everybody and everything. . . . Sometimes I am afraid of the terrible things that are real, in the darkness, and of the entire unreality of these things I see. It becomes like a madness at last, to know one is all the time walking in a pale assembly of an unreal world – this house, this furniture, the sky and the earth – whilst oneself is all the while a piece of darkness pulsating in shocks, and the shocks and the darkness are real. . . . This day time reality becomes more and more unreal, as if one wrote from a grave or a womb.

(D. H. Lawrence, Letter to Bertrand Russell, 15 March 1915)

Early in 1956 the Poetry Centre of the Young Men's and Young Women's Hebrew Association of New York sponsored a competition for a first book of poems in English. The prize was immediate publication by Harper. Hughes would never have dreamed of entering, but Sylvia typed up a manuscript of his pieces and sent it off. There were 287 entries. The judges, W. H. Auden, Stephen Spender and Marianne Moore, chose *The Hawk in the Rain*. In a brief Introduction to the American edition, Marianne Moore wrote: 'Hughes' talent is unmistakable, the work has focus, is aglow with feeling, with conscience; sensibility is awake, embodied in appropriate diction.'

The early fifties had been a thin time for English poetry. Dylan Thomas was dead; Eliot no longer writing poetry. We think of Eliot and Dylan Thomas as at opposite poles – classical and romantic. But what they had in common is far more important than what superficially distinguished them. Each handled the biggest themes he could reach – the relation of man to time, Nature and God; each knew poetry to be a unique language capable of supra-rational insights and more akin to music than to purely rational forms of discourse; each relied heavily on symbolism as the most powerful weapon in poetry's armoury; each assumed the poet to be a privileged being with a god's eye view of the world; each wrote complex, allusive, often obscure poetry with no concessions to the common reader.

The fifties brought a reaction against all this 'pretentiousness', a deflating scepticism. The mood of the post-war poets was best caught in Robert Conquest's 1956 anthology *New Lines*. The poets of the fifties, Conquest claimed, were 'down to earth', rooted in common experience with a reverence for the real person or event; men speaking to men in a manner in which they could hope to be generally understood about matters human, humane and rational. Clearly poetry must not be allowed to disappear into the clouds. Some poets may need someone to hang on to their legs. But isn't this a function for critics rather than other poets? And a man whose feet are on the ground need not fix his eyes upon his feet. Many of the poems in *New Lines* were not rooted in experiences one could feel to be important; they were commonplace. Too many of the poets represented there spoke like common men speaking to common men of common things in common language, all congratulating each other on their refusal to be taken in, aggressively provincial and slangy, disenchanted to the point of affectation. Most disabling was their refusal to handle or even acknowledge a dimension of human experience beyond the merely local and day-to-day. In the words of Charles Tomlinson: 'They show a singular want of vital awareness of the continuum outside themselves, of the mystery embodied over against them in the created universe' (*Essays in Criticism*, April 1957). The anthology, he concluded, testified to 'a total failure of nerve'.

A poem typical of *New Lines* was 'Against Romanticism' by Kingsley Amis, which reads like a prophetic attempt to keep Ted Hughes at bay:

A traveller who walks a temperate zone
– Woods devoid of beasts, roads that please the foot –
Finds that its decent surface grows too thin:
Something unperceived fumbles at his nerves.
To please an ingrown taste for anarchy
Torrid images circle in the wood,
And sweating for recognition up the road,
Cramming close the air with their bookish cries.
All senses then are glad to gasp: the eye
Smeared with garish paints, tickled up with ghosts
That brandish warnings or an abstract noun;
Melodies from shards, memories from coal,
Or saws from powdered tombstones thump the ear...
Over all, a grand meaning fills the scene,
And sets the brain raging with prophesy...

Hughes was younger than any of the contributors to *New Lines*, on average by several years. With the exception of Thom Gunn, who was already famous at university and whose poems Hughes greatly liked, he was quite unaware of them, wrapped up as he was in the exclusive world of *The White Goddess*.

They had come to maturity during the war, and that, perhaps, had something to do with the sense one gets from so much of *New Lines*, of having had enough of the big themes of Nature and metaphysics. Philip Larkin records no 'Blinding theologies of flowers and fruits' ('I Remember, I Remember'), and Kingsley Amis asks:

> Why drag in
> All that water and stone?
> Scream the place down *here*,
> There's nobody *there*.
> ('Here is Where')

Hughes, on the other hand, had not had enough:

I was all for opening negotiations with whatever happened to be out there.
(*London Magazine*, January 1971)

It might seem then, if Conquest was right, that the time was unpropitious for *The Hawk in the Rain*. But, in the event, the reviewers, in the words of Calvin Bedient, 'flocked to the book like ghosts to a pit of blood'. Here was no deficiency of force, rather a superabundance. The poems crackle with surplus energy. The words leap off the page to strike or grapple the reader. Even the most grotesquely exaggerated poems are inordinately there, and alive.

Hughes is a master of hyperbole. Hyperbole is deliberate exaggeration, not intended to be taken literally, to express strong feeling or make a strong impression. It is as essential to poetry as metaphor, and is responsible for the power of many of the most admired passages of English poetry, particularly in the sixteenth and seventeenth centuries. Its rarity in the twentieth is part of the failure of nerve. The metaphysical conceit is both metaphor and hyperbole. The first lines of the first poem in Hughes' first book plunge us into hyperbolic verse of a kind scarcely heard since Marvell:

> I drown in the drumming ploughland, I drag up
> Heel after heel from the swallowing of the earth's mouth,
> From clay that clutches my each step to the ankle
> With the habit of the dogged grave...

Here the exaggeration in the description of a man walking through mud seems to generate its own conceit: the earth is so habituated to its primary relationship with man – his grave – that it knows no reason to wait for him to die, but is, from the start, hungry for him, pulling him down with a force stronger than gravity–mortality. Yet so closely does the language mime the physical experience of dragging across a ploughed field in a rain-storm that we are hardly aware of it becoming either hyperbole or metaphor until it is too late to resist.

'The Hawk in the Rain' stands appropriately at the threshold of the book, for it announces the major themes – man in relation to the animals, the earth, the weather, time and mortality. As in many poems by Hopkins the imagination is hauled from the depths to the heights, from pole to pole, in this case from the turbulent circumference to the still centre. The 'I' of the poem, the narra-tor, is completely overwhelmed by the elements. He flounders like one drowning at sea, or struggles like the prey already in the pre-dator's mouth. In contrast the hawk effortlessly rides the storm:

> His wings hold all creation in a weightless quiet,
> Steady as a hallucination in the streaming air.

The man envies the hawk its apparent centrality and poise. The hawk exhibits a mastery over those forces which threaten its survival and identity, that the poet's heart stirs for. The hawk cannot drown or lose its bearings, since its pole star, the stable fulcrum of the universe, is within it. Man, with his burden of consciousness, does not know who he is or what his purpose. But he does know that he will die. Finding nothing unquestionable within himself, he must look outwards into the dark for a fixed point from which to take his bearings, as a shipwrecked man might search the heavens for the polestar, as the man seeking experience watches the blue immensity for angels:

> and I,
> Bloodily grabbed dazed last-moment-counting
> Morsel in the earth's mouth, strain towards the master-
> Fulcrum of violence where the hawk hangs still.

The 'eye' of the hawk hangs as still as a polestar, at the eye of the storm, the still centre round which all that violence threshes. The poet's eyes are his most vulnerable part, thumbed by wind and rain, but the hawk's eye seems as impervious as immortal

15

diamond. It is always the eye at which Hughes stares, from this hawk right through to Crow. The jaguar hurries 'after the drills of his eyes'; the macaw 'suffers the stoking devils of his eyes'; the thought-fox is 'an eye' –

> A widening deepening greenness,
> Brilliantly, concentratedly,
> Coming about its own business...

The eye is the 'I', the window of the soul, the outward expression of the hawk's innermost being, its unquestionable identity, its concentrated, inflexible purpose.

To the man, all too conscious of his own relativity, the hawk appears as an absolute, inviolable. We know that the hawk will ultimately die and enter the same grave as the man, 'the mire of the land'. The difference is that the hawk's time is up only by an internal clock. He does what he is programmed to do. Even as he plummets to a last suicidal kill, he believes that, by relaxing his will, he has let the earth fall upon his head.

> That maybe in his own time meets the weather
>
> Coming the wrong way, suffers the air, hurled upside down,
> Fall from his eye, the ponderous shires crash on him,
> The horizon trap him; the round angelic eye
> Smashed, mix his heart's blood with the mire of the land.

To die in your own time and your own way and without knowledge of death as a violation, but simply as the next of the programmed instructions from life, is, relative to man, to be free of it. Or, as Yeats put it:

> Nor dread nor hope attend
> A dying animal;
> A man awaits his end
> Dreading and hoping all...
> Man has created death.
> ('Death')

The images of inviolability – diamond, polestar, master-fulcrum – culminate in that of 'the round angelic eye'. There is a strikingly relevant passage in Yeats' *A Vision*:

Even the drilled pupil of the eye, when the drill is in the hand of some Byzantine worker in ivory, undergoes a somnambulistic change, for its deep shadow among the faint lines of the tablet, its mechanical circle, where all else is rhythmical and flowing, give to Saint or Angel a look of some great bird staring at miracle.

Angels in Hughes are always staring and unseeing.[1] 'Angelic' suggests not only inviolability but also purity and innocence. But we know that the hawk's eye is rounded the better to see distant prey, so that the phrase becomes a paradox like Yeats' 'the murderous innocence of the sea'. The paradox is extended by 'smashed' – angels have no blood to spill.

What is unambiguous is the totally non-human vision of the hawk. 'Angelic' suggests that it is a superhuman vision seeing through life and death – staring at miracle. But it could equally be an inferior vision, the superior poise possible only through sheer ignorance or madness, so that what the man sees as absolute and enviable is only, after all, a 'hallucination'. In the very next poem the jaguar's eye is 'satisfied to be blind in fire'.

The poem owes a great deal, as we have seen, to Yeats, Hopkins and Dylan Thomas, and this is perhaps why Hughes has not included it in his *Selected Poems*. But it seems to me that he has succeeded in making a thoroughly Hughes poem, an expression of his distinct feel for life. No one else could have written it. A poet has no obligation to be an original thinker. The war between vitality and death goes on. There will always be a need for reporters to go to that front line.

It did not occur to any of the reviewers to discuss Hughes as an 'animal poet'. There are only five animal poems, the first five, in *The Hawk in the Rain*. Of these 'The Thought Fox', however vividly present in the poem the fox may be, is purely metaphorical. 'The Hawk in the Rain' and 'The Horses' are both primarily about the 'I', the narrator. The macaw is simply an image of what the Little Miss and her grandmother have done to the principle of maleness. Which leaves 'The Jaguar' as the nearest thing to an orthodox 'animal poem', but we find that the phrase fits it about as well as it fits Blake's 'Tyger':

> a jaguar hurrying enraged
> Through prison darkness after the drills of his eyes
>
> On a short fierce fuse. Not in boredom –
> The eye satisfied to be blind in fire,
> By the bang of blood in the brain deaf the ear –
> He spins from the bars, but there's no cage to him
>
> More than to the visionary his cell:
> His stride is wildernesses of freedom:
> The world rolls under the long thrust of his heel.
> Over the cage floor the horizons come.

The jaguar is enraged not only because he is caged, but because Nature has set him on this terrible treadmill, turning the world beneath his stride, following the drills of his eyes, blinded by the fire of his eyes, deafened by the beating of his own heart, with the fearful symmetry of some machine forged in furnace and on anvil, and with no more freedom than a machine, whether in prison darkness or the forests of the night. Or with the total freedom of a machine which is so self-contained that it cannot be imprisoned. The poem has it both ways. Either way this machine cannot be switched off, cannot be disconnected from the power source as man was disconnected at the Fall for the sake of that other freedom, the freedom to eat of the fruit of the tree of knowledge, knowledge (as Lawrence puts it) of the self-apart-from-God.

By invoking the jaguar the poet invokes also the God (or Goddess, or demon) of the machine:

A jaguar after all can be received in several different aspects...he is a beautiful, powerful nature spirit, he is a homicidal maniac, he is a super-charged piece of cosmic machinery, he is a symbol of man's baser nature shoved down into the id and growing cannibal murderous with deprivation, he is an ancient symbol of Dionysus since he is a leopard raised to the ninth power, he is a precise historical symbol to the bloody-minded Aztecs and so on. Or he is simply a demon...a lump of ectoplasm. A lump of astral energy. The symbol opens all these things...it is the reader's own nature that selects.

(*London Magazine*, January 1971)

And it is the poet's task, having invoked all these feelings and energies, to try to 'resolve the whole uproar into as formal and balanced a figure of melody and rhythm' as he can.

All great poetry is inspired; which is only another way of saying that it is a product of the imagination, not the intellect, though the imagination draws freely upon the intellect as it draws upon every other human faculty, and is subject, afterwards, to the judgement and ordering of the intellect.

In *Poetry in the Making*, the best book I know about the writing (and reading) of poetry in schools, Hughes compares writing poems to capturing animals:

The special kind of excitement, the slightly mesmerized and quite involuntary concentration with which you make out the stirrings of a new poem in your mind, then the outline, the mass and colour and clear final form of it, the unique living reality of it in the midst of the general lifelessness, all that is too familiar to mistake. This is hunting and the poem is a new species of creature, a new specimen of the life outside your own. (17)

The secret is to 'imagine what you are writing about. See it and live it.... Just look at it, touch it, smell it, listen to it, turn yourself into it. When you do this, the words look after themselves, like magic.' Thus you breathe your own life into the poem, whose words, images and rhythms 'jump to life as you read them'.

Most Hughes poems testify to the efficacy of this ancient magic. 'The Thought-Fox' is both a description of the process and a splendid example of it. The language mimes in sound and rhythm what it describes:

> Cold, delicately as the dark snow,
> A fox's nose touches twig, leaf;
> Two eyes serve a movement, that now
> And again now, and now, and now
>
> Sets neat prints into the snow
> Between trees, and warily a lame
> Shadow lags by stump and in hollow...

The delicacy is there in those light consonants – *d*s and *t*s and *f*s, and in the tentative rhythm of that second line. The poem has already set neat prints upon the page in the line before we are told that the fox sets them into the snow. The noun 'shadow' has to drag itself across that gap between the lines which separates it from its adjective. And the alliteration of 'lame' and 'lag' upon a long palatal consonant mimes the meaning to a degree which becomes obvious if we try to find a substitute for either word.

The poem is about writing a poem, about poetic inspiration, not about a fox at all. But the blank page is like a snowy clearing in the middle of a dark forest inhabited by 'things which have a vivid life of their own, outside mine'. The marks he makes on his paper as he records himself imagining this remind him of footprints in snow moving more and more boldly towards him. Suddenly, out of the unknown, there it is, with all the characteristics of a living thing – 'a sudden sharp hot stink of fox'. A simple trick, like pulling a kicking rabbit from a hat, but only a true poet can do it: 'And I suppose that long after I am gone, as long as a copy of the poem exists, every time anyone reads it the fox will get up somewhere out in the darkness and come walking towards them' (20).

Not all Hughes' animal poems are about predators. But his horses share with his hawk their stillness and their trust in nature, even in its most extreme manifestations. 'The Horses' begins with the world, an hour before dawn, 'cast in frost', 'A horse sheltering from the rain', says Hughes in 'The Rain Horse', 'generally goes into a sort of stupor, tilts a hind hoof and hangs its head and lets its eyelids droop, and so it stays as long as the rain lasts.' These horses have gone into just such a stupor against the cold, 'with draped manes and tilted hind-hooves' 'megalith-still', as though they had never moved and never would, with the invulnerability of huge stones.

From the ridge of the moor the narrator watches the dawn:

> Then the sun
> Orange, red, red erupted
> Silently, and splitting to its core tore and flung cloud,
> Shook the gulf open, showed blue,
> And the big planets hanging –

then stumbles away 'in the fever of a dream'.

If we have responded fully to the language of that description – 'red erupted', 'splitting to its core', 'tore and flung', 'shook open', all this done to the grey sky and about to be done to the grey world (the tops already kindling, the frost showing its fires, the stone horses stirring) – we can feel what might be done to a mere flesh and blood man exposed to such extremes, to such 'red levelling rays'.

> Dazzling and tremendous how quick the sun-rise would kill me

wrote Whitman,

> If I could not now and always send sun-rise out of me.
> ('Song of Myself', 25)

But Whitman is speaking for Nature herself. Hughes speaks for mortal man all too aware of the lack of anything in himself to set against the sun-rise. In him is no fire, but only a fever. The word has many strong associations for us: 'Life's fitful fever', 'the weariness, the fever and the fret'. . . He hopes that the memory of these patient all-suffering horses will sustain him, teach him patience, as he finds himself again caught up in the busy time-conscious world of men.

The poem is Hughes' most Wordsworthian. 'Resolution and Independence' is its model. That poem too begins with the evocation of a sun-rise and of all the creatures which seem to be at one with it. But Wordsworth thinks only of the years to come, of

Solitude, pain of heart, distress and poverty

madness and death. At this moment he comes upon the Leech-gatherer on the moor, an old man who seems, like the horses, to be in a 'sort of stupor' – 'not all alive nor dead, nor all asleep'. His stillness immediately reminds the poet of 'a huge Stone'

> Couch'd on the bald top of an eminence.

He seems like one met with in a dream. Wordsworth's poem ends in trite banality:

> 'God', said I, 'be my help and stay secure;
> I'll think of the Leech-gatherer on the lonely moor.'

And Hughes' ending

> May I still meet my memory in so lonely a place

though less tritely phrased, is almost as banal in sentiment, and sadly lets the poem down.

Hughes sees human beings as predatory not so much when they fight or kill as when they love. *The Hawk in the Rain* moves straight from animals to lovers. Men and women given over to desire are, almost by definition, incompatibilities:

> Each, each second, lonelier and further
> Falling alone through the endless
> Without-world of the other, though both here
> Twist so close they choke their cries.
> ('Incompatibilities')

To possess the other wholly, to penetrate to the very 'star that lights the face' (if that were possible), the innermost selfhood and integrity of the other, would be to extinguish that star. This kind of love is hardly to be distinguished from hate. Such love released is fire and flood, a hawk in a dovecote.

'The Dove-Breeder' had devoted his life to breeding and showing fantails and pouters (the very names suggest the spite and vanity of women, rejected by the rude Misanthrope of the previous poem). His doves are his carefully cultivated, perfected attitudes and complacencies which enable him to be so mild-mannered. He has known, perhaps, gentle affections, but has never been driven by the desperation which is love. Love, the raider, makes his well-groomed attitudes show their bones. But the dove-breeder does not then go to the opposite extreme and walk the town naked as the truth:

> Now he rides the morning mist
> With a big-eyed hawk on his fist.

He does not allow himself to become hawklike. He neither rejects the hawk nor surrenders to it. He trains it. He canalizes its violence into the controlled, civilized, ritualized activity of falconry.

We see the same process again in 'A Modest Proposal'. Here the lovers are like two wolves rending each other in their obsessive rivalry to possess each other, each rent showing 'the red smelting of hatred'.

> Suddenly they duck and peer.
> And there rides by
> The great lord from hunting. His embroidered
> Cloak floats, the tail of his horse pours,
> And at his stirrup the two great-eyed greyhounds
> That day after day bring down the towering stag
> Leap like one, making delighted sounds.

These beautiful measured lines, with all the stateliness of a medieval tapestry brought to life, are not what we have come to expect from Hughes. Suddenly the violence gives way to grace, the claustrophobia, heat and darkness of the thicket, to cool air, light and space. The two greyhounds embody what the wolves can hardly conceive, a relationship of absolute concord. The wolves for fear of each other are unable to hunt, and therefore to live. The greyhounds, in partnership, bring down the towering stag every day. Their freedom is a condition of their service to the great lord to whose leash of love they submit. He has tamed them, not by violating them, but by releasing creative energies through the discipline of co-operation and respect and ceremony. The embroidery, the stylization, the flourishes, are all part of the evocation of a life lived by a high chivalric code, all air, pride and plume.

The modest proposal of the title is, perhaps, the lover's proposal that they should try to become the greyhounds of his story, not the wolves, by submitting their desire ('a vicious separator') to the yoke and leash of marriage.

The belief that violent energies might be controlled and diverted into creative channels by ceremony is not one we find again in Hughes after 'The Dove-Breeder' and 'A Modest Proposal'. The insistence that every attitude must show its bone takes over.

THE HAWK IN THE RAIN

But here Hughes seems equally drawn to the lover who says

> Love you I do not say I do or might either.
> I come to you enforcedly –
> ('Billet-Doux')

and the more courtly lover who makes his modest proposal of marriage.

The destructive/creative 'love' of these poems is not only the love of man and woman; it is also the relationship between the poet and his Muse:

> The poet is in love with the White Goddess, with Truth: his heart breaks with longing and love for her. She is the Flower-goddess Olwen or Blodeu-wedd; but she is also Blodeuwedd the Owl, lamp-eyed, hooting dismally, with her foul nest in the hollow of a dead tree, or Circe the pitiless falcon, or Lamia with her flickering tongue, or the snarling-chopped Sow-goddess, or the mare-headed Rhiannon who feeds on raw flesh. Odi atque amo: 'to be in love with' is also to hate. (Graves, *The White Goddess*, 448)

The poems in the middle of the volume, 'Egg-Head' and 'The Man Seeking Experience Enquires his Way of a Drop of Water', are more overt in their metaphysic than the rest. 'Egg-Head' is a savage frontal attack on man's complacency and pride. The title refers not only to intellectuals, but to all men, for every man's brain is protected from 'the flash of the sun, the bolt of the earth' by a skull as fragile, in relation to those forces, as an egg-shell. Many men, heroes and poets, have taken the terrible risk of exposing their sense to the outside world:

> A leaf's otherness,
> The whaled monstered sea-bottom, eagled peaks
> And stars that hang over hurtling endlessness,
> With manslaughtering shocks
>
> Are let in on his sense:
> So many a one has dared to be struck dead
> Peeping through his fingers at the world's ends,
> Or at an ant's head.

Many have not dared, but have set out to wall in the brain, to seal up the senses, deliberately to blind, deafen and numb themselves, until the skull becomes a monad, a sealed world, feeding upon itself and feeling safe. It is not this Hughes derides. Man cannot help his 'dew-drop frailty'. What angers him is that such a creature, far from recognizing his frailty and peeping through his fingers if he dares to peep at all, sets himself up as master of the world, brags and preens, thinks to defeat mortality itself ('the looming mouth of the earth') with his tiny skull, his nonentity, his petty calculations:

> Spurn it muck under
> His foot-clutch, and, opposing his eye's flea-red
> Fly-catching fervency to the whelm of the sun,
>   Trumpet his own ear dead.

Unfortunately, the poem itself stupefies us with its sleights of syntax, benumbs us with its insistence, and deafens us with its trumpeting, so that the many incidental felicities are almost lost in the clamour. The language works mainly as a loud-hailer. What I tell you loudly enough is true! The meaning remains what could have been put in plain prose; was, in fact, put in plain prose by Shakespeare's Lafeu:

They say miracles are past; and we have our philosophical persons to make modern and familiar things supernatural and causeless. Hence it is that we make trifles of terrors, ensconcing ourselves into seeming knowledge when we should submit ourselves to an unknown fear.

(All's Well That Ends Well, III, ii)

'The Man Seeking Experience' is a much better poem. This man is the opposite of the egg-head, knowing himself 'all droplet kin', composed largely of water whose history is much the same as that of the drop he addresses, and containing within himself the accumulated experience of the race.

Every drop of water in the world contains water which has been through every possible experience and has existed in some form or other since the world began. The drop which has just condensed on his kitchen wall is thus an 'ancient eye' which has seen all

>   and there is no place
> His bright look has not bettered, and problem none
> But he has brought it to solution.

That last pun betrays him. The man's mistake is in assuming that such experience results in wisdom (or at least knowledge) which can be expressed in language. But the droplet has solved no problems, merely dissolved them. The droplet has been changed by experience not in the least:

> This droplet was clear simple water still.

His grand address is as lost upon it as upon a new-born baby.

Unconscious under the shock of its own quick,
After that first alone-in-creation cry
When into the mesh of sense, out of the dark,
Blundered the world-shouldering monstrous 'I'.

The droplet too is utterly self-contained and always new-born as what it always was – 'clear simple water'. Every new birth removes the skull for a moment from the egg-shell head, exposing 'the yolk's dark and hush' in all its 'dewdrop frailty' to an earth-staggering shock, a bolt from the blue, a descent of angels.

The man wants 'a plain lesson', the Word of God spelled out. Experience will never yield him that.

This poem has all the qualities its predecessor lacks. It is clear, coherent, progressive, powerful, varied and delicately handled in tone. No prose account could match this poetic evocation of the droplet's chequered history or of the miracle of birth (already that phrase has reduced it to cliché). In this little drama, this dialogue of one, Hughes finds a perfect objective correlative for his theme, an object and a situation to give it body and life. Yet if we compare this poem with 'How Water Began to Play' in *Crow* we will see how far Hughes has come since *The Hawk in The Rain*.

'Meeting' is essentially a much better version of 'Egg-Head'. But here the bragging, preening solipsist, instead of being merely subjected to Hughes' abuse, is exposed for a moment to the 'hurtling endlessness' of the universe, seen in the eye of a black goat. In 'Meeting' the man is content to think himself the measure of the universe. His image in a mirror seems to him that of Faustus, a demi-god to whom the secrets of the universe are an open book. So blind is he to 'the whelm of the sun' that 'the whole sun-swung zodiac of light' is no bigger to him than a trinket, the dazzling and tremendous sun-rise as nothing compared to 'the rise of his eye'. His arrogant eye reduces the world to the point where he can feel himself to be gigantic, a Gulliver in Lilliput, until the day when

A black goat clattered and ran
Towards him, and set forefeet firm on a rock
Above and looked down
A square-pupilled yellow-eyed look,
The black devil head against the blue air . . .

Nature confronts him in the form of a goat in whose utterly non-human eye he sees himself reduced to his real insignificance and frailty, like Gulliver in Brobdignag, in a giant hand under an eye

like a huge sun, but cold as a star, the eye of some god or demon
who has his fate in its hands.

> What gigantic fingers took
> Him up and on a bare
> Palm turned him close under an eye
> That was like a living hanging hemisphere . . .

He might well have cried like Faustus:

> O soul, be changed into little water-drops,
> And fall into the ocean – ne'er be found.

The whole meeting with the goat, occupying some fourteen
lines, is one sentence which accumulates great power without in
the least straining for it, using so many monosyllables that the
longer word, when it comes, has tremendous impact:

> And watched his blood's gleam with a ray
> Slow and cold and ferocious as a star . . .

The poem makes no attempt to interpret the man's experience.
The matter-of-fact last line

> Till the goat clattered away

trusts the poem to have done enough to make further comment
superfluous. Hughes' rhetoric is impressive; but he is even more
impressive when, as here, he generates equal or even greater
power without it.

In the best poems in *The Hawk in the Rain* we find a language
characterized by its faithfulness to the facts, the evidence of the
senses, shaped by a strong inspiration into images which, like
those of Henry Moore, seem to have been waiting for aeons within
the living rock, the living language, and now, released, will stand
for aeons and could not be otherwise. It is a language spiced with
great relish for experience, even when that experience is unpleasant or horrifying. Most distinctively it is a language able to
cope with the biggest things; it can generate energies equal to the
great primary energies of the world. In 'October Dawn' it is
the irresistible coming of winter. 'October is marigold'. (Mari is the
goddess of fruitfulness.) October is rich and mellow, but vulnerable as a solitary flower when the whole 'whistling green shrub-
bery' is doomed. Wine, that distillation of autumn's superflux,
left outside by careless evening revellers, dreams 'a premonition of
ice across its eye':

First a skin, delicately here
Restraining a ripple from the air;

Soon plate and rivet on pond and brook;
Then tons of chain and massive lock

To hold rivers. Then, sound by sight
Will Mammoth and Sabre-tooth celebrate

Reunion while a fist of cold
Squeezes the fire at the core of the world,

Squeezes the fire at the core of the heart,
And now it is about to start.

We know it is 'only' winter, but perhaps each winter is Nature
flexing its muscles, rehearsing for the next ice-age. Whatever reunion was celebrated here last night, we know that humanity is
doomed ultimately to hand back these lawns and shrubberies to
creatures of the great cold. But it is not in these dramatic mam-
moths and sabre-tooths that the poem's power lies so much as in
that relentless rhythm, that ruthless march of monosyllables, and
the stark finality of that last full rhyme after so many half-rhymes.
And all that weight falling on the word 'start'! No one since
Hopkins had used rhythm and rhyme so powerfully.

This is a language uniquely fitted to express a 'vital awareness
of the continuum' outside human life, of the mystery embodied in
the created universe. The mystery takes many forms. There is no
mistaking it when it takes the form of a gale. A house is a place of
refuge, keeping out the elements, creating a sheltered environment where man can pursue his civilized activities undisturbed.
A man's house is his impregnable castle. The earth under his
feet, terra firma, is the most solid, stable, permanent thing he
knows, a sure foundation of eternal rock. In 'Wind' this security
of houses and hills is without warning pulled from under our feet.

This house has been far out at sea all night,
The woods crashing through darkness, the booming hills,
Winds stampeding the fields under the window
Floundering black astride and blinding wet

Till day rose

The first stanza is a description of a storm-tossed ship at sea, but
the ship is this house, the sea these crashing woods, booming hills
and stampeding fields. The hills, so much more immovable than
the house built of their stones, seem as flimsy as a flapping tent
held by one guyrope.

> The fields quivering, the skyline a grimace,
> At any second to bang and vanish with a flap:
> The wind flung a magpie away and a black-
> Back gull bent like an iron bar slowly.

The wind has the strength to dent eyeballs, bend iron bars. It can shatter the house, it would seem, by sound alone.

Within the house, how can the occupants, their security gone, hearing those 'wandering elementals' outside, continue with their civilized and complacent reading, thinking and conversation.

> Now deep
> In chairs, in front of the great fire, we grip
> Our hearts and cannot entertain book, thought,
>
> Or each other. We watch the fire blazing,
> And feel the roots of the house move, but sit on,
> Seeing the window tremble to come in,
> Hearing the stones cry out under the horizons.

They can only grip their hearts, hold desperately onto their integrity which is under siege. If the window gave and the wind came in, the whole charade of civilization would be swept away.

The wind is representative of all those natural forces we try to shut out of our lives, which, if let in on our sense would leave us blind, floundering or mad. The wind is

> Flexing like the lens of a mad eye

and the window 'trembles' to come in. A window is, etymologically, the wind's eye. The eye we think of as the window of the soul. The window is like a delicate membrane holding back

> The huge-eyed looming horde from
> Under the floor of the heart, that run
> To the madman's eye-corner...
> ('Childbirth')

holding back demons, dark, anarchic forces which inhabit what we prefer to think of as the safely locked cellar of the unconscious.[2]

Hughes was only fifteen when the war ended. His knowledge of war derived almost entirely from his father's stories and the poems of Wilfred Owen, which is why his war poems all feel like the First World War. 'Bayonet Charge' is good imitation Owen. The second stanza generates deliberate, controlled formulations of a kind we are to grow familiar with in mature Hughes:

> He was running
> Like a man who has jumped up in the dark and runs
> Listening between his footfalls for the reason
> Of his still running...

But there is that false note of the 'patriotic tear' in the first stanza to which he returns in the last; and he doesn't know how to finish the poem, or rather, how to go through with it, as Owen would have done. To compare it with Owen at his best, as in 'Spring Offensive', is to recognize it as falling short of that deeper poetry of Owen's which is in the pity.[3]

Hughes is much better when he writes of war from a distance, when he writes of what we at home make of death in war when we are forced to confront it, either at the time or long after. 'Griefs for Dead Soldiers' is in three parts, each expressing a different form of grief. The mightiest grief is the public grief expressed at the unveiling of a cenotaph. Part I has the sonority and large gestures which are the order of the day. It resembles many another poem which might be spoken by some VIP on Remembrance Day – Binyon's 'For the Fallen', for example:

> Solemn the drums thrill: Death august and royal
> Sings sorrow up into immortal spheres.
> There is music in the midst of desolation
> And a glory that shines upon our tears.

'For the Fallen' is a tissue of lies and sentimentality and portentousness. There is nothing so blatant in Hughes' handling of the public grief, but one becomes uneasily aware that the large gestures are dwarfing or replacing the actual deaths. If the mere unveiling ceremony is like a 'cataclysm', an end-of-the-world 'terror', a 'monstrousness', what were the actual deaths like? There is a disproportion between the thin bugle, the 'dead drum tap', the marching and the shouting, all 'blown about by the wind', and the sheer size and weight of what, in theory, is being constructed, a block of stone which will

> Make these dead magnificent, their souls
> Scrolled and supporting the sky, and the national sorrow...

Between these extremes of air and stone, mere flesh is overlooked, discarded. This magnificent grief which so quickly transforms itself into stirring affirmations of

> Permanent stupendous victory

is part of the process whereby the nation promises to remember for one day a year in order to be able to forget with a clear conscience for the other three hundred and sixty-four; the process whereby the nation accepts with pride the slaughter of a whole generation of its youth. The rhetoric of the cenotaph ceremony is a continuance in solemn guise of the lying jingoism which prompted Wilfred Owen to write three months before his death: 'I wish the Boche would have the pluck to come right in and make a clean sweep of the pleasure boats, and the promenaders on the spa, and all the stinking Leeds and Bradford war-profiteers now reading John Bull on Scarborough sands.' The bitterness of that prose is clearly absent from this poem. The disproportion is detectable, but many readers will still be able to take the poem at its face value. Its inadequacy only becomes evident when we pass on to the other, truer, griefs.

The smallest, most secret grief is that of the lonely widow:

> She cannot build her sorrow into a monument
> And walk away from it.

Yet even hers is not the truest grief. Her sorrow is for the severing of their love. She grieves for the smashing of her world, not, purely, of his body. She never sees or imagines the smashed body. Her greatest horror is watching her own hands, automatic, numb with apprehension, opening the telegram. Her grief is private grief, true for herself alone.

There remains the truest grief, and the only grief which does justice to the dead by confronting the bald reality of their deaths:

> thud of another body flung
> Down, the jolted shape of a face, earth into the mouth

Here grief can be measured by its exact weight in corpse-flesh and calmly buried. There are no flags and trumpets, no monuments, yet the sight 'could annihilate a watcher'. Perhaps the poem fails, at this point, quite to substantiate that horror. The reader has to imagine for himself why he would find that moment annihilating. Hughes needs a whole poem to develop his thought. That poem is 'Six Young Men'.

In Parts II and III of 'Griefs for Dead Soldiers' Hughes shows that he is not dependent on sound and fury, on exaggeration and strenuous muscular language. The image of the telegram 'opening of its own accord' really is more terrible by far than that of a bomb 'that dives to the cellar and lifts the house'. Gradually Hughes is to gain confidence in the just style as sometimes truer than the mightiest.

In his Introduction to the *Selected Poems of Keith Douglas*, Hughes wrote of the truth which kills everybody:

The truth of a man is the doomed man in him or his dead body....The murderous skeleton in the body of a girl, the dead men being eaten by dogs on the moonlit desert, the dead man behind the mirror, these items of circumstantial evidence are steadily out-arguing all his high spirits and hopefulness.

In 'Six Young Men' Hughes adds his own evidence, a photograph of his father's, six young men on a Sunday jaunt, each as alive as any man you can confront

> And shake by the hand, see hale, hear speak loud.

Yet they all died within six months and forty years ago.

> To regard this photograph might well dement,
> Such contradictory permanent horrors here
> Smile from the single exposure and shoulder out
> One's own body from its instant and heat.

'Exposure' is a perfectly chosen word. The camera which cannot lie exposed them as forever alive and young. Six months later they were exposed to the horrors of war which exposed their bones. And one's own vivid life, for all its bulk and weight, is equally flimsy. We are no more alive than they were, than, here in this photograph, they still are, as by a bilberried bank, a thick tree, a black wall 'which are there yet and not changed' they listen to the waterfall that roars yet in that valley. Yet we know that they are as dead as dinosaur or dodo, dead and rotten. If I have my photograph taken today, someone will look at it forty years hence and be looking at the photograph of a dead man. It is like seeing one's own tombstone, like becoming aware of one's own skeleton which will one day shrug off its flesh.

War, childbirth, the weather, love, and animals, are Hughes' chosen themes here because they all afford us, whether as participants or witnesses, moments of contact with a deeper reality than that we normally inhabit, with a dimension of existence where life is not insulated against the vast currents of energy which flow and drive everywhere in the non-human world: 'Any form of violence – any form of vehement activity – invokes the bigger energy, the elemental power circuit of the Universe' (*London Magazine*, January 1971).

Such experiences don't have to be 'galvanized into the improbable' as one critic put it; they are already, if we can be made to confront them, miracles, manifestations of forces we do not in the least understand or control, which can destroy us, mind or body, in a flash.

At the moment of childbirth, for example,

> The commonplace became so strange
>
> There was not looking at the table or chair:
> Miracle struck out the brain
> Of order and ordinary...
>
> ('Childbirth')

The opening through which a new life can come, that breach in the barrier between being and not-being, he imagines as death's door through which all the dead might have got back from their underworld 'under the floor of the heart'. It is as though all barriers were, for a moment, down, all strongholds breached, the whole world let in upon the sense as though the skull had been removed. All to let one child pass through into this life out of the dark. One would have thought some monster had shouldered the earth out of its path. Perhaps each

> Frowning ten-toed ten-fingered birth

is monstrous in its assumption of arrogant selfhood as its birthright.

> This six-day abortion of the Absolute

he is later to call Man –

> This monstrous-headed difficult child!
> ('The Perfect Forms')

To watch an animal, particularly a predator, about its business; to watch a pair of lovers, or a woman in labour, or a man dead, dying, or at great risk, is, clearly, to be a watcher of violence, but not a voyeur. Hughes watches, and makes us watch, such violence, not for frisson, but for estrangement. He wants to undermine our sense of the ordinary and let in a sense of the miraculous, a shock of recognition of ourselves as animals, as killers, as newborn babies or as corpses. If the violence we are made to confront is reality, or even a fundamental part of it, then the reality most of us think we inhabit must be relatively or wholly unreal. For Hughes, the poet cannot see too much or experience too much. He tries to find 'words that live in the same dimension as life at its most severe, words that cannot be outflanked by experience', and out of them to forge a vision which evades as little as possible and which the soul must learn to bear as best it can.

At this date it is perhaps most instructive to look closer not at the many enthusiastic reviews but at the reservations some of the favourable critics expressed, and at the criticisms of the few unfavourable ones.

The commonest criticism was that so many of the poems were derivative. This is of course true, and to be expected in a first book. These influences are not diffuse, but tend to be concentrated in single poems, as if Hughes had consciously attempted to write in a manner close to that of Hopkins, Dylan Thomas, Yeats, the Jacobeans, Frost or Wilfred Owen, for the space of a poem or two, and why not? He had much to learn from all of them.

Hughes was well aware of the dangers in this respect, of 'the terrible, suffocating, maternal octopus of ancient English poetic tradition':

The archetypes are always there waiting...swashbuckling Elizabethan, earthy bawdy Merrie Englander, devastatingly witty Restoration blade and so on. And some of the great poets are such powerful magnetic fields they remake us in their own image before we're aware. Shakespeare in particular of course.

(*London Magazine*, January 1971)

But in comparison with the dangers or rather the impossibility of making poetry out of Queen's English, Shakespeare is still the greatest source of vitality. In his Introduction to *A Choice of Shakespeare's Verse* Hughes writes: 'Shakespeare's language is somehow nearer to the vital life of English, still, than anything written down since. One reason for this is that it is a virtuoso development of the poetic instincts of English dialect.' His language has

the air of being invented in a state of crisis, for a terribly urgent job, a homely spur-of-the-moment improvisation out of whatever verbal scrap happens to be lying around, and this is exactly what real speech is. The meaning is not so much narrowly delineated as overwhelmingly suggested, by an inspired signalling and hinting of verbal heads and tails both above and below precision, and by this weirdly expressive underswell of a musical near-gibberish, like a jostling of spirits. The idea is conveyed, but we also receive a musical and imaginative shock, and the satisfaction of that is unfathomable. (11)

At the Restoration those spirits were exorcized. And during the eighteenth and nineteenth centuries 'the desirable ideal of speech for all Englishmen became the shrunken, atrophied, suppressive-of-everything-under, bluffing, debonair, frivolous system of team-calls which we have inherited as Queen's English' (198).

It was to serve Hughes well to be so thoroughly grounded in Shakespeare and the still more ancient and archetypal forms he knew in nursery rhymes and ballads, in the dialect and Old English. Knowing 'the old language' so well, Hughes was later able to make innovations in the most valid way (perhaps the only valid way). In Pasternak's words: 'The most extraordinary discoveries are made when the artist is overwhelmed by what he has to say. Then he uses the old language in his urgency and the old language is transformed from within.'

Some of the reviewers pointed to general faults such as stridency and bravado, others conceded that there were some bad poems, but most were canny enough not to specify them. In the few who did specify, there was little consensus. Some poems ('The Martyrdom of Bishop Farrar' in particular) appeared in lists of both the best and the worst poems in the book.

The only thoroughly hostile review was by Alan Brownjohn, who saw, or affected to see, nothing but 'a dismaying badness' characterized by 'a raw, sex-and-violence imagery' and 'melodramatic and slapdash hyperbole'. Others have since followed Alan Brownjohn's lead. The most extreme statement of the position is Calvin Bedient's. He claims that there is nothing admirable in *The Hawk in the Rain*, that Hughes is, in it, a mere 'voyeur of violence':

Everything – war, childbirth, the weather, laughter, love – is galvanised into the improbable: even the prodigious wears a fright wig...Occasionally the phrases are welded in a series like brass knuckles...All together, it is as if Billy the giant had chosen to speak with the lexical mincingness of an Elizabethan page. The language attempts to squeeze every thrill out of its subjects and yet to be priggishly superior to them. It turns to Shakespeare as to stilts...

It must be conceded that passages can be adduced, and are adduced by Carr, Brownjohn, Rawson and Bedient, which support these charges. All are true of some poems and parts of others. Strain as he might, Hughes cannot always disguise the staleness or crudity of some of the underlying attitudes.

The phrase 'voyeur of violence' implies that Hughes likes to imagine scenes of violence for cheap thrills. The charge relates closely to that brought by C. J. Rawson, who argues that Hughes' positives imply a facile code of suicidal heroism, a cult of the big-hearted mindless hero of legend (that his hero is still, in other words, Carson McReared). The poem most open to this charge is 'The Ancient Heroes and the Bomber Pilot' where the poet shows every sign of sharing the pilot's admiration (or perhaps 'awe' would be a fairer word) of the 'huge chested braggarts', 'their chariot-wheels tumbling the necks of screams', 'restuffing their dear fame with fresh sacks-full of heads'. All this is offered as heroism, glory and grandeur, in contrast to the activity of the pilot who only has to press a button to raze a city, or the 'timorous poet' enlarging heroisms the heroes would have got nowhere listening to. That timorous poet was indeed a voyeur of violence. In his anxiety not to be like him, Hughes occasionally writes as Bedient describes (in 'Fair Choice' and 'Complaint', for example), with the overheated imagination of his own Little Miss, who dreams of a warrior 'smashing and burning and rending towards her loin'.

No doubt it can be useful to a young poet to have his faults pointed out to him at an early stage. But in the case of Hughes his faults are very closely related to his strengths and perhaps inseparable from them, as they must be in any poet who takes so many risks. To have taken such criticism too seriously would have been to emasculate himself.

On the whole, however, the reception of *The Hawk in the Rain* did the reviewers great credit. Robin Skelton spoke for the vast majority when he wrote: 'All looking for the emergence of a major poet must buy it.'

LUPERCAL

I saw
Too far into the sea, where every maw
The greater on the less feeds evermore. –
But I saw too distinct into the core
Of an eternal fierce destruction...
The Shark at savage prey, – the Hawk at pounce, –
The gentle Robin, like a Pard or Ounce,
Ravening a worm.
(John Keats, 'Epistle to John Hamilton Reynolds')

In the spring of 1957 Ted and Sylvia Hughes went to live in the
United States. That summer they spent in a cabin among pines on
Cape Cod. They would write in the mornings, cycle to the beach
in the afternoons, and read in the evenings. In the autumn Sylvia
took up a teaching appointment at Smith College, Northampton,
Massachusetts; but after a year decided to abandon her academic
career for the sake of her writing. Hughes, meanwhile, taught for
half the year at the University of Massachusetts. The next year
they lived from hand to mouth in a cramped apartment on
Beacon Hill in Boston. Here, in addition to much of *Lupercal*,
Hughes wrote *Meet My Folks!* and most of the stories later collected in *Wodwo*. In the spring of 1959 Ted Hughes received a
Guggenheim fellowship. They spent the summer camping all
over the States, and the autumn at Yaddo, where Sylvia finished
The Colossus and Ted *Lupercal* which appeared in March 1960.

There is no spectacular advance in *Lupercal*, rather a careful
pruning of the luxuriance of *The Hawk in the Rain*. Gone are all
the faults of the earlier book. Hardly a line in *Lupercal* is obviously derivative. The posturing has gone. The poems are no
longer overloaded, forced or hectoring. A few poems ('Fourth of
July', 'Historian') as a result seem threadbare, their clichés showing through. Others ('Nicholas Ferrer', 'The Good Life') are like
the good poems of a minor poet. But most of the poems ('Hawk
Roosting', 'View of a Pig', 'Pike', 'Crow Hill', 'Relic', 'Snowdrop',
and many more) gain great strength in simplicity.

To take 'Snowdrop' as an example, this perfect poem concentrates the vision of *Lupercal* into eight lines.

> Now is the globe shrunk tight
> Round the mouse's dulled wintering heart.
> Weasel and crow, as if moulded in brass,
> Move through an outer darkness
> Not in their right minds,
> With the other deaths. She, too, pursues her ends,
> Brutal as the stars of this month,
> Her pale head heavy as metal.

It is the depth of winter and life seems to have retreated to the centre. Those creatures which hibernate are in suspended animation; those which must continue to hunt do so mechanically, like zombies or automatons, in a world given over to cold, darkness and death. It seems that mere flesh and blood could not survive, only creatures 'moulded in brass'. Yet it is now that the snowdrop blossoms. How much more hard and single-minded and irresistible as a little bulldozer the snowdrop must be to break that frozen ground with its assertion of renewal against everything, yet we know that it is also utterly frail, and a miracle.

It may be that Hughes took to heart some of the criticism of *The Hawk in The Rain*. He may have learned from the American poets he came to know in his years in America. Or this may have been his natural development in any case. Having found his voice there is no need for imitation. Having got himself a hearing there is no need for the loud-hailer. Having found his strength there is no need to flex his muscles. The style is now wholly Hughes, as he moves deeper into his chosen themes.

Many reviewers and later critics assumed that the territory Hughes was rapidly staking out was the world of animals. We have only to look down the titles of *Lupercal* to see horses, cats, a hawk, a bull, a mouse, a pig, an otter, thrushes, a bullfrog and a pike.

No poet has observed animals more accurately, never taking his eyes from the object, capturing every characteristic up to the limits of language. So vivid is his rendering, so startling and true his insights, that the way one looks at a hawk, a thrush or a pike (or, in later poems, a jaguar, a skylark or a swarm of gnats) is permanently altered. But the description generates metaphors, and the metaphors relate the creature to all other creatures and to human experiences and concepts.

In nearly all his poems Hughes strives to find metaphors for his own nature. And his own nature is of peculiar general interest not because it is unusual, but because it embodies in an unusually intense, stark form the most typical stresses and contradictions of human nature and of Nature itself. The poems are bulletins from the battleground within.

In the early poems the metaphors he found were so often animals because animals live out in such naked extremity the primary struggles, particularly that between vitality and death. They roar or bellow the evidence which men wrap in sophistry or turn a blind eye to. Their reality seems less questionable than ours.

In any discussion of Hughes as an animal poet it is not long before the name of Lawrence occurs, and rightly so. 'Bullfrog' is a particularly Lawrentian poem. There is the affectionate direct address to the bullfrog,

> But you bullfrog, you pump out
> Whole fogs full of horn – a threat
> As of a liner looming.

the easy colloquial style flexible enough to heighten instantly to

> Disgorging your gouts of darkness like a wounded god,

the unexpected, slightly comical, metaphors and exaggerations

> I expected...
> A broken-down bull up to its belly in mud,
> Sucking black swamp up, belching out black cloud
> And a squall of gudgeon and lilies

the freshness and liveliness, the touches of wit which have nothing to do with showing off but are a direct, amused, wondering and wholly serious response to a new awareness –

> all dumb silence
> In your little old woman hands.

'An Otter', too, has the creature there in a couple of perfect lines

> With webbed feet and long ruddering tail
> And a round head like an old tomcat.

So much for the appearance of an otter. Another two lines suffice for its distinctive movements:

38

Gallops along land he no longer belongs to;
Re-enters the water by melting.

Then, like Lawrence, into the little myth:

Seeking
Some world lost when first he dived, that he cannot come at since.

The otter is 'neither fish nor beast...Of neither water nor land.' He wanders in search of the long-lost world he once ruled, where he knew himself and his kingdom.

The poem is less a description of an otter than an invocation of the spirit of an otter. The subject was suggested to Hughes by an Ouija board. The Ouija spirit liked poetry (particularly Shakespeare) and one hot day wrote a poem about 'a cool little spirit that wanted to live in the bottom of icebergs'. Hughes wrote Part I with great labour over a long period and was not really satisfied with it. The second part virtually wrote itself and seemed to Hughes to be the Ouija spirit's revision of the first part – and very much better. Here the otter is not just dispossessed, but hunted. As he hides under water, his dual nature forces him to breathe the air tainted by men and dogs. 'The otter belongs'

In double robbery and concealment –
From water that nourishes and drowns, and from land
That gave him his length and the mouth of the hound.

So, in exile, the water's surface ('the limpid integument') is where he thrives. If he ventures on land he must not linger:

Yanked above hounds, reverts to nothing at all,
To this long pelt over the back of a chair.

The otter is the opposite of the hawk who rules his element imperiously, the kingdom of daylight. The otter is also a predator, giving short shrift to the trout, but, since man arrived on the scene with his trained dogs, is also prey, dual again in this.

No analogues are offered. But the otter, crying without answer for his lost paradise, is surely, in part, an image of the duality of man, neither body nor spirit, neither beast nor angel, yearning for his Eden home where death was not.

In 'The Bull Moses', a boy leaning over the half-door of the byre can at first see nothing but a 'blaze of darkness' – a darkness which strikes the eye as rich with dangerous potencies. Though he cannot see the bull, his other senses register very strongly the bull's presence:

> But the warm weight of his breathing,
> The ammoniac reek of his litter, the hotly-tongued
> Mash of his cud, steamed against me.

Then gradually, as if his mind's eye were giving the evidence of the other senses their appropriate embodiment, he begins to make out

> The brow like masonry, the deep-keeled neck:
> Something come up there onto the brink of the gulf,
> Hadn't heard of the world, too deep in itself to be called to...

Moses belongs to another world beyond the world of human consciousness, a gulf between. He looms up out of that potent darkness and now stands in a bovine twilight at the brink, the meeting point of the two worlds.

There was a time when bulls were undominated. Now

> Each dusk the farmer led him
> Down to the pond to drink and smell the air,
> And he took no pace but the farmer
> Led him to take it, as if he knew nothing
> Of the ages and continents of his fathers,
> Shut, while he wombed, to a dark shed
> And steps between his door and the duckpond;
> The weight of the sun and the moon and the world hammered
> To a ring of brass through his nostrils.

The bull meekly submits to servitude. The boy is vaguely aware of what sleeps within the bull – 'the locked black of his powers' which no bolt or ring of brass could hold in check should he revolt. And why doesn't he? Has he forgotten his wild ancestors who roamed continents? Of the jaguar in *The Hawk in the Rain* we were told:

> His stride is wildernesses of freedom:
> The world rolls under the long thrust of his heel.
> Over the cage floor the horizons come.

Moses, too, is like a visionary in his cell:

> Some beheld future
> Founding in his quiet.

The animal lives in a world without time or death. The consciousness of Moses is a racial consciousness. What redeems his servitude is that he 'wombs', that is, he fills the wombs of many cows with his progeny, passing on what Lawrence, also writing of a bull, called the 'massive Providence of hot blood'. He is but a link in the unbroken continuity from his wild ancestors to his wild descendants, when man has ceased to rule. He is progenitor, Patriarch, and, like the other Moses, he beholds the Promised Land he will never himself enter, satisfied that simply by ensuring the continuity of the race, he has played his part. His descendants will escape from captivity and inherit the earth. Providence will see to that – the powers which inhabit the darkness of his dream.

The blackness beyond the gulf is not only the other world of the bull, it is also 'depth beyond star', the outer darkness surrounding the small area lit by the lamp of human consciousness, the source of those imperatives by which non-human creatures live. There is a corresponding darkness within ourselves, for the look into the blackness of the byre is also 'a sudden shut-eyed look Backwards into the head'. The gulf between man and animal is also the gulf between civilized man and his animal self, which is also his angelic self – the only self capable of recognizing a divinity in the darkness and being at one with it.

'Pike' is another fine poem, with Lawrentian passages which are yet pure Hughes:

> silhouette
> Of submarine delicacy and horror.
> A hundred feet long in their world.

The horror is in the pitch of specialization this fish has reached as killer:

> The jaws' hooked clamp and fangs
> Not to be changed at this date;
> A life subdued to its instrument;

as though the whole creature existed purely to enable its jaws to go about their business. Two marvellously economical anecdotes substantiate the claim:

> Three we kept behind glass,
> Jungled in weed: three inches, four,
> And four and a half: fed fry to them –
> Suddenly there were two. Finally one
>
> With a sag belly and the grin it was born with.
> And indeed they spare nobody.
> Two, six pounds each, over two feet long,
> High and dry and dead in the willow-herb –
>
> One jammed past its gills down the other's gullet:
> The outside eye stared: as a vice locks –

> The same iron in this eye
> Though its film shrank in death.

When, at the end, the narrator fishes in terror at night

> For what might move, for what eye might move

he is no longer fishing for pike, but for the nameless horror which night's darkness frees to rise up from the legendary depth of his dream, his unconscious.

> Prehistoric bedragonned times
> Crawl that darkness with Latin names...

These lines are from 'To Paint a Water Lily' where again there are two worlds, that above and that below the surface, a world of daylight and a world of living darkness:

> Now paint the long-necked lily-flower
>
> Which, deep in both worlds, can be still
> As a painting, trembling hardly at all
>
> Though the dragonfly alight,
> Whatever horror nudge her root.

In 'Fish' Lawrence has a passage about a pike:

> But watching closer
> That motionless deadly motion,
> That unnatural barrel body, that long ghoul nose,...
> I left off hailing him.
>
> I had made a mistake, I didn't know him,
> This grey, monotonous soul in the water,
> This intense individual in shadow,
> Fish-alive.
>
> I didn't know his God.
> I didn't know his God.

But the thought of that unknown God does not make his hair freeze on his head with terror. Lawrence has not noticed 'the malevolent aged grin'. The other, smaller fish know fear, when the pike comes, but it is

> gay fear, that turns the tail sprightly, from a shadow.

None are eaten, and what their own bellies gulp we are not told.

> Food, and fear, and joie de vivre,
> Without love.
>
> The other way about:
> Joie de vivre, and fear, and food,
> All without love.

In Hughes' pond there is little room for joie de vivre. Lawrence not only insists on its presence, he insists on its primacy. It is essential to his metaphysic.

In his poems Lawrence seldom writes of predators (his mountain lion is seen as victim rather than killer) and shows little interest in the eating habits of the beasts he does describe. Yet in his prose he shows a full awareness:

> Food, food, how strangely it relates man with the animal and vegetable world. How important it is! And how fierce is the fight that goes on around it. The same when one skins a rabbit, and takes out the inside, one realizes what an enormous part of the animal, comparatively, is intestinal, what a big part of him is just for food-apparatus; for *living on* other organisms. ('Reflections on the Death of a Porcupine')

This is also the main theme of Hughes' 'Mayday on Holderness':

> What a length of gut is growing and breathing –
> This mute eater, biting through the mind's
> Nursery floor, with eel and hyena and vulture,
> With creepy-crawly and the root,
> With the sea-worm, entering its birthright.

Hughes muses on Holderness as Joyce's Stephen Dedalus mused among the seawrack on Sandymount strand: 'A misbirth with a trailing navelcord, hushed in ruddy wool. The cords of all link back, strandentwining cable of all flesh....' And the links are alimentary as well as navel: 'God becomes man becomes fish becomes barnacle goose becomes featherbed mountain. Dead breaths I living breathe, tread dead dust, devour a urinous offal from all dead' (*Ulysses*, 'Proteus').

Hughes evokes the same continuity. As the Humber feeds the North Sea with its dregs and refuse, including dung, corpses and misbirths, so his body, he feels, is a mere sheath for that 'mute eater' the intestine, designed, like an incinerator, like any scavenger, to receive all remains.

The same pattern is endlessly repeated.

> There are eye-guarded eggs in these hedgerows,
> Hot haynests under the roots in burrows.
> Couples at their pursuits are laughing in the lanes.

> The North Sea lies soundless. Beneath it
> Smoulder the wars: to heart-beats, bomb, bayonet.
> 'Mother, Mother!' cries the pierced helmet.

The eggs, so carefully watched over by the parent birds, are to produce new prey, if they are not sucked dry before they hatch. The laughing couples produce cannon-fodder for the next war. It is all like a madness, a frenzy. When Hughes writes of

> The expressionless gaze of the leopard,
> The coils of the sleeping anaconda,
> The nightlong frenzy of shrews...

he is writing not out of wonder and admiration, but out of horror, a horror he can evoke in a single line:

> The crow sleeps glutted and the stoat begins.

To call this pattern unredeemable would imply a concept of redemption. To call it mad would imply a concept of sanity. But here

> The stars make pietas. The owl announces its sanity.

There is nothing outside the pattern from which any other standard of holiness or sanity could be drawn.

When Lawrence was sickened by the war, he wrote: 'It isn't my disordered imagination. There is a wagtail sitting on the gatepost. I see how sweet and swift heaven is. But hell is slow and creeping and viscous and insect-teeming; as is this Europe now, this England' (*Collected Letters*, 338). The sanity announced by Lawrence's wagtail is 'sweet and swift' having nothing whatever in common with the madness and obscenity of men marching to war. But the 'sanity' of Hughes' owl is indistinguishable from its 'nightlong frenzy'. If the natural is the sane, then killing is sane. Wagtails also kill to live. Of course men need not kill each other to live. But slaughter is slaughter. If it is mad and obscene in men, why is it sweet and swift in a wagtail? In fact, one realizes, it is not the killing Lawrence finds mad and obscene so much as the regimentation. Killing as such he does not seem to mind: 'Leave me my tigers, leave me spangled leopards, leave me bright cobra snakes, and I wish I had poison fangs and talons as good. I *believe* in wrath and gnashing of teeth and crunching of cowards' bones. I believe in fear and pain and in oh, such a lot of sorrow' (*Collected Letters*, 651). Or again: 'The tiger, the hawk, the weasel, are beautiful things to me; and as they strike the dove and the hare, that is the will of God, it is a consummation, a bringing together of two extremes, a making perfect one from the duality' ('The

44

Crown'). This is very close to the position Hughes comes through to in 'Crow's Table Talk':

> The tiger
> Kills like the fall of a cliff, one-sinewed with the earth,
> Himalayas under eyelid, Ganges under fur –
> Does not kill.
>
> Does not kill. The tiger blesses with a fang.
> The tiger does not kill but opens a path
> Neither of life nor of death:
> The tiger within the tiger:
> The tiger of the earth.
>
> O tiger!
> O brother of the viper! O beast in blossom!

But Hughes earns the right to this hard-won position as Lawrence does not, by confronting and living through in his work the fear and pain and sorrow. He hears the inaudible

> battle-shouts
> And death-cries everywhere hereabouts
> ('To Paint a Water Lily')

He shares the terror of the mouse 'staring out the chance it dared not take' and knows that a man stands in God's eye no better than the mouse in the cat's:

> Whether to two
> Feet or four, how are prayers contracted!
> Whether in God's eye or the eye of a cat.
> ('Cat and Mouse')

When Lawrence's cat torments a chipmunk 'it is a game, and it is pretty'.

Lawrence is not only callous in comparison with Hughes, he is also, in his animal poems, frequently sentimental. In 'A Living' for example:

> A bird
> picks up its seeds or little snails
> between heedless earth and heaven
> in heedlessness.
>
> But, the plucky little sport, it gives to life
> Song, and chirruping, gay feathers, fluff-shadowed warmth
>
> and all the unspeakable charm of birds hopping and fluttering and
> being birds.
> – And we, we get it all from them for nothing.

45

Hughes sees nothing heedless or sporting or charming about a
bird eating snails:

> Terrifying are the attent sleek thrushes on the lawn,
> More coiled steel than living – a poised
> Dark deadly eye, those delicate legs
> Triggered to stirrings beyond sense – with a start, a bounce, a stab
> Overtake the instant and drag out some writhing thing.
>
> ('Thrushes')

The thrushes are terrifying not only for their ravening of
writhing things, but for the too streamlined efficiency with which
they pursue their unwavering purpose – the efficiency of a bullet
(whose one path is direct through the bones of the living). Whitman thought he could 'turn and live with animals':

> They do not lie awake in the dark and weep for their sins.
>
> ('Song of Myself', 32)

Hughes draws the same distinction, but does not choose the
animals or even admire them. Their efficiency is too horribly
automatic, like

> The shark's mouth
> That hungers down the blood-smell even to a leak of its own
> Side and devouring of itself...

What a man does neither defines nor deifies him, nor can he, unless he is that hardly human thing, a genius, crash straight through
doubts, obstructions, temptations, sin, guilt and despair:

> how loud and above what
> Furious spaces of fire do the distracting devils
> Orgy and hosannah, under what wilderness
> Of black silent waters weep.

Beyond the little area lit by his consciousness, his desk-lamp, is
a vast darkness peopled by demons. The distracting devils which
sin, praise, or despair are those suppressed powers within any man
which will not let him be satisfied with the heroisms he invents at
his desk, or with any enclosed self-worshipping activity. A man
totally given over to those powers, genius or hero, is a madman or
automaton. A man totally cut off from them denies, trivializes or
perverts the life that is in him, drops out of the divine circuit from
which alone come the energies to destroy or create.

The poem which really established Hughes' reputation and got into all the anthologies was 'Hawk Roosting'. This poem, we were told, was a brilliant *tour de force* in entering the consciousness of a hawk. At one level it is certainly that. The whole poem is in the first person – a hawk's eye view of the world. The hawk, taking himself to be the exact centre, assumes that trees, air, sun and earth are there for his convenience; that the purpose of creation has been solely to produce him; that the world revolves at his bidding; that all other creatures exist only as prey; that his eye is stronger than change or death:

> It took the whole of Creation
> To produce my foot, my each feather:
> Now I hold Creation in my foot
>
> Or fly up, and revolve it all slowly –
> · · ·
> The sun is behind me.
> Nothing has changed since I began.
> My eye has permitted no change.
> I am going to keep things like this.

At a deeper level the hawk becomes a spokesman for Nature herself and speaks in accents close to those of Whitman when he permits Nature ('without check, with original energy') to speak through him:

> I know I am solid and sound,
> To me the converging objects of the universe perpetually flow...
> I know I am deathless...
> I see that the elementary laws never apologize...
> I exist as I am, that is enough...
> My foothold is tenon'd and mortis'd in granite...
> ('Song of Myself', 20)
> All forces have been steadily employ'd to complete and delight me,
> Now on this spot I stand with my robust soul
> (*Ibid.*, 44)

Nature speaks through Tennyson too, a Nature 'red in tooth and claw', a loveless, careless, ravenous Nature:

> She cries 'A thousand types are gone:
> I care for nothing, all shall go.
>
> Thou makest thine appeal to me:
> I bring to life, I bring to death:
> The spirit does but mean the breath:
> I know no more.'
> ('In Memoriam', LV)

47

Tennyson had built his faith on the assumption that love was Creation's final law. When Nature undeceived him he could only cry

> Are God and Nature then at strife?

In Hughes we find neither the admiration of Whitman nor the anguish of Tennyson. All these animal and nature poems get their characteristic tension from the attempt to fuse into a unified response both admiration and horror. The reconciling spirit might be described as one of awe. This was certainly the spirit in which the ancient Egyptians saw the hawk:

> Under the name Hor – which in Egyptian sounds like a word meaning 'sky' – the Egyptians referred to the falcon which they saw soaring high above their heads, and many thought of the sky as a divine falcon whose two eyes were the sun and the moon. The worshippers of this bird must have been numerous and powerful; for it was carried as a totem on prehistoric standards and from the earliest times was considered the pre-eminent divine being. The hieroglyph which represents the idea of 'god' was a falcon on its perch. (Larousse *Encyclopaedia of Mythology*, 21)

In other words, a hawk roosting was 'god'. In his *London Magazine* interview (January 1971) Hughes said of his hawk:

> That bird is accused of being a fascist...the symbol of some horrible totalitarian genocidal dictator. Actually what I had in mind was that in this hawk Nature is thinking. Simply Nature. It's not so simple maybe because Nature is no longer so simple. I intended some Creator like the Jehovah in Job but more feminine. When Christianity kicked the devil out of Job what they actually kicked out was Nature...and Nature became the devil. He doesn't sound like Isis, mother of the gods, which he is. He sounds like *Hitler's familiar spirit*. There is a line in the poem almost verbatim from Job. (8)

Indeed Job's god is the god of hawks:

> Doth the hawk fly by thy wisdom, and stretch her wings
>   toward the south?
> Doth the eagle mount up at thy command, and make her nest
>   on high?
> She dwelleth and abideth on the rock, upon the crag of the
>   rock, and the strong place.
> From thence she seeketh the prey, and her eyes behold afar off,
> Her young ones also suck up blood: and where the slain are,
>   there is she.
>
> (Job 39: 26–30)

And Job's God speaks like Hughes' hawk:

48

Whatsoever is under the whole heaven is mine.
(Job 41: 11)
I kill where I please because it is all mine.
('Hawk Roosting')

That was before Jehovah became the God of Love; before he became Jehovah, for Job called him such primitive names as El, Eloah and Shaddai.

In Job we find God still acknowledges as his own the most crude and savage powers of nature – behemoth and leviathan. Behemoth is clearly phallic:

> Lo now, his strength is in his loins, and
> his force is in the navel of his belly.
> He moveth his tail like a cedar: the
> sinews of his stones are wrapped together.
> He is the chief of the ways of God.
> (Job 40: 16ff)

Leviathan represents the unkillable, untameable dragon (libido) of the sea (unconscious):

> Behold, the hope of him is in vain:
> shall not one be cast down even at the
> sight of him?
> (Job 41: 9)

Later the Hebrews, to accommodate their God to human morality, handed Nature over to the devil. For in terms of the Christian ethic, or of any sort of human morality, the hawk is evil or mad. An example the poem more directly evokes than Hitler is Shakespeare's Richard of Gloucester:

> For the one path of my flight is direct
> Through the bones of the living

is a paraphrase of Richard's

> For many lives stand between me and home.
> (3 *Henry VI*, iii, iii, 173)

The hawk's solipsism is also Richard's:

> I am myself alone. (v, vi, 83)

By attributing to the hawk a consciousness which can express itself in our language and concepts, the poem also invites us, though we envy the hawk his centrality, his freedom from the falsifying dreams, sophistries and arguments which distract and deflect men, to count the cost of letting such energies loose in a man.

Speaking of Job 38–41, the Voice out of the Whirlwind, I. A. Richards, says: 'It is not well to reflect whether more than two thousand years' adoration of this utterance (however magnificent its phrases) might not have something to do with the sad state of the world and with the mad and abominable tyrannies which have so mercilessly infected it?' (*Beyond*, 73) Perhaps Job himself was suppressing similar doubts when he put his hand over his mouth.

> Though he slay me, yet will I trust in him:
> but I will maintain mine own ways before him.
>
> (Job 13: 15)

The chief of the ways of Job is his sense of justice. How can he hope to maintain that against a god of whom he has already said

> For he is not a man, as I am, that I should answer him,
> and we should come together in judgment.
>
> (Job 9: 32)

This god is not interested in justice or morality. When Job tries to negotiate, God shouts him down, smashing straight through his arguments with sheer brute force. What is left for him? A choice of capitulation, futile rebellion, or putting his hand over his mouth?

(The same choice confronts Crow, who is both Job and hawk, and Prometheus on his cr· whose unjust God daily sends his vulture out of the sun to torment him – a bird whose manners are tearing out livers.)

All efforts to understand Nature in terms of human morality are as doomed as Job's effort to understand his God. His successors decided to remake God in their own image, separating out and exalting the Logos, leaving the dark side of God, unacknowledged, marauding destructively as Satan, serpent, dragon, Gog, unredeemable Nature and the ghosts of all the Pagan gods and goddesses. And it is this process which Hughes sees as having more to do with the sad state of the world than the adoration of Job's savage God which Richards strangely imagines to have characterized the last two thousand years.

In *Lupercal* Hughes gives us a few figures who escape the destruc-

tive extremes. There is Dick Straightup 'strong as the earth', a
living legend because impervious to those forces to which Hughes
feels himself most vulnerable:

> But this one,
> With no more application than sitting,
> And drinking, and singing, fell in the sleet, late,
> Dammed the pouring gutter; and slept there; and, throughout
> A night searched by shouts and lamps, froze,
> Grew to the road with welts of ice. He was chipped out at dawn
>
> Warm as a pie and snoring.

The tramp in 'November' also withstands the worst that weather
can do. Then there are the 'Acrobats'. It is gravity they defy as
they fling

> Out onto nothing, snap, jerk
> Fulcrumed without fail
> On axes immaterial as
> Only geometry should use.

Hughes wonderfully mimes their 'hurtle and arc'

> somersaulting
> (As might hardly be dared in the head)
> Bodily out on space,
> Gibboning, bird-vaulting . . .

The verbs themselves launch out into space with their heavily
stressed first syllables. And that parenthesis achingly arrests the
somersault in mid-air. Such defiance of natural laws is 'unearthly', miraculous. But the watching crowd have no share in it.
It makes them only the more conscious of their insecurity and
vulnerability and mortality

> bearing
> Plunge of that high risk without
> That flight; with only a dread
> Crouching to get away from these
> On its hands and knees.

The acrobats are the exception which proves the rule. The world
of nonchalant ease, freedom and grace which they inhabit ('a
hundred feet above ground') is as remote from ordinary men as
heaven itself. Ordinary men can but dream of such a world, or
strive by means of vigil, ordeal, prayer and spiritual disciplines at
the body's expense, towards it. But

The acrobats flashed
Above earth's ancient inertia,
Faltering of the will,
And the dullness of flesh –
In the dream's orbit; shone, soared,
Mocking vigil and ordeal,
And the prayer of long attempting
Body had endured
To break from a hard-held trembling seat
And soar at that height.

When Hughes was a boy, his brother told him the story of a tramp sleeping in the heather, who stirred at an unlucky moment and was shot dead for a fox by an alert farmer. Already the tramp, in his imagination, was associated with those creatures we call vermin, shoot at will and hang on gibbets 'pour encourager les autres'. Other meanings of the tramp figure emerge in *Lupercal*. In 'Things Present' the tramp in his sodden ditch is defined by what he lacks – fire, cat, bread, shoes, honour and hope. His ancestors who gradually acquired these appurtenances of civilized living 'honed their bodies away' in the effort, that is, lost the stability and centrality that goes with a sense of the bulk and weight, the instant and heat, of one's own body. Most significantly he lacks 'a roof treed to deflect death'. Imagine those characters in 'Wind' deprived of their roof and fire.

In 'November' we learn why the tramp is willing to forego these things. The speaker is the same speaker as in 'The Hawk in the Rain', desperately conscious of his own exposure, vulnerability and mortality, running for shelter from the 'drilling rain'. The tramp embodies a less spectacular, more passive form of the same mastery of the elements which characterizes the hawk in the earlier poem.

In a let of the ditch a tramp was bundled asleep:
Face tucked down into beard, drawn in
Under its hair like a hedgehog's. I took him for dead,

But his stillness separated from the death
Of the rotting grass and the ground. A wind chilled,
And a fresh comfort tightened through him,
Each hand stuffed deeper into the other sleeve.

His secret is his 'strong trust'.

I thought what strong trust

Slept in him – as the trickling furrows slept,
And the thorn-roots in their grip on darkness;

And the buried stones, taking the weight of winter;
The hill where the hare crouched with clenched teeth.

What, exactly, does the tramp trust? That Nature will look after him, like the Babes in the Wood? That spring cannot be far behind, and better days? The speaker runs into a wood for shelter and there finds himself confronted by a gibbet:

The keeper's gibbet had owls and hawks
By the neck, weasels, a gang of cats, crows:
Some, stiff, weightless, twirled like dry bark bits

In the drilling rain. Some still had their shape,
Had their pride with it; hung, chins on chests,
Patient to outwait these worst days that beat
Their crowns bare and dripped from their feet.

These creatures share the patience of the tramp, even his posture 'chins on chests'. Is their patience misplaced, since they are not, like the tramp, the furrows and the thorn-roots, merely asleep? Nature has no spring or better days in store for them.

The tramp, like them outcast, dispropertied, unaccommodated, has nothing to lose. He is willing to forego even a roof, because being without hope he is not prepared to devote his life to the doomed attempt to deflect death. His trust is in all life's purposes or processes, including death.

In 'Crag Jack's Apostasy' Crag Jack is another tramp or outsider. His name implies his toughness, the qualities he shares with Heathcliff: 'an unreclaimed creature, without refinement, without cultivation'. Apostasy is the abandonment of religious faith. The opening lines –

The churches, lord, all the dark churches
Stooped over my cradle once:

evoke an image of witches suffocating the new born child with sterile blessings, obscuring the light; also, perhaps of the Calder Valley, the cradle of a Methodism which often took an extremely repressive Calvinistic form. (Joseph and the Reverend Jabes Branderham in *Wuthering Heights* are caricatures of this.) Crag Jack has come clear of the world (power, wealth, comfort, security) and the churches with their dogmas, theologies and traditional imagery.

> I came clear, but my god's down
> Under the weight of all that stone:
> Both my power and my luck since
> Have kicked at the world and slept in ditches.

Though he has no desire to be reclaimed, Crag Jack fears to become, like Heathcliff, a 'wolfish man'. He has retained a deep need to worship, but not the god of the churches.

> I do not desire to change my ways,
> But now call continually
> On you, god or not god, who
> Come to my sleeping body through
> The world under the world; pray
> That I may see more than your eyes
> In an animal's dreamed head...

Exposed as he is to life at its most severe, his imagination can find no appropriate image for the forces which control life other than that of a wolf's head or eagle's feet. Crag Jack is like The Toughest in *Recklings* who also survives the collapse of church-towers and hears 'the laughter of great outer darkness' threatening 'to close its teeth on the skull'. The Great Outer Darkness is a name for God. It is also, in 'The Toughest', 'the same as the small inner darkness'. The images of organized religion do not match those of the violent world Crag Jack inhabits. They are supplanted by his dream images. The only god who reveals himself to Crag Jack is the god of predators, the god of ruthless killing; or, if this god has other aspects, it is only in this aspect that he ever reveals himself. 'Plum Blossom' III in *Recklings* might be one of Jack's dreams:

> Inside the head of a cat
> Under the bones, the brains, the blood-tissue,
> Bone of the bone and brain of the brain,
> Blood of the blood and tissue of the tissue,
> Is God's head, with eyes open.
> And under that my own head, with wide eyes.
> And under that the head of a cat, with eyes
> Smiling and closed.

These images, wolf's head, eagle's claws, shark's mouth, the curved jawbone which did not laugh

> But gripped, gripped and is now a cenotaph
> ('Relic')

dominate *Lupercal*. Crag Jack's god is the god of death, of the

54

underworld. If we must name him he is Pluto or Dis, or Februus, to whom the month of February was sacred. In 'February' the dominant image is again the wolf – winter gripping the world with vice-like jaws. The word 'wolf' throws up several images in the poet's mind – the wolves he remembers from those horrific nursery stories *Red Riding Hood* and *The Wolf and the Seven Little Kids*, the wolves of Norse legends, 'gibbet-hung wolves' he has seen in engravings, or the caged wolves he has seen at the zoo. But none of these images suffices to personify the spirit of February, none captures the pure spirit of wolf as it is captured in

> A photograph: the hairless, knuckled feet
> Of the last wolf killed in Britain. . .

These feet run and run in the darkness of his dream, and

> By day, too, pursue, siege all thought. . .

There are no wolves in Britain, no large predators at all to make the nights dangerous. And we like to think that we have got rid of the wolfishness in our own natures. But these feet run

> Through and throughout the true world

disdaining the storied, pictured or tamed world, searching

> For their vanished head, for the world
> Vanished with the head, the teeth, the quick eyes –

the world in which wolves roamed at will before man rifled the forests. And man, meanwhile, is terrified that these disembodied feet will choose his head, will occupy the brain they lay siege to, driving out his 'reasonable ways'.

> Now, lest they choose his head,
> Under severe moons he sits making
> Wolf-masks, mouths clamped well onto the world.

Making wolf-masks is the attempt to divert the wolf-spirit into the false world of art or fiction, where it can be dealt with. But that final image of the world held between the teeth of a wolf-mask through whose eye-holes the quick eyes of the savage god might look out is far from reassuring.

'Fire-Eater' is yet another variant on 'Egg-Head' (in *The Hawk in the Rain*). The poem falls into two halves (the second a mirror-image of the first). The first half is about the stars as fire-eaters, the second about the speaker's claim to be himself a fire-eater on a much vaster scale.

> Those stars are the fleshed forebears
> Of these dark hills, bowed like labourers,
> And of my blood.
> The death of a gnat is a star's mouth: its skin,
> Like Mary's or Semele's, thin
> As the skin of fire:
> A star fell on her, a sun devoured her.

The stars are like materialized fires, the gods making themselves visible to men. We give them the names of gods. These gods gave life, and they snuff it out as easily as swallowing the tiny spark which is the life of a gnat. Mere skin is no protection. Both Mary and Semele were pierced by stars, that is by gods. When Semele rashly persuaded Zeus to let her see him in all his glory, the vision killed her. But from her body Zeus took the unborn child and fostered him in his own body until he was born as Dionysus. Semele is a counterpart of Persephone, a virgin seduced by Pluto in the form of a snake and possibly with the aid of an apple. She also 'died' but gave birth in fire to a divine son, Dionysus again, who brought the gift of wine, as Demeter, mother and counterpart of Persephone, brought the gift of grain. Thus, in the pagan myth, the Fall, the crucifixion of the god and the birth of the god are one divine event. To be pierced by the god may be death, but it is also the guarantee of immortality. And in Jerusalem two thousand years after Christ as at Eleusis a thousand years before, the miracle is celebrated by the leaping of fire from the Holy Sepulchre.

There is a legend that the sacred fire at Eleusis once restored a blind man's sight, as Orion restored his by gazing at the sun. To expose oneself to 'the whelm of the sun' is to risk death, but also to let in restoration and fertility.

However, the speaker in the poem, far from showing a due reverence and humility before these powers, claims to be himself a fire-eater capable of managing whole constellations:

> My appetite is good
> Now to manage both Orion and Dog
> With a mouthful of earth, my staple.
> Worm-sort, root-sort, going where it is profitable.
> A star pierces the slug,

The tree is caught up in the constellations.
My skull burrows among antennae and fronds.

This is Faustus again, whose first request to Mephistophilis was for knowledge of astronomy. But before he can swallow stars, this man must eat earth as staple, burrowing downwards like any worm or root into inert matter. (We think of Blake's Newton at the bottom of the sea of materialism, his back to the sun and stars, putting the universe on paper.)

Even the slug is 'pierced' by the divine fire. Even the trees are 'caught up in the constellations', even the insects reach up their antennae, the plants their fronds towards the vivifying stars. But the last we see of our hero he is still underground, still eating earth not fire, and now a skull emptied of what fire it ever had. So much for his arrogant appetite to contain the universe.

'Fire-Eater', like 'Urn Burial', seems to me a bad poem, though Sylvia Plath thought it the best poem in *Lupercal*. These poems are so cryptic and oblique that they can only be read as puzzles to be solved. The images are clues which send us groping far from the poem. There is insufficient continuity, coherence or realization for us to have much faith in any answers we might ultimately come up with. It would not surprise me to learn that my interpretation of 'Fire-Eater' is completely wide of Hughes' intention. It would not much trouble me either, since I believe a poet has the obligation to give his intentions rather more flesh and bone than this.

A specific example of a failed fire-eater is given in 'Strawberry Hill'. Strawberry Hill was the name of the house which Horace Walpole bought in 1747 and converted into a monument to the Gothic tastes of the time. He added battlements, pinnacles and all the other vulgarities which were supposed to suggest wild Nature, the supernatural, and the romantic, heroic past. The forces such writers as Walpole trivialized and sought to tame in their architecture and 'Gothick' novels, in that same age when the last wolf was killed in England, are here represented by a stoat which they expected to dance to their tune.

A stoat danced on the lawns here
To the music of the maskers;
Drinking the staring hare dry, bit
Through grammar and corset.

Blood, skulls, horror, death, the supernatural were all treated as mere playthings easily contained by artificial stylistic devices.

> They nailed to a door
> The stoat with the sun in its belly,
> But its red unmanageable life
> Has licked the stylist out of their skulls,
> Has sucked that age like an egg and gone off. . .

That life is unkillable. It killed them and their age. It 'got into some grave', returned to the underworld, but

> Emerges, thirsting, in far Asia, in Brixton.

Emerges, that is, wherever and whenever violence breaks out, for all our assurance that we are highly civilized and that civilization means having it well under control.

The god of the underworld may be the god of death, and February the month of the dead, but Persephone in the underworld is fertilized by Pluto and gives birth to Dionysus, who is Pluto himself in his creative, life-giving aspect. The wolf and the stoat cannot be exorcised from the human world, and if they could, along with the goat and all the other beasts of our being, there would be an end to the race.

One way to negotiate with these powers is through ritual. We call the animals fauna. Fauna was, in Roman mythology, the wife or daughter of Faunus, the fertility god, who corresponds closely to Pan or Dionysus. Under the name of Lupercus he was worshipped in Rome at a temple on the Palatine called the Lupercal. This temple was so called (*lupus* being Latin for wolf) because it was believed to be on the site of the cave where the she-wolf (which is the symbol of Rome) suckled Romulus and Remus, founders of the city. The rituals, the Lupercalia, were celebrated on the 15th of February. The purpose of the rituals was to restore fertility to barren women. Goats and dogs were sacrificed. Young men, athletes, were touched with blood and milk by the priests, then raced through the streets striking the waiting women as they passed with whips of goat-skin. Calphurnia, wife of Julius Caesar, once stood there, and one of the runners was Mark Anthony:

> Forget not, in your speed, Antonius,
> To touch Calphurnia; for our elders say,

> The barren, touched in this holy chase,
> Shake off their sterile curse.
>
> (*Julius Caesar*, I, ii)

The athletes run not to distinguish themselves but to snatch the lowliest, the barren women 'flung from the wheel of the living', back into that wheel, into 'the figure of the racers'.

'Lupercalia' fittingly ends the volume, for it offers to resolve in ritual the dilemma of Crag Jack and the horrors evoked in so many of the poems. It is made up of four short poems, each describing one of the participants – the dog, the barren woman, the goats and the racers.

The dog, though its blood is declined from the days when it was wolf, still 'held man's reasonable ways between its teeth'. There is still the 'old spark of the blood-heat' in him. And it is this, 'the brute's quick' which will be tinder, it is hoped, the touch of life on the woman's barren body. What gave the bull Moses his foothold in life, his sense of the continuity of his race, both heir and progenitor, is what she lacks, what makes her a hostage to death:

> The past killed in her, the future plucked out.

The dog dies that she might live again.

The goat has always been thought of as an embodiment of libidinousness, the lower half of the satyr, and of Pan the goat-god, and of the devil.

> Goats, black, not angels, but
> Bellies round as filled wine-skins
> Slung under carcase bones.

That marvellous image is so right purely as a visual image, descriptive, yet also suggests prodigality and licence, Dionysus and the Bacchic rites. The god is even more evident in the goat's eyes:

> Yet that's no brute light
>
> And no merely mountain light –
> Their eyes' golden element.

The goat is also characterized by the 'stink of a rank thriving'. All these are to pass to the women through the goat-skin thongs.

In 'Acrobats' the performers are

> Fulcrummed without fail
> On axes immaterial as
> Only geometry should use.

The racers in their blessed fury achieve an unearthly access of power and become

> A theorem of flung effort, blades:
> Nothing mortal falters their poise.

But where the circus crowd were merely spectators excluded from the 'grace' of the acrobats, here the crowd are all participants as they urge on the athletes, their representatives. The racers become conductors of energy between earth and sky:

> The earth's crammed full,
> Its baked red bellying to the sky's
> Electric blue.

Through the ritual they are blessed by dog and goat, caught up in the intercourse of earth and sky, and as they strike a woman they draw her into their pattern, the divine circuit:

> And deliberate welts have snatched her in
> To the figure of racers.

So the poem and the book end with a prayer for life, for the miraculous fertilizing touch of the god:

> Maker of the world,
> Hurrying the lit ghost of man
> Age to age while the body hold,
> Touch this frozen one.

WODWO

The roaring of lions, the howling of wolves, the raging of the stormy sea, and the destructive sword, are portions of eternity, too great for the eye of man.
(William Blake, 'Proverbs of Hell')

In December 1959 Ted and Sylvia Hughes returned to England for good, and, after a few weeks at Heptonstall, settled in February in a small flat near Primrose Hill where their first child Frieda was born in April. It was impossible to work in the flat, but the W. S. Merwins lent them a room in theirs. Sylvia would use it in the morning while her husband looked after Frieda. His turn would come in the afternoon. Sylvia worked mainly on *The Bell Jar*; Hughes wrote poems, some of which later appeared in *Recklings* and some in *Wodwo*, several radio plays, and a grand oratorio of the *Bardo Thodol* for the Chinese composer Chou Wen Chung, which was never used.

The following summer they moved to the thatched cottage in Devon where Hughes still lives, with an orchard on one side and a churchyard on the other. There Nicholas Farrar Hughes was born in January 1962. Hughes wrote rapidly – poems, stories, plays, reviews for the *New Statesman*. Sylvia Plath entered upon the phase of her *Ariel* poems. Their creative partnership was flowering, but their marriage was under strain. Sylvia was exhausted and could not face another winter in Devon. She found a flat at Primrose Hill and took a five-year lease. It was the coldest winter for half a century. She was ill and depressed. On 11 February 1963 she committed suicide.

Later that month Hughes wrote 'The Howling of Wolves' and in March 'Song of a Rat', then nothing (except a long play from which 'Ghost Crabs', 'Waking' and Part III of 'Gog' were salvaged) until 1966, when he went to Ireland and started with 'Gnat Psalm' and 'Skylarks'.

Recklings are the smallest and weakest animals in a litter – runts, wasters. Perhaps Hughes thought of these poems as throwouts and failed experiments, but hadn't the heart to burn them. Many of

61

them give the impression of being exercises in new styles, not quite brought off. And some are opaque in their dense symbolism – private poems. Almost all are very different from anything we have had before, stripped-down, skeletal poems, with little rhetoric and few animals. Some have a moving simplicity and understatement like the compassionate 'Small Events'; some, like 'Poltergeist', an epigrammatic wit; some a terse colloquial vigour. Ideas are now being handled as confidently as experiences. The most powerful poem, 'Logos', was carried over into *Wodwo*; 'A Match', 'On the Slope' and 'To be a Girl's Diary', all fine, went into the American *Wodwo* as 'Root, Stem, Leaf'. But there were several other poems well worth saving in *Recklings* – 'Memory', 'Thaw', 'Plum Blossom', 'Unknown Soldier'.

But to compare *Recklings* with *Wodwo* is to recognize that Hughes is a good judge of his own work. Here we have ample justification for those experiments, and for calling those thin years fallow, not sterile. Here Hughes comes into his own as a poet with a great range of themes and styles, and, if he must be labelled, a 'metaphysical' poet.

The reviewers of *Wodwo* were again (with very few exceptions) impressed, though several admitted their bafflement. It was not a reviewable book. These poems need to be lived with for years, not days, before it becomes possible to see *Wodwo* whole, not just as a collection of marvellous though often enigmatic poems.

The unenthusiastic reviewers wanted Hughes to be a different kind of poet, with different themes. They entirely missed the point that an inspirational poet like Hughes (or any great poet) does not choose what to write or how to write. He writes what he must. And they missed what some other reviewers tried to point to: 'He comes face to face with those forces in the physical world which are outside the range of moral choice or rational control, forces we have to live with or die with' (Norman Nicholson). 'Often pieces read like the tales of the stranger from beyond normal bournes, returning with a renewed clarity of vision, sharp as toothache, as uninvited as Lazarus' (Barbara Lloyd-Evans).

From the first poem, 'Thistles', on, we meet poetic utterance perfectly at one with its subject:

> Every one a revengeful burst
> Of resurrection, a grasped fistful

Of splintered weapons and Icelandic frost thrust up
From the underground stain of a decayed Viking.

Look at those spiky clusters of consonants, 'sp', 'spl' and, especially, 'st'. It is impossible to read the lines other than spitefully.

Or the subject may be a harebell and the language fragile and tender:

> That trembles, as under threats of death,
> In the summer turf's heat-rise,
> And in which – filling veins
> Any known name of blue would bruise
> Out of existence – sleeps, recovering,
>
> The maker of the sea.
>
> ('Still Life')

This is the voice of a man who speaks poetry as his first language. Despite the absence of rhyme or regular rhythms it never approaches prose. In the whole of *Wodwo* I can find only one stanza which could have been written by a bad poet – the conclusion of 'Ludwig's Death Mask':

> . . .
> Caused himself flee seventeen feet down
> Through the church-floor into dumb earth touched
> His ears dead to continue complete
> In union with the communion of angels.

Within the unity of his vision of life, presented most starkly in such poems as 'Pibroch', there are many different kinds of poem. There are poems about landscapes (owing much in their powerful simplicity and brevity to Eliot's 'Landscapes'); about specific animals and plants and people; about what Lawrence calls 'the animal, in all its animal difference and potency, its hinterland consciousness which circles round the isolated consciousness of man' (*Apocalypse*, 41); about the two worlds, the natural and the supernatural, a gulf between; about the first and last things, sometimes handled in the abstract, sometimes in agonizingly concrete images, sometimes in myths. The myths are, I think, the most impressive. The best description of them is Hughes' own, though he is speaking of Vasko Popa's ability to make miniature myths out of two bones or a quartz pebble:

It is in this favourite device of his, the little fable of visionary anecdote, that we see most clearly his shift from literary surrealism to the far older and

THE ART OF TED HUGHES

deeper thing, the surrealism of folklore. Folktale surrealism is always urgently connected with the business of trying to manage practical difficulties so great that they have forced the sufferer temporarily out of the dimension of coherent reality into that depth of imagination where understanding has its roots and stores its X-rays. (Introduction to Vasko Popa's *Selected Poetry*, 14–15)

There is also a great deal of variety in style and technique, and in tone. Nearly every poem is witty, as the Metaphysicals were witty, in perceiving new connections. Description generates metaphor. Then the metaphor takes over and becomes the meaning. From the thistle as 'a grasped fistful of splintered weapons' we move to:

> Then they grow grey, like men.
> Mown down, it is a feud. Their sons appear,
> Stiff with weapons, fighting back over the same ground.
> ('Thistles')

The wit is usually a means of deepening the seriousness of a poem. Occasionally it conveys a savage irony:

> Desertion in the face of a bullet!
> ('Bowled Over')

or a metaphysical dilemma:

> He is a man in hopeless feathers
> ('Kafka Writes')

or it can be epigrammatic, gnomic, as in 'The Bear' or 'Theology'. At other times it is frankly humorous without the humour in any way compromising the seriousness, as in 'Gnat Psalm'.

Some poems are expansive and free, in the Lawrence manner ('Skylarks'), others extremely concentrated, with regular stanzas. Some progress by narrative, some by argument, some by what looks like the spontaneous generation of images ('Cadenza') or sound patterns. Hughes is trying to recapture 'Some sort of language or set of sounds I can hear going on in the bottom of my mind, that's not quite English and not quite music. It's probably some sort of forgotten inherited language' (*The Poet Speaks*, 88). Perhaps a language better fitted to express the deepest rhythms and tensions of experience.

The tension, in *Wodwo*, is in the struggle for meanings, not for effects, the struggle to part meanings from their bedrock in the physical world. The eye strains to focus further, but the voice now has the calm assurance of the man who says what he must say, whether or not anyone listens or understands or applauds. If the men in the public bar fail to comprehend the hazy diminished images which flicker on the TV screen, the reality those images derive from is not diminished and must be witnessed afresh by the poet:

> On a flaked ridge of the desert
> Outriders have found foul water. They say nothing;
> With the cactus and the petrified tree
> Crouch numbed by a wind howling all
> Visible horizons equally empty.
>
> The wind brings dust and nothing
> Of the wives, the children, the grandmothers
> With the ancestral bones, who months ago
> Left the last river,
>
> Coming at the pace of oxen.
>
> ('Public Bar TV')

Ted Hughes is, of course, no philosopher. Few of his ideas are original. He takes what he can from diverse sources. (The same could be said of Shakespeare, Donne, Eliot, Beckett...) What we are primarily interested in is not the meanings themselves, as they can be paraphrased, but the new relationship between these perennial meanings and the raw materials – the world, experience, language. It is symbolism which most potently makes these new connections. The symbol has a foot in each world, one in the world of experience, one in the world of meanings.

In our efforts to extract meanings we must guard against the assumption that whatever meanings we extract are in some way the equivalent of the poem, or replace it, or the equally dangerous assumption that the best poems are those which elicit the lengthiest explication. These may be poems where the meaning is too near the surface, so that one is invited to discuss the meaning almost independently of the poem, or too far from it, so that one is obliged to tease it out.

Some of the poems in *Wodwo* are perfectly transparent, others perfectly solid – so much of a piece, so self-sufficient that there is no point at which the probe can enter. 'The Green Wolf', for example, is a good poem, but 'The Bear' is much finer. The symbols here are not pointing towards meanings outside themselves. They are the meanings and they resist translation into any other terms. Yet the poem is in no way obscure. We don't feel that meanings are being deliberately withheld or hidden, or that something is being said obliquely which could just as well be said directly. The poem derives from a much longer narrative poem called 'The Brother's Dream'. It is, presumably, the dream of a Christian brother, who goes, of his own will, in search of the embodiment of his terror. In an eternal mountain landscape with blasted bristling pine-trees, the savage spirit of that place manifests itself as a huge bear which the frail brother calls out of its cave, and, transformed into 'a steel madman', stabs to the heart. George MacBeth describes this poem (in *Poetry 1900 to 1965*, p. 332) as 'a reworking of the legend of St George and the Dragon in modern psychological terms. The bear is perhaps an image for our animal nature, or more precisely the emotion of fear, which can only be controlled by the ruthless cruelty of the will.'[1]

In 'The Bear' all the externals and particulars fall away. The bear is no longer seen, it is seen through – to the spirit and essence of bears and of the world which created them. If a mountain cave is the pupil in the sleeping eye of the mountain, the cave-bear is 'the gleam in the pupil', the spirit of the mountain. The oldest chapels on earth are those of Neanderthal man in high mountain caves, filled with cave-bear skulls and sacred to the bear as mountain god. Part of the initiatory ordeal of the Eskimo shaman is the acquisition of a mystical faculty for contemplating his own skeleton, and in this he needs the help of a bear to devour his flesh. 'The Bear' is part of Hughes' initiation into the secrets of the earth, a confrontation with that which seems capable of swallowing all we are.

Wodwo differs from the earlier books most obviously in its much bleaker vision, a vision now much closer to Beckett's than to Lawrence's:

> Within seconds the new born baby is lamenting
> That it ever lived.
>
> ('Logos')

In 'Lines To A Newborn Baby', written shortly after the birth of Frieda, Hughes tells her:

> You will find a world tossed into shape
> Like a hatful of twisted lots; locked in shape
>
> As if grown in iron: a stalagmite
> Of history under the blood-drip.

The child will cry all its life in vain

>   for milk
>   From the breast
>   Of the mother
>   Of the God
>   Of the world
>   Made of Blood.
>   ('Karma')

The evidence is everywhere. In 'The Green Wolf' your neighbour lies paralysed

>   While somewhere through a dark heaven
>   The dark bloodclot moves in

like a predator. 'The Green Wolf' is a strange title for a poem in which no wolf appears, and in which there is nothing to explain how a wolf can be green.[2] The wolf, as we saw in discussing *Lupercal*, is one of Hughes' primary symbols of savage, destructive nature. But green is the colour of vegetation and growth. The oxymoron corresponds closely to Dylan Thomas's 'green age':

>   The force that through the green fuse drives the flower
>   Drives my green age.

'The Green Wolf' continues:

>   The punctual evening star,
>   Worse, the warm hawthorn blossoms, their foam,
>
>   Their palls of deathly perfume,
>   Worst of all the beanflower
>   Badged with jet like the ear of the tiger
>
>   Unmake and remake you.

The White Goddess is both Queen of May, when the hawthorn, a tree sacred to her, blossoms, and Queen of Death, both Demeter and Persephone. The scent of the hawthorn blossom is simultaneously deathly (it is still called 'mother-die blossom' in some parts of the country) and erotic. The association of beans with the White Goddess is even closer:

The Pythagorean mystics were bound by a strong taboo against the eating of beans and quoted a verse attributed to Orpheus, to the effect that to eat beans was to eat one's parents' heads. The flower of the bean is white and it blooms at the same season as the hawthorn. The bean is the White Goddess's... The reason for the Orphic taboo was that the bean grows spirally up its prop,

THE ART OF TED HUGHES

portending resurrection, and that ghosts contrived to be reborn as humans by
entering into beans and being eaten by women. (*The White Goddess*, 69)

Hughes would not call it resurrection; simply unmaking and re-
making in a pointless cycle:

> The lips of time leech to the fountainhead
>   ('The Force That Through the Green Fuse')

Hughes believes with Heraclitus that everything is born out of the
death of something else. Heraclitus wrote: 'Mortals are immortals,
and immortals are mortals, the one living the other's death and
dying the other's life.' Hughes quotes him in 'Ghost Crabs':

> They are the powers of this world.
> We are their bacteria,
> Dying their lives and living their deaths.

Heraclitus also believed that Nature was a perpetual flux: 'This
world was ever, is now, and ever shall be an ever-living Fire, with
measures kindling and measures going out.' In 'That Nature is a
Heraclitian Fire and of the Comfort of the Resurrection' Hopkins
wrote:

> Million-fueled, nature's bonfire burns on.

No doubt he knew that 'bonfire' originally meant 'bone-fire':

> Flesh fade, and mortal trash
> Fall to the residuary worm; world's wildfire, leave but ash.

He trusted the Resurrection to lift him out of the fire transformed
into immortal diamond. Hughes can find no such comfort:

>   all
> One smouldering annihilation.

'Still Life' might seem to be a more hopeful, even a religious
poem. Here Hughes takes stone as the most perfect, most self-
sufficient of substances, giving nothing of itself, eternal, itself the
measure of the transience of all other things.

> It expects to be in at the finish.
> Being ignorant of this other, this harebell...

But stone is poverty-stricken, 'hoarding its nothings'. In fact it is

>   imprisoned
> Like nothing in the Universe.
>   ('Pibroch')

There is no such thing as still life. Life 'trembles, as under threats of death'. There is nothing in stone to answer to the blueness of a harebell, which, for all its frailty, is a manifestation of energy, not matter; that is to say, a miracle:

> this harebell,
> That trembles, as under threats of death,
> In the summer turf's heat-rise,
> And in which – filling veins
> Any known name of blue would bruise
> Out of existence – sleeps, recovering,
> The maker of the sea.

The power which sleeps in the veins of the harebell is the power which made the sea, which made the stone, and will ultimately use the roots of the harebell to break the stone. In this cycle of making and unmaking what significance can we attach to beauty?

A companion-piece to 'Still Life' is 'Pibroch', perhaps the ultimate expression of Hughes' vision of the world in *Wodwo*. A pibroch is, in Hughes' words, 'a piece of music for bagpipes, part elegiac, part martial'. The power of this poem derives from its witty but deadly serious anthropomorphism, the attempt to find adequate human terms in which to describe the life of an archetypal landscape of sea, stone, wind and a tree. The sea is 'meaningless', 'bored', 'without purpose'. The stone is 'imprisoned', 'created for black sleep', 'blind'. The wind rushes senselessly over and round, incapable of any relationship.

> Drinking the sea and eating the rock
> A tree struggles to make leaves –
> An old woman fallen from space
> Unprepared for these conditions.
> She hangs on, because her mind's gone completely.

We are challenged, all the time, to reverse these metaphors, to see this landscape as an image of the human condition. If the tree is like a crazy old woman, isn't any person hanging on to barren life as tenaciously as the tree, as crazy as the old woman?

> Minute after minute, aeon after aeon,
> Nothing lets up or develops.
> And this is neither a bad variant nor a tryout.
> This is where the staring angels go through.
> This is where all the stars bow down.

This also is a miracle. The only angels are the forces which, staring without seeing, mad in human terms, pass this way unknowing, intent on other, unknowable purposes or on none, their one path direct through the bones of the living.

If we could see, in imagination or nightmare, these invisible powers, what would they look like? In 'Ghost Crabs' (a poem of great urgency and excitement) Hughes imagines, each nightfall, the sea uncovering

> Giant crabs, under flat skulls, staring inland
> Like a packed trench of helmets.
> Ghosts, they are ghost-crabs.

The comparison of the crabs with flat skulls and helmets suggests helmet crabs, which are not true crabs at all, but extremely primitive creatures of the spider family. Fossils have been found 400 million years old, little different from the living species. The same image reminds us also of the ending of 'Mayday on Holderness':

> The North Sea lies soundless. Beneath it
> Smoulder the wars: to heart-beats, bomb, bayonet,
> 'Mother, Mother!' cries the pierced helmet.
> Cordite oozings of Gallipoli,
>
> Curded to beastings, broached my palate,
> The expressionless gaze of the leopard,
> The coils of the sleeping anaconda,
> The nightlong frenzy of shrews.

Taken together, the two associations suggest the sea as cradle of primitive life-forms, permanent battleground where jaws

> Eat and are finished and the jawbone comes to the beach:
> ...and is now a cenotaph
>
> ('Relic')

and grave of all things. The sea, through all its 'accumulations and changes' ('The Voyage') simply continues the beginning:

> Time in the sea eats its tail, thrives, casts these
> Indigestibles, the spars of purposes
> That failed far from the surface.
>
> ('Relic')

Perhaps the pierced helmets, the broken shells, pursue their frenzied murderous purposes as ghosts, ghost crabs. They can be seen only with the mind's eye:

Their bubbling mouths, their eyes
In a slow mineral fury
Press through our nothingness where we sprawl on our beds,
Or sit in rooms.

They invade our dreams and nightmares.

These crabs own this world.
All night, around us or through us,
They stalk each other, they fasten on to each other,
They mount each other, they tear each other to pieces,
They utterly exhaust each other.
They are the powers of this world.
We are their bacteria,
Dying their lives and living their deaths.

Hughes here vividly dramatizes his sense that there are forces working in us and through us for which we are not ultimately responsible, historical forces, genetic forces:

They are the moil of history, the convulsion
In the roots of blood, in the cycles of concurrence.

The horror of the poem is not only in what the crabs are and do, but in the fact that they are so totally oblivious of the devastating effect they have on the human effort to live in this world:

Their hungers are homing elsewhere.

Crabs are peculiarly apt since they appear to be machines specialized for stalking, fastening, mounting, tearing, kept, in the daytime, at the bottom of the sea, which is also the unconscious. When Eliot's Prufrock cried out to be freed from his disabling self-consciousness so that he could simply grab what he wanted from life, he cried:

I should have been a pair of ragged claws
Scuttling across the floors of silent seas.
('The Love Song of J. Alfred Prufrock')

Though the crabs seem wholly destructive and demonic, they stare and 'go through' like the 'staring angels' of 'Pibroch'. If they are 'God's only toys', it follows that we are not God's toys. God is as unaware of us as the crabs are. For his toy soldiers the world is 'empty battleground'; for him it is empty playground as he childishly, pointlessly, unleashes these murderous toys.

Did God create them? Has he any control over them? A rather

different version of his role is offered in 'Logos'. The Logos, according to Robert Graves, is the secret name of God, the God who existed before creation. Graves suggests that this God was enthroned in place of the White Goddess as a result of a religious revolution initiated by Ezekiel:

> The result of envisaging this god of pure meditation, the Universal Mind still premised by the most reputable modern philosophers, and enthroning him above Nature as essential Truth and Goodness was not an altogether happy one. The new God claimed to be dominant as Alpha and Omega, the Beginning and the End, pure Holiness, pure Good, pure Logic, able to exist without the aid of woman; but it was natural to identify him with one of the original rivals of the Theme and to ally the woman and the other rival permanently against him. The outcome was philosophical dualism with all the tragi-comic woes attendant on spiritual dichotomy. If the True God, the God of the Logos, was pure thought, pure good, whence came evil and error.
> (*The White Goddess*, 465)

The first two stanzas are about this God, the God of perfect strength who is in control of creation. But they contain many suggestions that his creation of man 'was not an altogether happy one'. Creation is seen as the moulding of flesh and blood onto a radiant star, a mystical endless knot (Donne's 'subtil knot which makes us man'), a godly pattern of spiritual perfection (Yeats' 'ghostly paradigm of things'), onto, that is, the Logos itself. But the pentagram is 'blinding' and the body 'frail' – too frail to be able to look upon the radiance within. Far from sharing God's perfect strength, the odds are that the baby will not survive long enough to become a person. God gives us the freedom to have babies, but if our purpose in doing so is to assert a claim to everlasting life, then it is doomed from the start.

> Creation convulses in nightmare. And awaking
> Suddenly tastes the nightmare moving
> Still in its mouth
> And spits it kicking out, with a swinish cry – which is God's first cry.

We are now moving toward the universe of *Crow*, where a whole creation myth is generated by that question: 'whence came evil and error?' This third stanza gives us a version of the birth of God, where in the beginning was creation and nightmare. Even in creation's primeval sleep the nightmare is within it, and the beginning of everything, the first birth, is the spitting out of the nightmare, whose birth cry – gross and degraded – is the first cry of the now incarnate God, appropriately 'swinish' since his mother, creation, is none other than the White Goddess or Sow Goddess who eats her own young.

As soon as 'ancient law' and all the 'truths' of the well-meaning God of the Logos descend into matter, they are broken down by the still more ancient powers of nature which are inimical to all laws and truths and whose highest purpose is to streamline its killers so as to destroy the more efficiently everything it creates – creates, apparently, for the purpose of destroying.

> God is a good fellow, but his Mother's against him.

God has the best of intentions, but he is at odds with a goddess older and still stronger than himself.

'Reveille' is a rude awakening of Adam and Eve to sexuality and death.

> No, the serpent was not
> One of God's ordinary creatures.

God had never intended there to be this creature in the world, and its purpose was not God's. Eden was God's dream. The reality was the nightmare to which Adam and Eve awoke. The serpent is also the great dragon which holds the world in its coils, poisoning, crushing, burning, the principle of corruption in all things:

> The black, thickening river of his body
> Glittered in giant loops
> Around desert mountains and away
> Over the ashes of the future.

In 'Endgame' Hamm tells of a madman, a painter, who thought the end of the world had come:

I'd take him by the hand and drag him to the window. Look! There! All that rising corn! And there! Look! The sails of the herring fleet! All that loveliness! He'd snatch away his hand and go back into his corner. Appalled. All he had seen was ashes.

All the loveliness is in fact a mere dream, an illusion, to the artist or prophet, the man who is aware of the skull beneath the skin and the vanity of everything under the sun. The end of the world is always with us, since the principle of self-destruction was within it from the beginning, the worm in the bud, the serpent in Eden.

In 'Theology' (inspired by Popa's 'The heart of the quartz pebble') Hughes goes further. The serpent did not simply corrupt humanity, he swallowed it:

> Adam ate the apple.
> Eve ate Adam.
> The serpent ate Eve.
> This is the dark intestine.

'This', of course, is the world as we know it. God, it seems, cannot kill the serpent to release his prime creation from sin and death. He can only call, peevishly, 'Adam, where art thou?'

'Gog' is the fullest (and most difficult) exploration in *Wodwo* of the relationship between God, man and the serpent, here called Gog, who is identified with the Dragon of the Book of Revelation:

It ended by being about the dragon in Revelations that's waiting under the woman in heaven, between the sun and moon, waiting for her to deliver the child with its mouth open. (*The Poet Speaks*, 90)

> I awoke to a shout: 'I am Alpha and Omega'.

In *Revelation* Gog is awoken by Satan, but here it is God's claim to be the first and the last which wakes him. If God, the God of the Logos, is all, what is Gog? It is God's claim to be everything and yet to exclude the World, the Flesh and the Devil, which provokes into wakefulness and destructive activity the sleeping dragon, which is all that is not Logos.

> The dog's god is a scrap dropped from the table.
> The mouse's saviour is a ripe wheat grain.
> Hearing the Messiah cry
> My mouth widens in adoration.

Gog does not worship Holiness and Truth and Logic; he worships food, like all the creatures of earth. When he hears the birth-cry of Christ, 'the dragon stood before the woman which was ready to be delivered, for to devour her child as soon as it was born' (Book of Revelation, 12: 4). Lichens, air and dust have no mouths to fill. But Gog has no choice. He is not responsible for his massive bones, his teeth, his terrible appearance and jarring song, nor for the trail of destruction he leaves behind him.

The implication is that if God had not made his claim to be the Logos, Alpha and Omega, thus denying the existence of Gog, Gog would have slept on. His awakening is therefore like that of Yeats' 'rough beast' in 'The Second Coming':

> The darkness drops again; but now I know
> That twenty centuries of stony sleep
> Were vexed to nightmare by a rocking cradle,

> And what rough beast, its hour come round at last,
> Slouches towards Bethlehem to be born?

Part I of 'Gog' first appeared in 1961, Part III as 'The Knight' in 1966, and Part II not until *Wodwo* itself in 1967. The three parts are very difficult to relate. In Part II we have a vision of a world which belongs to death, dust and nothingness.

> Then whose
> Are these
> Eyes,
>   eyes and
> Dance of wants,
> Of offering?

The clue comes in the last line when we are told that all created things are 'her mirrors'. Who, then, is 'she'? The only woman in the poem so far is the weeping mother who has lost her son to Gog. She was neither dancing nor offering. Only Gog was dancing. Part III gives us some help. The Knight's enemy is woman and dragon, woman and dragon, it comes slowly clear, in alliance against him, virtually indistinguishable from one another. The woman's weeping turns into a secret laughter, a smile, a seductive glance, a 'ribboned gift', a kiss:

> Shield him from the dipped glance, flying in half light, that tangles
>   the heels,
> The grooved kiss that swamps the eyes with darkness.

The Knight is fighting to come clear of woman, whose smile is in her belly, whose womb is a 'tireless mouth', a 'fanged grail', an 'octopus maw', whose womb, in other words, is the mouth of Gog.

> Bring him clear of the flung web and the coil that vaults from the
>   dust.

The flung web is love, the coil is 'this mortal coil' (the body encircling and entangling the soul) and also the serpent or dragon reared up waiting to swallow the new-born child. The dragon is incarnation and therefore death and therefore reincarnation to keep the cycle going – Karma.

> Death is not failure and cease
> But clean back to a fresh start
> Laying the original wide open
> Like a bitch on heat
>   a secret laughter
>   ('As Woman's Weeping')

75

The Knight, like Crow after him, is taking the 'Examination at the Womb Door' the purpose of which is to close the womb door, to avoid reincarnation, to break out of the greedy dream, the illusion of the life of the senses, the dance, and try to reach the light, the Logos.

The main obstacle is Woman, woman as mother, as fallen Eve, as Whore of Babylon, as spurned Venus, as revengeful White Goddess, as Gog waking within her every Spring:

> My mouth is the despair of God
> Formed only for men.
>
> The serpent remains earthen, brutishly-veined,
> Rooted in crevices, living on flies and men –
>
> The serpent that should have strangled me
> And then eaten itself.
>
> I sing, stamping the gruelling drum-beat
> To renew fallen men.
>
> Love is weak to protect as webs.
>
> In April my body begins to frighten me
> And my sleep fills with weeping –
>
> Again and again the forced grave of men.
> ('Fallen Eve')

Thus the poem is a battle between Gog and woman on the one hand, God and man on the other, exactly the battle described by Graves in *The White Goddess*.

The Messiah who is born in the New Testament Revelation is to 'rule with a rod of iron', (or in Moffat's translation 'shepherd with an iron flail'). He grows up to be the horseman of iron:

And I saw heaven opened, and behold a white horse; and he that sat upon him was called Faithful and True, and in righteousness he doth judge and make war.

And he was clothed with a vesture dipped in blood: and his name is called The Word of God.

And out of his mouth goeth a sharp sword, that with it he should smite the nations: and he shall rule them with a rod of iron. (Book of Revelation, 19: 11, 13, 15)

The lance and the grail were the great male and female sexual symbols of the pagan fertility religions. As the serpent, another phallic symbol, was degraded and denied and thrown out of heaven as Lucifer, so in the new religion of the dead body, the lance and grail became mere relics of the crucifixion. Here the grail is restored to its original meaning, but becomes the enemy the Knight rides against. His phallus is transformed into a destructive lance-blade or gunsight. No doubt, like Calvin, he has iron arteries too. Like Blake's visionless crazed God, Urizen, this Messiah seeks to live by and impose on others

> the ruled slab, the octaves of order,
> The law and mercy of number.

As in Blake, as in Lawrence, the energies he denies rear up against him:

> The sun erupts. The moon is deader than a skull.
> ('Gog')

> My heavens are brass my earth is iron my moon a clod of clay
> My sun a pestilence burning at noon and vapour of death in night
> (Blake, *The Four Zoas*)

If we get out of contact and harmony with the sun and moon, then both turn into great dragons of destruction against us. (Lawrence, *Apocalypse*)[3]

He finds he cannot destroy the dragon without destroying life itself. Since the serpent's coil is 'under his ribs' the horseman is seeking to destroy an essential part of himself:

And the vital twist, the mysterious chemical change that converts the resisting high-minded puritan to the being of murder and madness, is that occult crossover of Nature's maddened force – like a demon – into the brain that had rejected her...

Coriolanus, looking at his wife and mother, sees the Roman mob who want to tear him to pieces, and begins to act like a madman...(*A Choice of Shakespeare's Verse*, 192–3)

> He will need to be strong
> To follow his weapons towards the light.
> Unlike Coriolanus, follow the blades right through Rome...
> ('Gog')

This Hughes sees as the basic psychology of Fascism (which is what 'Gog' began by being about). He will need to be strong to overcome

> The whorish dragon of the dark ages
> Helmed with a modern capital and devouring
> Virginal St George as a flower.
> ('Humanities')

She is 'the real deity of Medieval England, the Celtic pre-Christian goddess, with her tail wound round those still very much alive pre-Christian and non-Christian worlds'. She is 'the old Mediterranean serpent goddess, the Anathema of the Old Testament'. This 'Queen of Heaven who was the goddess of natural law and of love, who was the goddess of all sensation and organic life – this overwhelmingly powerful, multiple, primaeval being, was dragged into court by the young Puritan Jehovah' (*A Choice of Shakespeare's Verse*, 186–7). The trial of strength continues. But in the Queen's armoury there are many 'empty armours, at attention, loyal St Georges surviving the worm and the virgin, faces open for inspection' ('The Wound').

Despite the fact that it contains five stories and a play in addition to the poems, *Wodwo* is a far more unified work than its predecessors, as Hughes himself claims in his prefatory note:

> The stories and the play in this book may be read as notes, appendix and unversified episodes of the events behind the poems, or as chapters of a single adventure to which the poems are commentary and amplification. Either way, the verse and the prose are intended to be read together, as parts of a single work.

I propose to look now at the stories and the play, to try to determine what they have in common, and then to see to what extent the poems relate to the same 'single adventure'.

The earliest of these stories is 'The Rain Horse'. It is an exercise in the Lawrence manner, drawing heavily on Ursula's encounter with the horses at the end of *The Rainbow*.[4] Nevertheless it is distinctively Hughes. A young man returns nostalgically to a once familiar landscape. But he has changed a lot in twelve years. The land no longer recognizes him. He feels an outcast. He loses his way, ruins his shoes in mud, fears for his new suit as it begins to rain. – 'He had come too far' – too far from the comfort and familiarity of his ordinary urban life. He finds himself, like the protagonists of 'The Hawk in the Rain', and 'November', exposed to the elements. He can find some shelter from the rain, but none from the rain-horse, the malevolent spirit of this non-human world into which he has wandered. The horse murderously attacks him, again and again, with an occult foreknowledge of his movements.

The man insists on bringing his rational intelligence to bear, trying to account for the horse's malice, predict its movements and outwit it, while the horse obviously inhabits a reality not subject to such reasoning. 'Its whinnying snort and the spattering whack of its hooves seemed to be actually inside his head...' He is running from and fighting against something he carries within him, which he can only escape from by damaging his heart and cutting out an important part of his brain. In a sense he had already done that, and this is what provokes these powers to such malevolence against him. He is tame. He has taken it for granted that horses are tame, either working or making their contribution to the picturesque landscape. This landscape refuses to gratify him by being picturesque. It is part of his own life he has denied which turns against him.[5]

In 'The Harvesting' Grooby has waited far too long in the sweltering heat for the hare to break from the dwindling square of wheat. He has ignored all the signs of sunstroke and has already fallen almost under the blades of the cutter. At last the hare breaks and it is a race between Grooby and the colliers' dogs. He fires and falls, struck by blackness:

One need possessed him. It drove him to struggle up the hill. None of his limbs belonged to him any more, and he wondered if he still lay in the wheat and whether the cutter blades had indeed gone over him. But loudest of all he heard the dogs. The dogs were behind him with their inane yapping. He began to shout at them and shouted louder than ever when he heard the sound that twisted from his throat, the unearthly thin scream. Then the enormous white dog's head opened beside him, and he felt as if he had been picked up and flung and lost awareness of everything save the vague, pummelling sensations far off in the blankness and silence of his body.

The epigraph:

> And I shall go into a hare
> With sorrow and sighs and mickle care

is a witch spell for turning oneself into a hare. The next stanza begins:

> Hare, take heed of a bitch greyhound
> Will harry thee all these fells around.

Grooby, as his human consciousness blacks out with sunstroke and the blow of his gun's recoil, finds himself gone into the hare that moment caught by the dogs.

'Sunday' begins with an evocation of a stifling scrubbed Sunday morning in Mytholmroyd, the church-going slopes spotless and

THE ART OF TED HUGHES

harmless, forbidden grass in the Memorial Gardens, even the pavements 'untouchably proper'. The men wear 'tight blue pin-stripe suits' and Michael wears his 'detestable blue blazer'. Sitting in chapel is the situation of greatest constraint he knows, and he shuts his eyes, letting his imagination fill his mind (as it always does on such occasions) with the image of a wolf which 'urged itself with all its strength through a land empty of everything but trees and snow'. The wolf is that in him which refuses to be constrained, tamed, disciplined, like those Vikings, 'the snow's stupefied anvils', who spent themselves in 'beforehand revenge'.

> For the gruelling relapse and prolongueur of their blood
> Into the iron arteries of Calvin,
>   ('The Warriors of the North')

that which draws him away from chapel and the Sunday routine and respectability towards Top Wharf Pub, where, his father has told him, a man called Billy Red will kill rats in his teeth like a terrier. The thought of that savagery, that closeness of the human to the animal world, obsesses the boy and reduces everything else in his consciousness to unreality. When he hears the rat scream 'his stomach began to twist and flex like a thick muscle'. After its death 'he put his hand to his scalp and pressed the scorch down into his skull, but that didn't seem to connect with the dull, thick pain'. He runs, speechless, through a land empty of everything but that pain.

Michael's problem is partly sexual. He cannot relate the wolf which roams in his imagination or the killing of the rat to the Sunday world of respectability and demure girls in floral dresses. Billy Red's fascination for the watchers is the fascination of someone who is too close to the animal world for those who are too far from it. His counterpart is the girl who ignored Michael, 'perched on the last ten inches of the bench, arranged her wide-skirted, summery, blue-flowered frock over her knees, and busied herself with her mirror'. She cannot remain in Billy Red's world even as spectator. Michael cannot run away from it. He carries it within him.

'The Suitor' is about a boy, perhaps Michael a few years later, in the grip of an infatuation for a girl. Instinct has dragged him miles in the rain, late at night, to her street, in the hope of merely glimpsing her. But another man is also waiting in the rain for her.

Both stealthily, separately, enter her garden. As he crouches straining every sense, suddenly the boy hears, not a yard behind him,
the sound of a flute: 'I express my amazement by pulling a slow,
skin-stretching grimace, a contorting leopard-mask, in the pitch
darkness. I hold it, as the flute-notes play over my brain.' We
remember that the rain horse first appeared to the man 'like a
nightmarish leopard'. Hughes wrote of a jaguar: 'He is an ancient
symbol of Dionysus, since he is a leopard raised to the ninth
power' (*London Magazine*, January 1971, 8). To the Greeks the
panther was a mythical beast, half leopard, half lion, sacred to
Dionysus. Etymologically, 'panther' means, in Greek, 'all-beast'.
Its name also associates it with Pan, whose flute here plays over
the brain of his leopard-masked initiate.[6]

The poem 'Heatwave' in *Recklings* describes the uncharted
silence of sunstruck London and continues:

> Men can't penetrate it. Till sundown
> Releases its leopard
>
> Over the roofs, and women are suddenly
> Everywhere, and the walker's bones
>
> Melt in the coughing of great cats.

In 'The Wound'[7] the walker is a young soldier with a bullet hole
right through his head, accompanied by his sergeant who is dead.
The path crosses a black icy river. As they cross and approach a
ruined château they are watched by women who laugh. The
laughter turns to a wail, then a yap, a barking, which passes between them disembodied. As the Queen ushers them in to the
banquet, there is the baying and snarling and howling of dogs and
the screeching and squealing of pigs. The uproar turns into the
shrieking laughter of the women. The Queen offers them 'peacock,
snipe, woodcock, quail, black-cock, game-cock and cock starlings.
Dogfish, catfish and assorted shellfish. Cod and conger, gudgeon
and sturgeon...eels...duck, a hare, a boar and a roebuck.' Most
of these are either aphrodisiacs or creatures sacred to fertility
deities, or both. The quail, for example, was associated with lust.
Graves tells us 'that the Phoenician Hercules, Melkarth, died
yearly and that the quail was his bird of resurrection' (*White
Goddess*, 133). The hare was sacred 'because it is very swift, very
prolific – even conceives when already pregnant – and mates
openly without embarrassment' (*White Goddess*, 293). Pigs were

THE ART OF TED HUGHES

particularly sacred to the Moon-goddess because they 'vary between white, reddish and black, feed on corpse-flesh, are prolific but eat their own young, and their tusks are crescent-shaped' (*White Goddess*, 222). The roebuck was the guardian of the secret (the name of the deity) in the sacred grove. In the reaction away from the worship of the Moon-goddess many of these creatures became taboo foods in many cultures.

Ripley refuses the burnt offerings ('birds gone black, fish curling their ends up, fumigants not food'). He refuses red meat also: 'I get nightmares being eaten by bulls.'[8]

He is a vegetarian:

> Fearful of the hare with the manners of a lady,
> Of the sow's loaded side and the boar's brown fang,
> Fearful of the bull's tongue snaring and rending,
> And of the sheep's jaw moving without mercy,
> Tripped on Eternity's stone threshold.
>   Staring into the emptiness,
> Unable to move, he hears the hounds of the grass.
>
> ('A Vegetarian')

The hounds of the grass are what Ripley also hears at the château. He, like all creatures, is doomed ultimately to be dismembered. At one point the women, like the frenzied Bacchantes in *The Bacchae*, dismember Sergeant Massey. The men have crossed the Styx. This Queen is also 'the Queen of Hell, in which aspect her wild boar is the demon of destruction and death. In that form she is also Hecate, Goddess of witchcraft, all magical operations, the underworld, spirits, the moon, darkness, hounds, etc.' (*A Choice of Shakespeare's Verse*, 189). She is the leprosy-white goddess, nightmare and incubus; her other colours are the red of shed blood and the black of the grave and nothingness. But this triple-Goddess is dual in all her colours. White is also the colour of the new shoot, red of love, and black of divination. It is a girl who leads Ripley out of the château and gets him walking again. He is found muttering 'Will you marry me.'

Unlike Sergeant Massey, Ripley has not, in fact, died. 'What are you doing here?' the Queen asks him. And the women never touch him. 'I came back without a hand, but my comrade was devoured' says the epigraph. Ripley comes back with his terrible wound, leaving Massey and all his other comrades to be devoured by the women, their partners in the Dance of Death. 'He must have walked over nine miles with that lot, straight towards us. That's animal instinct for you.'

'The Wound' moves into and out of a surrealistic world. 'Snow' is wholly surrealistic and calls in question the very existence of a normal world to return to. The protagonist is an even worse case than Ripley. He has been wandering through a perpetual snowstorm for five months without food. He has no memory of a time when he was not walking through a twilight of snow. He seems to have 'dropped out of nothing casually' as Wodwo puts it. But, unlike Wodwo, he has a highly developed mind which he seeks to anchor in his 'reasonable hopes', his 'system of confidence' based on the facts which he takes to be on his side. The facts are that there is something firm enough to support him under his feet from which he deduces that he is on a planet and not in the gulf. The atmosphere is breathable, from which he deduces that he is on Earth. His physical shape is what he feels it ought to be – it corresponds to the images of his dreams. And then there is his excellent clothing and his chair, from which he deduces another world than this world of snow, a world of civilization, of purposive human activities and relationships. This is the world he dreams about and is obliged to think of as 'the world as it is' – reality, because if the world of snow were the real world 'I could have known no purpose in continuing the ordeal. I could only have looked, breathed and died, like a nestling fallen from the nest.' But in 'the world as it is' nestlings do fall from the nest:

So this year a swift's embryo, cracked too early from its fallen egg –
There, among mineral fragments,
The blind blood stirred,
Freed,

And, mystified, sank into hopeful sleep.

('Small Events')

Mystified is what this man refuses to be. Logic is his lifeline. The chair testifies to the reality of the world it comes from, predicates the entire Universe. How can there be a chair without a carpenter? How can there be consciousness without identity? At this point the story becomes a Kafkaesque satire on rationalism. In *Metamorphosis* Gregor Samsa, having woken up to find himself turned into a beetle, says to himself: 'I'd better get up, since my train goes at five.'

Hughes' hero, having described his hands and feet as 'so black and shrunken on the bone' that 'one could believe I was several hundred years old, or even dead', goes on 'I have my job to get back to, and my mother and father will be in despair'. Yet he realizes that he must not trust logic too far:

> If I were to take this drift of thoughts to the logical extreme there is no abso-lute proof that my job, my parents, Helen and the whole world are not simply my own invention, fantasies my imagination has improvized on the simple themes of my own form, my clothes, my chair, and the properties of my present environment.

He falls back on 'conviction, faith', his last defence against 'a huge futility' which threatens to grip him. He has reached, in Nietzsche's words in *The Birth of Tragedy*, 'those outer limits where the optimism implicit in logic must collapse. When the inquirer, having pushed to the circumference, realizes how logic in that place curls about itself and bites its own tail, he is struck with a new kind of perception.' He is on the brink of the Absurd.

'Cogito ergo sum' proves nothing, since the 'I' which is to be proved is already present in the proposition 'I think'. The argu-ment is circular. Descartes nowhere proves that thought requires a thinker. That Hughes should use the phrase 'this drift of thoughts' surely leads us to relate the man's thoughts to the snow-flakes (which he begins to call to and give the names of people). The snowflakes are thoughts, words, people, experiences, mo-ments. In Beckett's *Endgame* they are the millet grains of Zeno's paradox, which can never be completely transferred from one pile to another, half the pile at a time, since, there being no highest number, there can be no smallest fraction:

> Then babble, babble, words, like the solitary child who turns himself into children, two, three, so as to be together, and whisper together, in the dark. Moment upon moment, pattering down, like the millet grains of... that old Greek, and all life long you wait for that to mount up to a life. (*Endgame*)

And that life is 'a vast grey dissolution' and a patter of small events half of which are deaths. Hamm calls, as though to the man in the snow: 'Use your head, can't you, use your head, you're on earth, there's no cure for that' (*Endgame*). Pozzo calls to him: 'One day like any other day, one day he went dumb, one day I went blind, one day will go deaf, one day we were born, one day will die, the same day, the same second, is that not enough for you?

(*Waiting for Godot*). Hughes calls to him: 'Where are you head-ing? Everything is already here' ('You Drive in a Circle').

The 'single adventure' in these prose pieces is clear. In each case the protagonist, in a moment of crisis or state of extremity, loses his hold on habit, on the day-to-day 'reality' of work and play, peaceful Sundays, chapel, pin-stripe suits, suburban streets; loses his hold on the mind which insists on the reality of this world. Thus diminished and defenceless, another reality invades the vacuum of his brain. The man in 'The Rain Horse' only escapes when he submits to the 'superior guidance' of his most primitive instinct. Afterwards he 'just sat staring at the ground, as if some important part had been cut out of his brain'.

In 'The Harvesting' the brain is blacked out by the sun, then supplanted by the consciousness of a hunted hare. In 'Sunday' the screeching of the rat is not in the same world as the pleasant Sunday scene:

> supplanting every human brain inside its skull with a rat-body that knots and unknots.
>
> ('Song of a Rat')

In 'The Suitor' Pan himself fills the boy's brain with an 'inane ecstasy'. In 'The Wound', Ripley's brain is supplanted first by a bullet, then by 'animal instinct', then by images of the powers of the Great Outer Darkness, ('which is the same as the small inner darkness'). And in 'Snow' the protagonist's brain hangs on, madly refusing to acknowledge the void.

The boy Michael in 'Sunday' grew up to write 'Song of a Rat'. The rat in extremity, in the grip of death, stands on the threshold between two worlds, the world of dogs, traps, and a vulnerable body, meaning living and dying, and the world of disembodied spirits and powers which know nothing of space and time, life and consciousness. Here

> The rat is in the trap...
>
> Iron jaws, strong as the whole earth
> Are stealing its backbone.

The rat cannot reconcile itself to suffering as man has tried to do, by inventing some larger purpose in terms of which suffering, even one's own, can be accepted, by inventing such evasive sophistries as:

'This has no face, it must be God'

or

'No answer is also an answer'.

The rat can only confront the horror, which is all pain and death.
For him there can be no distinction between understanding and
experience. He can understand death only by dying.

> The rat understands suddenly. It bows and is still,
> With a little beseeching of blood on its nose-end.

Section II, 'The Rat's Vision', expands on that understanding.
What the rat sees at that moment is the earth as a vast design of
dereliction, like a no-man's-land, in mourning for its losses, anti-
cipating nothing but further losses. The land is 'widowed'. The
old barbed wire and 'trenched' gateway complete the suggestion
of a deserted battlefield given over to wind and snow.

> The rat screeches
> And 'Do not go' cry the dandelions, from their heads of folly
> And 'Do not go' cry the yard cinders, who have no future, only their
>   infernal aftermath
> And 'Do not go' cries the cracked trough by the gate, fatalist of star-
>   light and zero
> 'Stay' says the arrangement of stars
> Forcing the rat's head down into godhead.

The dandelions are finished, mere clocks now caught in the one-
way process, the trap. The cinders are already burned out. The
trough holds no water and so is doomed to futility and emptiness.
They cry, 'do not go' to the rat, but they have gone themselves,
for going is the system. The Universe is so arranged that life, in
saying 'stay', opens its iron jaws for the kill.

The final section 'The Rat's Flight', follows the rat beyond
death into his godhead. 'The horned Shadow of the Rat' crosses
into power, leaving the rat's body as

> A bloody gift for the dogs
> While it supplants Hell.

It needs the whole weight of universal law to force his head
down. He puts up such resistance that when he does let go, his
soul catapults from him across the gulf with such velocity that it
jolts the stars in their sockets and consumes the flames of hell. The
fires of hell are continually recharged thus with the flames of
Nature's bonfire.

Gnats are living sparks of that bonfire. 'Gnat-Psalm' is one of the most successful poems in *Wodwo*. At one level it is a marvellous evocation of a swarm of gnats:

> Scribbling on the air, sparring sparely,
> Scrambling their crazy lexicon.

The very words of the title, 'gnat' and 'psalm', with their clusters of surplus consonants, are a joy to players of Lexicon or Scrabble. Half the letters are quite without substance and seem to have come together by a process of shuffling. The dance is interpreted as the writing of illegible ephemeral messages on the air, then as

> Immense magnets fighting around a centre

but finally not as dancing or writing or fighting but as singing the song of themselves and of 'all the suns', the song of themselves as suns, as sources of brimming energy not to be blotted out by the earth's sun.

Their vision is very like the rat's vision, a vision of a world emptied of life, through which the wind howls and dances its death dance. But their song is quite unlike the rat's song. The rat's body anchors him in that world; the separation from it is an agony and a violation. The gnat-god, like every other, has been crucified, nailed to the cross of the physical world, which holds the body while the soul is torn from it. But it is so almost-bodiless ('its skin thin as the skin of fire' as 'Fire-Eater' put it), its connection with the solid world so tenuous that the cross is but air. It is nailed to nothing and the nails in its hands and feet do not stop them from dancing.

Gnats are nailed to their own dancing bodies, which with their mummy faces and the dangling legs of victims are already ridden to death. Their dance is not a violation or an agony. It is what they live for – to burn themselves up, to ride their own bodies to death. The vegetarian

> Tripped on Eternity's stone threshold

and heard 'the hounds of the grass'. But the gnats, living on air, are so insubstantial and weightless

> their agility
> Has outleaped that threshold
> And hangs them a little above the claws of the grass...

The rat had to cross into power over that terrible threshold of death. The gnats' hold on life is so tenuous that death is no matter. They are spirits already

> You are the angels of the only heaven!
> And God is an Almighty Gnat!

In Ionesco's *The Chairs*, the orator arrives to bring to a world whose cities 'faded right away' four hundred thousand years ago the secret of life, the occult doctrine, the key to the mystery. He turns out to be dumb, but chalks on a blackboard the word ANGEPAIN, Angelbread, then, as if equally significant, NNAA NNM NWNWNW V. Then, rubbing all this out, he writes ΛΑDIEU ΛDIEU ΛPΛ. Getting no reaction, since the room is empty, he leaves, disgruntled.

The gnats shuffle their 'dumb Cabala' (an oxymoron, since the Cabala was a purely oral tradition), rub out everything they write, jerk their letters into knots and tangles. Thus God reveals himself and his secrets, in the paradoxes of angels and pain, angels and bread, spirit and substance, power and helplessness, godhead and absence. What can human hands, tongue, brain accomplish in the face of such a God.

The poem ends with these vivid and expressive images and freely mimetic rhythms:

> My hands fly in the air, they are follies
> My tongue hangs up in the leaves
> My thoughts have crept into crannies
>
> Your dancing
>
> Your dancing
> Rolls my staring skull slowly away into outer space.

'Skylarks' is the most assured and accomplished of the larger poems in *Wodwo*. It is one of the great poems of the language. Quickly the poem is into its striking descriptive metaphors:

> Barrel-chested for heights,
> Like an Indian of the high Andes,
>
> A whippet head, barbed like a hunting arrow...

But before it can generate any rhythmic impetus and really launch the skylark, the rhythm drags it down again with struggling, leaden lines:

> But leaden
> With muscle
> For the struggle
> Against
> Earth's centre.

Shelley, assuming the skylark's song to be an expression of care-less rapture, and feeling that no creature of earth could know such pure delight and 'ignorance of pain', is driven to call his skylark an 'unbodied joy', a 'blithe Spirit'. Hughes, on the contrary, starts from the bird of muscle, blood and bone, feathers thrashing, lungs gasping, heart 'drumming like a motor', voicebox grinding like a concrete-mixer, and cannot believe that such climbing and sing-ing can be done for joy.

> And singing still dost soar, and soaring ever singest

wrote Shelley. Why, and at what cost, Hughes asks.

Lead is the heaviest of the earth's substances, the most inimical to flight. But in its struggle against gravity the lark needs sub-stantial muscles; it needs ballast if it is not to be wrecked by the storms of its own breath as the gaspings 'rip in and out':

> Leaden
> Like a bullet
> To supplant
> Life from its centre.

Life's centre, its only home, is the earth. Insubstantial ephemeral creatures such as gnats seem almost independent of it, but most creatures hang on, with mindless grip. The rat, try as it might, cannot uproot itself into its screeching. When its grip is broken by death, it rockets away from the earth. But the skylark can, with-out dying, launch off from earth in the body, uproot itself into its song, then fling that song like a sacrifice to the sun. But life's centre is also within, and to supplant that with a bullet is suicidal. Skylarks are 'crueller than owl or eagle' because their 'one path is direct through the bones of the living' ('Hawk Roosting') but, unlike a predator, the bones are their own. And what

> Gives their days this bullet and automatic
> Purpose?   ('Thrushes')

The image of the head 'barbed like a hunting arrow' now generates the deeper image 'shot through the crested head'. The barb is what fixes there the command

> Not die
>
> But climb
>
> Climb
>
> Sing
>
> Obedient as to death a dead thing.

Why should the command begin 'Not die', as though the command to die might have been expected? The earth is sending the skylarks to be 'burned out', 'sucked empty' by the sun. In 'The Crown', Lawrence describes it thus: 'It is a leap taken into the beyond, as a lark leaps into the sky, a fragment of earth which travels to be fused out, sublimated, in the shining of the heavens' (*Phoenix* II, 374). 'Fused out', 'sublimated', 'burned out' – what Lawrence and Hughes are both here trying to convey is surely a process of separating out the physical and the spiritual, body and soul, the soul to be taken up into the heavens, the body flung back to earth ('a gift for the dogs'), a process of breaking down

> Like a breaker of ocean milling the shingle,

of total abandonment:

> I suppose you just gape and let your gaspings
> Rip in and out through your voice box

of giving up the ghost. But the skylark is commanded to do this *without dying*, and to live at that pitch is agony, self-immolation, crucifixion. By the time we come to the song itself

> Joy! Help! Joy! Help!

it is 'Joy!' not 'Help!' which needs explaining.[9]

The watching poet loses sight and sound of the lark, now given over to the sun. It is as though the lark has crossed, for a moment, the threshold, the impossible gulf, leaving the earth also 'fused out' to its dross, irredeemably mere dust and clay, and the poet, wingless, enfolded by it:

> The lark is evaporating
> Till my eye's gossamer snaps
> and my hearing floats back widely to earth
>
> After which the sky lies blank open
> Without wings, and the earth is a folded clod.

Is it fanciful to hear an echo in these lines of Keats' 'Ode to a Nightingale':

Now more than ever seems it rich to die,
To cease upon the midnight with no pain
While thou art pouring for thy soul abroad
In such an ecstasy!
Still wouldst thou sing, and I have ears in vain –
To thy high requiem become a sod.

The word 'folded' has several layers of suggestion: the earth folded in its time-bound geological strata; the earth with folded arms, ignoring the lark's cries for help with a foolish smile; but primarily, the earth with folded wings, pretending that flight is impossible, that there are no such things as skylarks. Is the earth hoping that its little missionaries will convert heaven to its own pointless processes?

At last the earth recalls them

and they stoop

And maybe the whole agony was for this

The plummeting dead drop

With long cutting screams buckling like razors

These lines describe quite literally the most spectacular but least familiar phase of the lark's flight. But the language takes us also beyond the literal. 'Stoop' is normally used of birds of prey stooping for the kill. The primary meaning of the word, in any case, is 'to bow down'. Razors would normally be folded or closed like wings. Here they are cutting to kill. What is being described here is a suicide-dive. 'The earth gives them the O.K.' means that they need no longer climb and sing but may now die and end their agony. But as their singing itself was, in its total self-abandonment, a little death, a miming of death, so too the suicide-dive is a mime, stopping just short of mixing their heart's blood with the mire of the land, able to stop short only perhaps, because they are now 'weightless', already sucked empty by the bloodthirsty sun.

I have deliberately ignored so far the poem's wit and humour, never more evident than in section VII. It is a sign of Hughes' new assurance that he feels he can afford not to be portentous or bullying, that he can be assumed to be taking himself seriously without having to be seen to be doing so. The poem itself is 'folded' in that it can be read simply as the record and rendering of the experience of watching and listening to larks 'all the dreary Sunday morning', or as a little myth as I have read it. And the two are not kept apart. Hughes weaves in and out. At the end, for example, he suddenly flares and glides off from the suicide-dive to witty, accurate observation of the skylarks in a tone of affectionate anthropomorphic banter.

> But just before they plunge into the earth
> They flare and glide off low over grass, then up
> To land on a wall-top, crest up,
>
> Weightless,
> Paid-up,
> Alert,
>
> Conscience perfect.

If the agony was not for suicide, then it was for *this*, for just being skylarks at one with the world. Hughes exploits the disparity between the real birds and the symbolic drama he has cast them in for comic purposes. But the disparity is there outside the poem and won't go away. What does it mean to be a skylark? Are they mad or are we?

So evocative and lucid and accessible is this poem at one level that many reviewers and critics have been betrayed into praising it for its charm. Possibly in order to make this response impossible Hughes added two new sections in *Selected Poems*. The new section IV describes the lark at the top of his flight as

> Like a mouse with drowning fur
> Bobbing and bobbing at the well-wall
>
> Lamenting, mounting a little –

stressing again the death theme. The other new section, section VIII, transforms the poem by giving it a new ending which, instead of returning us reassuringly to the self-satisfied larks, opens out the myth to relate directly to Celtic mythology in the figure of Cuchulain.

> Manacled with blood,
> Cuchulain listened bowed,
> Strapped to his pillar (not to die prone)
> Hearing the far crow
> Guiding the near lark nearer
> With its blind song
>
> *'That some sorry little wight more feeble and misguided than thyself*
> *Take thy head*
> *Thine ear*
> *And thy life's career from thee.'*

Cuchulain is the type of the hero, blinded by honour, who uses his superhuman strength to resist death. Though he is doomed from the start, his death foreknown, he believes that his courage will win him undying fame. He is invincible, but not invulnerable. He can only be overcome by magic or treachery. Even when he is strapped to a pillar and bleeding his life away, his enemies dare not approach to finish him (by beheading him) until Morrigu, the crow-headed Goddess of War, perches on his shoulder.

Cuchulain is like 'The Contender' in *Crow*:

> There was this man and he was the strongest
> Of the strong.
> He gritted his teeth like a cliff.
> Though his body was sweeling away like a torrent on a cliff
> Smoking towards dark gorges
> There he nailed himself with nails of nothing
>
> ('The Contender')

It is a 'senseless trial of strength'. He is as mad as the old woman in 'Pibroch' who 'hangs on because her mind's gone completely'.

The skylarks have also been 'sucked empty', have battered out their last sparks at the limit, but not for fame, not in resistance to life's imperatives, but in blind obedience and self-abandonment. Their song tells Cuchulain that, though he is 'the strongest of the strong' he is feeble in relation to the non-human powers he resists and totally misguided in that resistance. The lark blinded by the sun and guided by the bird of death, the crow, curses him with the curse he most dreads – that his death shall not be glorious, but humiliating.[10] The lark's words are a translation of part of a Gaelic charm.

This new closing section seems to be a Crow poem, or even a Prometheus poem (Prometheus and Cuchulain having much in common) arbitrarily tacked on to the ending of 'Skylarks' and different from it not only in subject matter but also in style and tone.

Perhaps Hughes wanted to guard against the possibility of a sentimental reading of 'Skylarks' or a reading which takes it to be no more than a very fine descriptive poem. The whole poem must be read differently with this ending. Much more weight must be given to the skylarks as living sacrifices and to their 'agony'.

But I feel that in trying to redress the balance Hughes has gone too far in the opposite direction and violated the unity of the poem with an ending quite lacking the wit which plays in the rest of the poem in the space between the vivid description and the symbolic significance.

Wings, as we saw in 'Skylarks', are for leaping off from earth towards the sun. They are for escaping from the weight of mortality. They are for gnats, birds and angels. Perhaps man flew once

> With unearthly access of grace,
> Of ease: freer firmer world found
> A hundred feet above ground.
> ('Acrobats')

Then came the fall. The only vestige of flight is the shadow of a huge broken wing man now trails behind him. The fall was from the grace of total self-abandonment into self-consciousness and blind rationality. As Blake chose real men, Newton and Locke, as exemplars of fallen man in his age, so Hughes chooses, in 'Wings', Sartre, Kafka and Einstein as exemplars in ours.

The pre-Christian prototype of fallen man was Icarus, who strained the resources of intellect and science to reach the sun on artificial wings. Hughes is concerned with the spiritual wings the soul miserably flaps in its cage, and with the blindness of men who substitute knowledge for vision.

All these parts of 'Wings' are marvellous purely physical descriptions of their subjects, Sartre's globular head and 'extinct eyeball', Kafka's big-eyed owlishness, like a pallid night-creature exposed to the glare of the photographer's lights, and Einstein's

> tired mask of folds, the eyes in mourning,
> The sadness of the monkeys in their cage—

In 'M. Sartre Considers Current Affairs', having fallen from that true vision which enables you

> To see a World in a Grain of Sand
> And a Heaven in a Wild Flower,
> Hold Infinity in the palm of your hand
> And Eternity in an hour
> (Blake, 'Auguries of Innocence')

Sartre regrows the world inside his skull, like the spectre of a flower. 'Spectre' is a term used by Blake in a very special sense which fits 'Wings' perfectly and adds greatly to its coherence.

94

(The half-quotation from Blake in 'single sandgrain' invites us to make the connection.) John Beer explains Blake's terms as clearly as they allow:

The unified personality is unified by the vision which is allowed to shine through it; self-love is equivalent to the setting up of an inward barrier. It creates a new force, the selfhood, which stands between the vision and its free expression.

As the selfhood begins to assume a life of its own, appropriating to its own use the energies of the individual, it becomes, in Blake's terminology, the 'spectre'; the imagination which remains is called the 'emanation'.

The terms may perhaps be associated with Blake's critique of eighteenth-century mathematical thought as a way of thinking which divided the forces of the universe into two distinct phenomena – the 'spectre' sun, the spherical body which provides a focus for laws of gravitation, and the 'emanation' of vivifying light, which is mysteriously produced by this apparently dead body. If men saw even the sun as a divided image it was not surprising that they should conform to the same pattern, becoming what they beheld: each man became centre of his own mechanically organized little universe, disregarding his imagination as a meaningless accessory except in moments when he wished to relax from the serious clockwork of life. Blake felt, evidently, that if men saw the sun as he saw it, a form which is imposed on that infinite energy of the universe which shouts 'Holy, holy, holy is the Lord God Almighty, – and necessarily imposed if human life is to survive at all – they would see their own humanity in the same light. Spectre and emanation would disappear, their functions being integrated back into a human nature which acted no longer as a moonlit mechanism but as an expressive unity of vision and desire, seeing every thing that lives as holy.

Until such an awakening, the spectre retains power in the individual, per-mitting his vision to linger on as impotent emanation. In representing the two split forces pictorially, Blake usually gives them both wings: the spectre has the dark sinister wings of the bat, the emanation the coloured irridescent wings of the butterfly. (*Blake's Visionary Universe*, 39–40)

The intellectual defines the world as the contents of his own brain, which has no miracles to reveal:

> Angels, it whispers, are metaphors, in man's image,
> For the amoeba's exhilarations.

His 'extinct eyeball' can see only facts, all of which are subsumed by the fact of mortality:

> His eyes are imprisoned in the fact
> That his hands have sunk to the status of flies.
>
> With skull-grins, the earth's populations
> Drift off over graves...

The only wings he sees are those of carrion-eaters, flies and skate.

His spirit, imprisoned in rationalism, denies Heaven, Infinity, Eternity. He sinks, like Blake's Newton, to the bottom of the sea of materialism.

> Pondering on the carrion-eating skate.
>
> And on its wings, lifted, white, like an angel's,
> And on those cupid lips in its deathly belly,
> And on the sea, this tongue in his ear, licking the last of pages.

Kafka, for Hughes,

> is an owl, 'Man' tattooed in his armpit
> Under the broken wing...

The tattoo can only be seen when the wing is lifted in flight, but the broken wing cannot be lifted. Similarly the owl's large eyes are for peering into the darkness, but Kafka is condemned by his flightlessness to live in the stunning glare, under the arc-lamp of man's rational consciousness.

> He is a man in hopeless feathers

given the need to fly, commanded by his own nature to fly, without the means to fly. It is the predicament of the artist as described by Beckett in his *Dialogues with Georges Duthuit* 'The expression that there is nothing to express, nothing with which to express, nothing from which to express, no power to express, no desire to express, together with the obligation to express.' It is the predicament Kafka expressed in his diaries, his aphorisms, his fiction:

There is a goal, but no way. (*Reflections*)

Writing is a form of prayer. (*Reflections*)

Sometimes I think I understand the Fall of Man better than anyone else. (*Letters to Milena*)

Still unborn and already compelled to walk around the streets and speak to people. (*Diaries*)

The Castle in particular expresses the futility of the attempt to approach grace by the experience of reason. There may be a way from God to man, but there is no way from man to God. Yet Kafka felt the obligation to keep up his hopeless 'assault on the last earthly frontier' (*Diaries*).

Man has no other equipment for this assault but logic, language and mathematics. Perhaps Einstein flew highest of all, far into space, but without ever escaping from the prison of his own intellect:

> Star peering at star through the walls
> Of a cage full of nothing.

And he saw no miracles in space such as had sustained his ancestors in the desert:

> And no quails tumbling
> From the cloud. And no manna
> For angels.
> Only the pillar of fire contracting its strength into a star-mote.

Indeed he sought not the miracle of sweet water, but salt, stagnant knowledge:

> Now the sargasso of a single sandgrain
> Would come sweeter than the brook from the rock
> To a mouth
> Blasted with star-vapour.

The nearest he gets to prayer is in his playing of Bach. But music is also mathematics:

> But it is the cauldron of the atom.
> And it is the Eye of God in the whirlwind.
> It is a furnace, storming with flames.

We are back to the Heraclitian fire of the material world, and to mortality, and the human consequences of mathematics in our time:

> It is a burned-out bottomless eye-socket
> Crawling with flies
> In fugues...

His prayer for motherly love is answered not by angels but by a rising cloud of flies, not by the pillar of cloud by day, but by the mushroom cloud of nuclear explosion.

The inability to weep or love is symptomatic of a shifting of the centre of gravity away from 'man's sense of himself,...his body and his essential human subjectivity' and a surrender of his individuality to an 'impersonal abstraction'. For a physicist 'the centre of gravity is...within some postulate deep in space, or leaking away down the drill-shaft of mathematics'. (Introduction to Vasko Popa's *Selected Poetry*, 10–11.)

The poet and the physicist are concerned to explore 'the same gulf of unknowable laws and unknowable particles', but the poet must do it very differently. Hughes' metaphor for the poet's way is 'Wodwo'.

Sir Gawayn, in his journey through the Wirrall, fought with, among other creatures of that remote region, wodwos:

> Sumwhile with wormes he werres, and with wolves als
> Sumwhile with wodwos, that woned in the knarres,
> Bothe with bulles and beres, and bores otherwhile,
> And etaines, that him anelede of the heghe felle.
> *(Sir Gawayne and the Grene Knight*, 720–4)

> (Sometimes with serpents he fought, and with wolves also
> Sometimes with wodwos, that lived in the rocks,
> Both with bulls and bears, and at other times with boars,
> And giants that pursued him on the high fells.)

'Wodwos' is sometimes translated 'trolls', sometimes 'satyrs', sometimes 'wildmen of the woods'. It is this uncertainty of status – man or beast or monster or goblin – which attracts Hughes. Introducing a reading of the poem Hughes described his wodwo as 'some sort of satyr or half-man or half-animal, half all kinds of elemental little things, just a little larval being without shape or qualities who suddenly finds himself alive in this world at any time'.

In 'Wodwo' the speaker is himself a wodwo finding himself at large in a world inhabited by other creatures whose relation to himself he does not in the least understand, without roots ('dropped out of nothing casually'), not knowing why his nose leads him to water or his hands pick bark off a rotten stump, not knowing who he is or what he is doing there, supposing himself to be the exact centre of 'all this' and seeking to discover the circumference of himself. 'Very queer', he concludes, 'but I'll go on looking.'

Hughes is a wodwo in all his poems, asking these same questions of the world in which he finds himself, looking at that world and its creatures to discover where he ends and the other begins, and what relationship exists between the naked self and 'the endless without-world of the other'.

That Hughes is here expressing the activity of the poet, or of any man 'trying to find out what does exist, and what the conditions really are' is evident if we compare the poem with this prose passage:

> ...the living suffering spirit, capable of happiness, much deluded, too frail, with doubtful and provisional senses, so undefinable as to be almost silly, but palpably existing, and wanting to go on existing...homing in tentatively

on vital scarcely perceptible signals, making no mistakes, but with no hope of finality, countinuing to explore.

It could be a paraphrase of 'Wodwo' but it is not. It is from Hughes' Introduction to Vasko Popa's *Selected Poetry* and it describes the efforts of a generation of East European poets to come to terms through poetry with the hostile world in which they are obliged to live and to salvage their humanity and self-respect.

The poet is the humble Man Seeking Experience, who looks at the world without arrogance, recognizes it as neither bad variant nor tryout, but what we are stuck with, sees the absence of clear signs and certainties (except for the mass of evidence of his own fragility), sees dangers and horrors, beauties and miracles in the way (though not the difference between them), and then, alert in all his faculties, moves forward to confront the world.

If he can come to terms with the facts of life and the fact of death, he will become the still centre within the violence. In 'Full Moon and Little Frieda', for the first time, there is a moment of harmony:

A cool small evening shrunk to a dog bark and the clank of a bucket –
And you listening.
A spider's web, tense for the dew's touch.
A pail lifted, still and brimming – mirror
To tempt a first star to a tremor.

Cows are going home in the lane there, looping the hedges with their
    warm wreaths of breath –
A dark river of blood, many boulders,
Balancing unspilled milk.

'Moon!' you cry suddenly, 'Moon! Moon!'

The moon has stepped back like an artist gazing amazed at a work
That points at him amazed.

The poem testifies in its delicacy of utterance, its utterly fresh sense of wonder, to the possibility of knowing 'the redeemed life of joy' in normal daily experience, when, with an unspectacular access of grace, the elements of a scene – human, animal, domestic, rural, cosmic – suddenly cohere to express a plenitude, all the 'malicious negatives' miraculously melted away.

The evening has shrunk not only because the light is failing but also because, as it does so, time seems to slow down, as it approaches that crucial moment of nightfall, dewfall, the first tremor of the first star. And the poet is aware that his daughter is the hand pointing to that moment because she is utterly open, without defences, without distracting consciousness of past and future, to the scene, her fine web of senses perfectly tuned to it, tense as a spider's web, brimming as a lifted pail.

The cows, too, are part of the scene, the condensation from their 'warm wreaths of breath' falling like dew on the hedges, their udders brimming like the pail of water, their blood like a river flowing darkly through, bringing fertility, their bony haunches like boulders ballasting the moment, balancing its fragility and delicacy with permanence and solidity.

Perhaps it needs the child to register and hold all this because the poet cannot open himself, cannot jettison his knowledge of past and future, his knowledge that blood can be spilled as easily as milk and run in rivers outside the body, that boulders in a river are dangerous, that darkness is dangerous, that the moon is a fickle murderous goddess, that, as an earlier version ended:

> Any minute
> A bat will fly out of a cat's ear.

The poem as we have it holds all this at bay, submerges all darker knowledge which might disturb the perfect harmony of man and nature the child experiences.

With no self-consciousness to close her, she points at the moon with an amazement the moon can only reciprocate, like an artist whose work has come to life or perfectly reflects the life of its creator.

Sylvia Plath said of her poem 'Nick and the Candlestick': 'A mother nurses her baby son by candlelight and finds in him a beauty which, while it may not ward off the world's ill, does redeem her share of it' (*The Art of Sylvia Plath*, 171). 'Full Moon and Little Frieda' is without irony because, through his child, Hughes is able to see the world with the eyes of unfallen vision. It is the first of his *Songs of Innocence*.

CROW

The man of theory, having begun to dread the consequences of his views, no longer dares commit himself freely to the icy flood of existence but runs nervously up and down the bank. He no longer wants to have anything entire with all the natural cruelty of things: to such an extent has the habit of optimism softened him. Wisdom, unmoved by the pleasant distractions of the sciences, fixes its gaze on the total constellation of the universe and tries to comprehend sympathetically the suffering of that universe as its own.

(Friedrich Nietzsche, *The Birth of Tragedy*)

In 1957 Ted Hughes met the American sculptor, engraver and publisher Leonard Baskin. Baskin was obsessed by corpses, and a variety of other things attended this obsession, including crows (which he engraved with disturbingly anthropoid characteristics). A later invitation from Baskin to Hughes to write a few little poems to accompany his engravings was the cause of the first Crow poems. Up to 1964 Hughes had never written about crows, though he was familiar with the prominent and rather grim part they play in so much of the world's folklore.

The first appearance of a crow was in a dialogue from *Eat Crow* (written in 1964):

SHE: A crow is a sign of life. Even though it sits motionless.

MORGAN: And a man, lying alone, among stones, with a rifle, lying limply, in a waterless land, in a grey desert of tumbled stone, with one bullet, a man dryer than a lizard, is a sign of life. Even though he does not move.

SHE: The crow watches the man.

MORGAN: Between the crow and the man, across three hundred yards of primaeval stone, a horrible connection has found its way. Now these two can never separate. The stones are in their usual trance, rapt to the circles of galactic dust. They hear nothing of the song of silence these two sing together, these two silent living ones, alone with each other in the stone land...The furnace roars in the silent man, and the crow glitters, in the early grey light, molten bronze and phosphors settling in his darkness, set out to cool, fresh from the furnace. The crow ruffles.

SHE: The crow is composed of terrible black voice. He is neither stone nor light. But voice that can hardly utter. He looks this way and that. The forms of the stones, the fractures of heavenly accident, the resolute quality of light, hold the crow anaesthetized, every hour in more skilled patience, resigned to the superior stamina of the empty horizon, limber and watchful.

MORGAN: The laws are still with the living.

SHE: The crow arrived before dawn, smelling the man, and settling to watch at extreme range.

MORGAN: And when he saw the crow, in the blue thinning light, the man gave thanks to the studded, baleful pallor of the heavens, and to this strange-faced company of stones. His prayer has produced not quails and not manna. A crow has come up from the maker of the world.

SHE: The crow watches the man.

Crow and man are signs of life because life is neither stone nor light, neither matter nor spirit; it is that which must struggle to preserve itself at the expense of others. The man must eat. He cannot eat stone nor drink light; he cannot become other than he is, needing to kill some other living thing to survive. So he waits with his rifle and one bullet for the crow to come within range. The crow too must eat, and cannot kill a man; but he can outwait him. This is the horrible connection between creature and creature: kill to live. Is it a god of love who has thus answered the man's prayer for food?

Several poems in *Wodwo* clearly announce the coming of Crow. In 'Logos', 'Reveille' and 'Theology' all the main characters of *Crow* except Crow himself are assembled – God, Adam, Eve and the Serpent. And all the conditions for his annunciation, the conviction that this cannot be the world God sought to create, perhaps not even the world he did create ('this is the dark intestine'), that there must be something outside God, prior to him, unimpressionable, inimical to his purposes, perhaps itself the creator of God or a precondition of his existence, or his necessary incarnation:

> Creation convulses in nightmare. And awaking
> Suddenly tastes the nightmare moving
> Still in its mouth
> And spits it kicking out, with a swinish cry – which is God's first cry.
>
> . . .
>
> God is a good fellow, but His mother's against Him.
>
> ('Logos')

The blackbird in 'Stations' III is almost Crow. And Crow has something in common with the wodwo, who asks:

> Why do I find
> this frog so interesting as I inspect its most secret
> interior and make it my own?

Crow

plucked grass-heads and gazed into them
Waiting for first instructions.
He studied a stone from the stream.
He found a dead mole and slowly he took it apart,
Then stared at the gobbets, feeling helpless.
He walked, he walked
Letting the translucent starry spaces
Blow in his ear cluelessly.
                    ('Crow Hears Fate Knock on the Door')

'Dawn's Rose' is, in its way, a perfect poem, a distillation of the spirit of *Crow*, as 'Pibroch' is of *Wodwo* or 'Snowdrop' of *Lupercal*. It has a mood of quiet thrilling loneliness:

Dawn's Rose

Is melting an old frost moon.

Agony under agony, the quiet of dust,
And a crow talking to stony skylines.

Desolate is the crow's puckered cry
As an old woman's mouth
When the eyelids have finished
And the hills continue.

A cry
Wordless
As the newborn baby's grieving
On the steely scales.

As the dull gunshot and its after-râle
Among conifers, in rainy twilight.

Or the suddenly dropped, heavily dropped
Star of blood on the fat leaf.

The crow's 'puckered cry' is equally like an old woman's death-rattle or a new-born baby's 'grieving' as its body is first brought into contact with cold steel. The cry is like the gunshot which perhaps wounded the crow and caused the cry.

So real is that sudden spattering of red on green in the last lines that we forget it is 'only' a metaphor for the wordlessness of the crow's cry, itself 'only' a giving voice to the general desolation. The poem itself is laminated, 'agony under agony', the dust quickly settling on yesterday's millionth layer.

But the language of 'Dawn's Rose' is too musical, its imagery too traditional to be typical of *Crow*. It is recognizably in the same tradition as, for example:

> The woods decay, the woods decay and fall,
> The vapours weep their burthen to the ground,
> Man comes and tills the field and lies beneath,
> And after many a summer dies the swan.
>
> (Tennyson, 'Tithonus')

Hughes is well aware of the power and beauty which are at his command in the more traditional modes, but the overriding consideration is the necessity to 'Sing one's own tune':

I think it's true that formal patterning of the actual movement of verse somehow includes a mathematical and a musically deeper world than free verse can easily hope to enter...and the very sound of metre calls up the ghosts of the past and it is difficult to sing one's own tune against that choir. It is easier to speak a language that raises no ghosts. (*London Magazine*, January 1971, 20)

The rejection of musical language and traditional imagery which Hughes feels his theme demands is evident in 'Crow and the Birds'.

In 'Cape Ann' Eliot lists for ten lines the appropriate responses to all the 'delectable' birds seen and heard at that place. All are easy to appreciate, empathize with, anthropomorphize –

> But resign this land at the end, resign it
> To its true owner, the tough one, the sea-gull.
> The palaver is finished.

Only the seagull does not pretend to be 'sweet' or to be concerned with anything but his own survival and that of his species. 'Crow and the Birds' opens with fourteen lines in which the distinctive sounds and movements of many birds are inscaped, and it is claimed for them that they are able, by being so wholly themselves, to get clear of the complexities and ugliness which characterize human life in an age of technology and pollution. They do not share man's smudge and smell. The images they generate are all of purity and naturalness. The reader who is despairing of finding beauty at this point in *Crow* will come with pleasure upon the opening lines of this poem:

> When the eagle soared clear through a dawn distilling of emerald
> When the curlew trawled in seadusk through a chime of wine-
>   glasses
> When the swallow swooped through a woman's song in a cavern
> And the swift flicked through the breath of a violet

But it is all 'palaver'. They are not doing these things to gratify man's aesthetic sensibilities. The eagle soars to scan the earth for prey, and the swift, as we know from 'Crow Tyrannosaurus', is

> Pulsating
> With insects
> And their anguish...

Crow, the tough one, does not hide behind a disguise of beauty:

> Crow spraddled head-down in the beach-garbage,
> guzzling a dropped ice-cream.

The rejection of the palaver is also a crucial stylistic decision, like Eliot's

> The poetry does not matter
> ('East Coker').

The first idea of *Crow* was really an idea of a style. In folktales the prince going on the adventure comes to the stable full of beautiful horses and he needs a horse for the next stage and the king's daughter advises him to take none of the beautiful horses that he'll be offered but to choose the dirty, scabby little foal. You see, I throw out the eagles and choose the Crow. The idea was originally just to write his songs, the songs that Crow would sing. In other words, songs with no music whatsoever, in a super-simple and a super-ugly language which would in a way shed everything except just what he wanted to say without any other consideration and that's the basis of the style of the whole thing. I get near it in a few poems. There I really begin to get what I was after. (*London Magazine*, January 1971, 20)

Why does Hughes choose a crow as his protagonist? The prevalence of ravens and crows in folklore derives largely from the real bird's characteristics. The crow is the most intelligent of birds, the most widely distributed (being common on every continent), and the most omnivorous ('no carrion will kill a crow'). Crows are, of course, black all over, solitary, almost indestructible, and the largest and least musical of songbirds. It is to be expected that the Songs of the Crow will be harsh and grating. He kills a little himself, and, as carrion eater, is dependent on the killing of others and first on the scene at many disasters.

Eskimo legend tells that in the beginning the raven was the only creature and the world was, like him, black. Then came the owl and the world became white like him, with the whiteness of unending snow. Hughes' mythology of Crow is deeply rooted in such legends. Within it are several little contradictory apocryphal accounts of the creation of Crow. The most central goes like this:

God, having created the world, has a recurring nightmare. A huge hand comes from deep space, takes him by the throat, half-throttles him, drags him through space, ploughs the earth with him then throws him back into heaven in a cold sweat. Meanwhile man sits at the gates of heaven waiting for God to grant him audience. He has come to ask God to take life back. God is furious and sends him packing. The nightmare appears to be independent of the creation, and God cannot understand it. The nightmare is full of mockery of the creation, especially of man. God challenges the nightmare to do better. This is just what the nightmare has been waiting for. It plunges down into matter and creates Crow. God tests Crow by putting him through a series of trials and ordeals which sometimes result in Crow being dismembered, transformed or obliterated, but Crow survives them all, little changed. Meanwhile Crow interferes in God's activities, sometimes trying to learn or help, sometimes in mischief, sometimes in open rebellion. It is, perhaps, his ambition to become a man, but he never quite makes it.

The whole myth was to be told as an epic folk-tale in prose with songs by and about Crow interspersed. A good deal of unpublished material exists, but it is unlikely that the project will ever be completed. Very few of the poems in *Crow* demand a knowledge of the mythic framework, a good deal of which can, in any case, be deduced from the poems themselves.[1]

Crow has a distinguished lineage in mythology. The God of healing known variously as Cronos, Saturn, Aesculapius and Apollo, was a Crow-god. A Celtic name for him was Bran. Crow is a totem of England because Bran, when he knew himself to be dying, ordered his head to be severed and buried on 'The White Hill' (now Tower Hill) as a charm to protect England from invasion. This tradition has persisted to such an extent that when, during the Second World War, the Tower ravens died out, new ones were immediately supplied and their wings clipped to prevent them escaping.

The Celtic death-goddess, the Morrigu, was, as we have seen, a crow. She is the underground form of the original life-goddess. The crow is prominent in many other mythologies from America to China, and in alchemy. All these are ancestors of Hughes' Crow. *Crow* could easily have been as overtly syncretic as *The Waste Land*, a history of religion and ideology from Babylonian creation myth, through Middle Eastern religions to the collision of Judaism and its neighbours, the Manichees, the early Christians and the Roman Empire, the Reformation and its impact in England, Puritanism, down to the sickness of England now. It is not syncretic because

My main concern was to produce something with the minimum cultural accretions of the museum sort – something autochthonous and complete in itself, as it might be invented after the holocaust and demolition of all libraries, where essential things spring again – if at all – only from their seeds in nature – and are not lugged around or hoarded as preserved harvests from the past. So the comparative religion/mythology background was irrelevant to me, except as I could forget it. If I couldn't find it again original in Crow, I wasn't interested to make a trophy of it.

This method makes life very difficult for the reader, who, in the less successful poems, is confronted with something which, in the absence of clues to its antecedents, looks merely random and slapdash. For example, the beginning of 'A Kill':

> Flogged lame with legs
> Shot through the head with balled brains
> Shot blind with eyes
> Nailed down by his own ribs
> Strangled just short of his last gasp
> By his own windpipe
> Clubbed unconscious by his own heart

look like nothing more than a lame attempt to revamp Marvell's splendid lines:

> O who shall, from this Dungeon, raise
> A Soul inslav'd so many wayes?
> With bolts of Bones, that fetter'd stands
> In feet; and manacled in Hands.
> Here blinded with an Eye; and there
> Deaf with the drumming of an Ear.
> A Soul hung up, as 'twere, in Chains
> Of Nerves, and Arteries, and Veins.
> ('A Dialogue between the Soul and Body')

Not many readers will be reminded by the phrase 'balled brains' of Conchubar, who was sling-shot in the head by a missile made of the dried brains of an enemy (an ancient Celtic missile). To keep the wound closed, the missile was allowed to stay in. Eventually, hearing of the crucifixion, Conchubar went mad with rage against Christ's crucifiers, and attacked a forest. The brain-ball then burst from his skull, his brains followed it, and he died. The lines also contain references or parallels to Norse sacrificial executions ('Nailed down by his own ribs'), folk-tales, and a Manichean text. In all these sources the physical mutilations involve psychic positives, but little sense of this gets into the poem. A rather more successful handling of the same subject (with the Celtic source actually quoted at some length) is 'Crow's Battle Fury'.

But when the method works well, as in many of the poems I shall later discuss, the resultant concentration and nakedness evokes a response in the reader very similar to that which Raymond Williams noted in reading Blake's *Songs of Experience*: 'Very quickly, if not always overtly, inquiry breaks beyond the texts, and it is easy to feel that there is no stopping-point short of the history of the world.' (*Guardian*, 29 November 1973)

The absence of 'music' and 'poetry' of the kind we are familiar with in English verse since the sixteenth century does not involve any lack of rhetorical force and vitality. The language and poetic technique is more varied than before. And there is much more use than ever before of the oldest poetic devices (such as survive in nursery rhymes and ballads, folksongs and charms) – repetitions and refrains, parallelism, catalogues and catechisms, incantations and invocations.

Crow opens with a statement of the book's basic dichotomy, that between blackness and light; and an introduction, as in an overture, to several of the primary themes:

> Black was the without eye
> Black the within tongue
> Black was the heart
> Black the liver, black the lungs
> Unable to suck in light
> Black the blood in its loud tunnel
> Black the bowels packed in furnace
> Black too the muscles
> Striving to pull out into the light
> Black the nerves, black the brain
> With its tombed visions
> Black also the soul, the huge stammer
> Of the cry that, swelling, could not
> Pronounce its sun.
>
> ('Two Legends' 1)

The eye at least we would expect to reflect some light from the world about him or, as the window of the soul, show some spark from within. But Crow is not yet born, and birth is not a release from the tunnel, the furnace, the tomb, into light; rather it is when everything goes black. For the tunnel is the circulatory system, the furnace the alimentary system, the tomb the skull, and death owns them all.

The fire within Crow is heat without light. The lungs strive to suck in light, the muscles to pull out into the light, the brain to release its visions from the body's tomb, the cry to pronounce such words as light and love. Light is enlightenment, freedom, joy, fulfilment, atonement. Life is the incarnation of the spirit, which is the absolute need for light, within the physical universe which totally excludes it.

> Black is the earth-globe, one inch under,
> An egg of blackness
> Where sun and moon alternate their weathers
>
> To hatch a crow, a black rainbow
> Bent in emptiness
>   over emptiness
>
> But flying
>   ('Two Legends' II)

A rainbow is a sign of creative interchange between heaven and earth, of fertility, of all the varied colours of experience. It is the token of the covenant between God and every living creature of all flesh, for perpetual generations. But Crow flies over a universe empty of God, given over entirely to Death. Crow bends over the world, under the weight of the world, like an unholy ghost. The poem is an inversion of the ending of Hopkins' 'God's Grandeur':

> The Holy Ghost over the bent
> World broods with warm breast and with ah! bright wings.

But Crow's flying is at least a sign of life and selfhood ('flying the black flag of himself'). Crow cannot be crushed whatever is done to him. He is the unkillable urge to keep trying in spite of everything. He is energy itself, infinitely corruptible, infinitely educable and transformable. In that sense he is stronger than death.

In the beginning was not the Word, God, the light that shineth in darkness. In the beginning was nightmare and chaos. Fear was the mainspring of the evolutionary process which produced man.

Man created God, who, like King Lear, handed his kingdom over to death, who is stronger than hope, the will, love and life:

> Adam
> begat Mary
> Who begat God
> Who begat Nothing
> Who begat Never
> Never Never Never
>
> Who begat Crow
> Screaming for Blood
> Grubs, crusts
> Anything
> Trembling featherless elbows in the nest's filth
> ('Lineage')

God's first cry, when he is born into such a world, is a 'swinish cry' ('Logos'). Life, in such a world, becomes 'that pushing, self-protective, malodorous, carnivorous, lecherous fever which is the very nature of the organic cell' (Campbell, *The Hero with a Thousand Faces*, 121). Only the belief that mere existence, on any terms, however brief, is a triumph of self over death, could enable Crow to pass the 'Examination at the Womb Door' and enter once more the cycle of physical life.

The Tibetan Book of the Dead teaches techniques for closing the Womb Door. The whole point of all the disciplines of Buddhism is to 'become the light', to avoid reincarnation into the illusory world of desires and appearances. To pass through the Womb Door is to fail the examination. Crow's attachment to self is so total that he strives to open the Womb Door through which he can enter the blackness, the blindness of physical vision.

The next poem 'A Kill' is, in fact, the birth of Crow (or anyone), as he is delivered into the waiting hands of the gravedigger.

Crow is a developing character. Starting from 'nothing', his quest is to learn how to live according to the laws of creation. He confronts the evidence without evasion or sophistry, (he has a bird's eye view of it), and draws the obvious conclusions. In 'Crow Alights'

> Crow saw the herded mountains, steaming in the morning.
> And he saw the sea
> Dark-spined, with the whole earth in its coils.
> He saw the stars, fuming away into the black, mushrooms of the
>   nothing forest, clouding their spores, the virus of God.

And he shivered with the horror of Creation.

As he approaches from deep space Crow sees the earth to be composed entirely of living things – mountains pushing up to each other and steaming like cows on a chilly morning, the sea like a sea-serpent wound about the continents, the stars sowing their baleful influences upon the world like mushrooms broadcasting their invisible spores upon the air, sparks from the fire of God or viruses from his diseased body. It all seems horrible to Crow; so horrible that it must be a hallucination. But at least it is all vividly alive and interrelated, if only as predator and prey or virus and victim are related. But when Crow alights and sees what man has done to himself and the living body of the earth he sees something less dramatic and nightmarish, something so stark and common-place and unchanging and unmistakably there that it must be reality, but something more horrible because utterly drained of life, utterly disconnected from the source, rootless, solitary, alienated.

He saw this shoe, with no sole, rain-sodden,
Lying on a moor.
And there was this garbage can, bottom rusted away,
A playing place for the wind, in a waste of puddles.
There was this coat, in the dark cupboard, in the silent room, in the
    silent house.
There was this face, smoking its cigarette between the dusk window
    and the fire's embers.
Near the face, this hand, motionless.
Near the hand, this cup.
Crow blinked. He blinked. Nothing faded.
He stared at the evidence.

The light fails at the window, heat fails in the hearth. Life burns away like a smoking cigarette. Nothing is in a vital relationship with anything else. Motionless hand cannot connect with blank face even by lifting a cup to it. Without relatedness the human being cannot function any more than a disconnected electrical machine. He is as absurd as and redundant as a shoe with no sole or a can with no bottom. But his garbage covers the earth and his cigarettes pollute the atmosphere.

But for all that Hughes is compassionate. The man is an image of loneliness and despair. The verse is moving in its bare scrupulousness and objectivity, like Beckett's prose.

Crow's response is to blink and stare. He cannot believe his eyes. He is not moved to sympathy. Even in 'That Moment', a poem to which the poet's own compassion gives great poignancy, Crow has the more important matter of his next meal to think of.

His first sign of conscience appears in the next poem 'Crow Tyrannosaurus':

> Crow thought 'Alas
> Alas ought I
> To stop eating
> And try to become the light?'
>
> But his eye saw a grub. And his head, trapsprung, stabbed.
> And he listened
> And he heard
> Weeping
>
> Grubs   grubs   He stabbed   he stabbed
> Weeping
> Weeping
>
> Weeping he walked and stabbed
>
> Thus came the eye's
>   roundness
>   the ear's
>   deafness.

Crow is not free to become a vegetarian. Stabbing grubs is what it is to be a crow. He has evolved a round eye the better to see grubs and an ear deaf to the universal weeping. But for the first time he has used the word 'ought' and wept for his own victims.

In 'Crow's Account of the Battle' reality gives Crow another lesson. 'Its mishmash of scripture and physics' (heaven and earth nailed together) results in a pattern of recurring war (scripture providing the motive and physics the means) for which no one seems responsible, since 'everything took the blame' and which comes to be accepted as inevitable, normal. If this is really Crow's account, then Crow is coming to feel a genuine outrage:

> And when the smoke cleared it became clear
> This had happened too often before
> And was going to happen too often in future
> And happened too easily
> Bones were too like lath and twigs
> Blood was too like water
> Cries were too like silence
> The most terrible grimaces too like footprints in mud
> And shooting somebody through the midriff

Was too like striking a match
Too like potting a snooker ball
Too like tearing up a bill
Blasting the whole world to bits
Was too like slamming a door
Too like dropping in a chair
Exhausted with rage
Too like being blown to bits yourself
Which happened too easily
With too like no consequences.

Crow's outrage finds its outlet in the superstition that there is some external evil being responsible for all this, who can be hunted down and killed, like the Beast in *Lord of the Flies* (who is not only in the evil Jack, but in the thoroughly decent and civilized boys, Ralph and Piggy), like the killer in Ionesco's *Tuer Sans Gages* who, while the idealist Berenger dashes about the city in search of him, sits in Berenger's own chair in his own locked room.

Where is the Black Beast?
Crow sat in its chair, telling loud lies against the Black Beast.

The Beast must be inside your enemy. Or inside your brother (Abel). In his pursuit of the Black Beast Crow destroys everything he wanted to save from the Beast and looks everywhere but within himself. This is Crow as Trickster:

The so-called civilized man has forgotten the trickster. He remembers him only figuratively and metaphorically, when, irritated by his own ineptitude, he speaks of fate playing tricks on him or of things being bewitched. He never suspects that his own hidden and apparently harmless shadow has qualities whose dangerousness exceeds his wildest dreams. As soon as people get together in masses and submerge the individual, the shadow is mobilized, and, as history shows, may even be personified and incarnated. (C. G. Jung, 'On the Psychology of the Trickster Figure', Radin, *The Trickster*, 206)

It was also Jung who suggested, in *Answer to Job*, that God hid the devil from his own consciousness in his own bosom.

Crow's progress continues through 'Crow on the Beach':

He knew he grasped
Something fleeting
Of the sea's ogreish outcry and convulsion.
He knew he was the wrong listener unwanted
To understand or help –

His utmost gaping of brain in his tiny skull
Was just enough to wonder, about the sea,
What could be hurting so much?

until, in 'Crow's Nerve Fails', he finally recognizes himself as the
Black Beast.

The strange combination of roles we find in Crow – all-suffering
Everyman, culture-hero, clown-devil – links him unmistakably
with one of the oldest figures in all mythology, Trickster: 'a
clown figure working in continuous opposition to the well-
wishing creator. . . as accounting for the ills and difficulties of
existence this side of the veil.' (Campbell, *The Hero With a
Thousand Faces*, 292). Paul Radin, in *The Trickster*, tells us about
the Winnebago Trickster, Wakdjunkaga. After Earthmaker has
created the universe and all its inhabitants, he discovers that evil
beings, led by the Satan figure Hereshguina, not created by
Earthmaker and existing since the beginning of time, are about to
exterminate man, and sends Wakdjunkaga to teach man how to
survive. But Wakdjunkaga is completely incompetent and selfish:
'He was like a small child crawling about. He accomplished no
good and in fact injured Earthmaker's creation.' Because of him
men die and steal and abuse women and lie and are lazy and unreliable. Sometimes he is even equated with Hereshguina. 'He
does not at first accept responsibility for his actions, holding the
world outside of himself as compelling him to behave as he does.'
But later he shows signs of 'an awaking consciousness and sense of
reality, indeed, the beginning of a conscience'.

All this could be describing Crow. In fact on the north-west
coast of America the Trickster is Raven, who differs from Wakdjunkaga primarily in his insatiable appetite. The Eskimo of Bering
Strait also have a Raven as trickster-hero.

Joseph Campbell records the following Trickster myth:

The black Tatars of Siberia say that when the demiurge Pajana fashioned the
first human beings, he found that he was unable to produce a life-giving spirit
for them. So he had to go up to heaven and procure souls from Kudai, the High
God, leaving meanwhile a naked dog to guard the figures of his manufacture.
The devil, Erlik, arrived while he was away. And Erlik said to the dog: 'Thou
hast no hair. I will give thee golden hair if thou wilt give into my hands these
soulless people.' The proposal pleased the dog, and he gave the people he was
guarding to the tempter. Erlik defiled them with his spittle, but took flight the
moment he saw God approaching to give them life. God saw what had been
done, and so he turned the human bodies inside out. That is why we have
spittle and impurity in our intestines. (Campbell, *op. cit.* 294)

In 'A Childish Prank', God, having created Adam and Eve without souls, is beaten by the problem of how to invest them with any kind of purpose or stimulate them to any activity. Crow steps in and invents sexuality which has kept the race in perpetual motion ever since.

Christianity, for Hughes, is 'just another provisional myth of man's relationship with the creator' (*London Magazine*, January 1971, 16). Its inadequacies, as such, give rise to much of the comedy in *Crow*, where the God of Genesis often figures as something of a well-meaning booby. 'Apple Tragedy', for example, is also apple farce. Hughes here interprets the connection between the apple and original sin as cider, invented by God, drunk by Adam, Eve and the Serpent, and responsible for all our subsequent transgressions. If we imagine the Genesis story having derived from the interpretation or, more likely, the misinterpretation of an ancient icon on which the dumb images of God, serpent, man, woman, apple, hanged man, crucified man or God appeared, this reinterpretation is as good as any.

Sometimes, however, Crow's pranks or ineptitudes have consequences of full tragic proportions. In 'Crow's First Lesson', God tries to teach Crow to say Love, but the word is not in him:

> Crow gaped, and the white shark crashed into the sea

The incident is straight out of trickster mythology:

To Karvuvu admired the Thum-fish and wanted to make one, but when he was taught how, he carved a shark instead. This shark ate the Malivaran-fish instead of driving them ashore. To Karvuvu, crying, went to his brother and said: 'I wish I had not made that fish; he does nothing but eat up all the others.' 'What sort of fish is it?' he was asked. 'Well,' he answered, 'I made a shark.' 'You really are a disgusting fellow,' his brother said. 'Now you have fixed it so that our mortal descendants shall suffer. That fish of yours will eat up all the others, and people too. (Campbell, *op. cit.*, 293)

Love is the first word God tries to teach Crow because God wishes all creation to be founded on it. But Crow can only express the principle of his own being, which is 'entire with all the natural cruelty of things'. God curses and weeps, for the effect of a world of sharks, blueflies, tsetses, mosquitos and stifling sexuality upon man

> Who trusted God was love indeed
> And love Creation's final law –
> Though Nature, red in tooth and claw

With ravine, shrieked against his creed.
(Tennyson, 'In Memoriam')

An even more serious intervention occurs in 'Crow Blacker Than Ever':

> When God, disgusted with man,
> Turned towards heaven.
> And man, disgusted with God,
> Turned towards Eve,
> Things looked like falling apart.
>
> But Crow   Crow
> Crow nailed them together,
> Nailing Heaven and earth together –
>
> So man cried, but with God's voice.
> And God bled, but with man's blood.
>
> Then heaven and earth creaked at the joint
> Which became gangrenous and stank –
> A horror beyond redemption.

Man cannot be man, cannot live in this world, because his spirit strains towards heaven (a world without darkness, suffering and death). God cannot be God, for he must share the sufferings of this world. But Crow can be Crow

> Flying the black flag of himself.

His intervention, perhaps misguided, is nevertheless an effort towards wholeness, an effort to live simultaneously on earth and in all the heavens and hells rather than allow things to fall apart and life to be polarized into irreconcilable extremes. Here is an example of the ease with which Hughes can move from comedy to deepest seriousness, of how Crow's wildly improbable escapades can dramatize the biggest theological issues. The incongruity is already there in the gap between the world as it is and the world as a loving God must have intended it. What has this earth to do with that heaven, that men must strain to become light and God be nailed to a cross in a vain attempt to teach man to pronounce the word 'love'?

'Crow Communes', one of the most tightly organized poems in *Crow*, is another variation on the same theme.

> 'Well,' said Crow, 'What first?'
> God, exhausted with Creation, snored.
> 'Which way?' said Crow, 'Which way first?'

God's shoulder was the mountain on which Crow sat.
'Come,' said Crow, 'Let's discuss the situation.'
God lay, agape, a great carcase.

Crow is willing to accept instruction from God, but God's silence
obliges him to let his own instincts point the way.

Crow tore off a mouthful and swallowed.
'Will this cipher divulge itself to digestion
Under hearing beyond understanding?'

The title implies not only that Crow attempts to converse with
God and is reduced to talking to himself, but also that he parti-
cipates in the rite of Holy Communion, or an unholy parody of it.
In the Eucharist man becomes God by eating his body and drinking his blood. But if the body of God is merely this world, there
can be nothing redemptive about eating it:

The dripping blood our only drink,
The bloody flesh our only food:
In spite of which we like to think
That we are sound, substantial flesh and blood...
(T. S. Eliot, 'East Coker')

The great carcase of God from which Crow tears off a mouthful is
not only the unredeemed world. It is also the corpse of that redemptive love – 'agape' – which was also the name of a love-feast
held by the early Christians in connection with the Lord's
Supper. Crow feels much stronger for his meal. That is his only
illumination, his only claim to be 'the hierophant', the expounder
of sacred rites and mysteries.

Crow, the hierophant, humped, impenetrable.
Half-illumined. Speechless.
(Appalled.)

Crow is so appalled by the secret he has half-perceived that he is
struck dumb. Humped like a stone, impenetrable as stone, silent
as stone, covered with the pall of his own blackness, he stands at
the end more like a gravestone than a priest.

The God Crow has to deal with is neither God the Creator nor the
God who spoke to Job out of the whirlwind. That God, who in-
corporated Satan and serpent, hawk and shark, could easily have
coped with Crow.

Finding the right speech for Crow involved me in inventing a longish series of episodes, beginning in traditional fashion, in heaven, where Crow is created, as part of a wager, by the mysterious, powerful, invisible prisoner of the being men called God. This particular God, of course, is the man-created, broken down, corrupt despot of a ramshackle religion, who bears about the same relationship to the Creator as, say, ordinary English does to reality. He accompanies Crow through the world in many guises, mis-teaching, deluding, tempting, opposing and at every point trying to discourage or destroy him. Crow's whole quest aims to locate and release his own creator, God's nameless hidden prisoner, whom he encounters repeatedly but always in some unrecognisable form. (*Crow*, Claddagh Records CCT 9–10, 1973)

The account is by Hughes himself, but it describes largely a part of the Crow story Hughes never reached in the poems. I can find no hint in *Crow* that the creator of Crow is God's prisoner or that Crow has a quest to locate and release him.

The form in which Crow most frequently encounters his own creator is the serpent, which is God's prisoner only in the sense that it is imprisoned within its serpent form in which it cannot be seen by man or Crow as other than ugly and destructive. In 'A Horrible Religious Error' Crow blames the serpent for the deplorable condition of fallen man and woman, and thinks he has saved them by eating it. He thinks he is swallowing death, but he is swallowing something much bigger (creation itself, mother of all), something he is already inside ('this is the dark intestine').

In Hughes' adaptation of Seneca's *Oedipus* Jocasta says:

> I carried him for disease
> for rottenness and dropping to pieces
> I carried him for death bones dust   I knew
> but I carried him not only for this I carried him to be king of this
> and my blood didn't pause
> didn't hesitate in my womb
> considering the futility
> It didn't falter reckoning the odds
>   . . .
> and what was I   what cauldron was I
> what doorway was I   what cavemouth

Her womb is the cave of the sphinx in 'her nest of smashed skulls and bones'. She is like the woman in 'Fleeing from Eternity' who, 'lying among the bones on the cemetery earth', sang out of her belly. The song is the hope that the mother invests, that the gods and the whole earth invest in every new birth. The new-born baby Jocasta delivered into the blackness of the sphinx's maw was 'a bag of blood a bag of death a screaming mouth', but also

> he was a king's son   he was a man's shape
> he was perfect
>
> . . .
>
> he was the warrant of the gods
> he was their latest attempt
> to walk on the earth and to live
> he only had to live.

But Oedipus cannot live without solving the sphinx's riddle –

> Four legs three legs two legs one leg
> Who goes on them all.

The correct answer – 'Man' – would imply an acceptance of a definition of man's life in terms of its stages within time towards death, and that would be to admit that we are already inside the sphinx – 'as if we were living inside her carcase'.

'Song for a Phallus' is a savagely comic rendering of the Oedipus story. Oedipus here pits himself against his mother, his fate, the facts of life. He seeks to counter the riddle of the sphinx (the serpent is 'the sphinx of the final fact') with sheer brutality:

> Oedipus took an axe and split
>   The Sphinx from top to bottom
> The answers aren't in me, he cried
>   Maybe your guts have got 'em.

The answer indeed emerges in the form of his own mother. But Oedipus is ruthless, crazed, in his determination to smash his way out of the darkness, the cycle of birth and death and replacement represented by the mother:

> He split his Mammy like a melon
>   He was drenched with gore
> He found himself curled up inside
>   As if he had never been bore.
>   Mamma   Mamma

This symbolic violation of the mother, and the infantile 'Mamma Mamma' at the end of every stanza, suggest that his fury is a transference of the repressed incest-wish. Jung gives an interpretation of the spinx which exactly fits the use Hughes makes of it and enables us to relate it to many of his other theriomorphic images:

In consciousness we are attached by all sacred bonds to the mother; in the dream she pursues us as a terrible animal. The Sphinx, mythologically considered, is actually a fear animal, which reveals distinct traits of a mother derivate. In the Oedipus legend the Sphinx is sent by Hera, who hates Thebes on account of the birth of Bacchus; because Oedipus conquers the Sphinx, which is nothing but fear of the mother, he must marry Jocasta, his mother, for the throne and the hand of the widowed queen of Thebes belonged to him who freed the land from the plague of the Sphinx. The genealogy of the Sphinx is rich in allusions to the problem touched upon here. She is a daughter of Echnida, a mixed being; a beautiful maiden above, a hideous serpent below.

In this she is all women:

> Above – the well-known lips, delicately downed.
> Below – beard between thighs.
>
> Above – her brow, the notable casket of gems.
> Below – the belly with its blood-knot.
>
> Above – many a painful frown.
> Below – the ticking bomb of the future.
>
> Above – her perfect teeth, with the hint of a fang at the corner.
> Below – the millstones of two worlds.
>
> Above – a word and a sigh.
> Below – gouts of blood and babies.
>
> Above – the face, shaped like a perfect heart.
> Below – the heart's torn face.
>
> ('Fragment of an Ancient Tablet')[2]

Jung continues:

This double creature corresponds to the picture of the mother; above, the human, lovely and attractive half; below, the horrible animal half, converted into a fear animal through the incest prohibition. Echnida is derived from the All-mother, the mother Earth, Gaea, who, with Tartaros, the personified underworld (the place of horrors), brought her forth. Echnida herself is the mother of all terrors, of the Chimaera, Scylla, Gorgo, of the horrible Cerberus, of the Nemean Lion, and of the eagle who devoured the liver of Prometheus; besides this she gave birth to a number of dragons. One of her sons is Orthrus, the dog of the monstrous Geryon, who was killed by Hercules. With this dog, her son, Echnida, in incestuous intercourse, produced the Sphinx. (*Psychology of the Unconscious*, 112–13)

Several other poems link Crow with Oedipus. In 'Oedipus Crow', Crow in his pride wants to deny his own mortality, to cut himself off from all mortal things, to measure time by his own pulse. Oedipus too regarded himself as the measure of all things and sought to evade his fate. But every step brought him closer to it, until, mutilated, he served as a living warning to mankind.

In 'Revenge Fable'

> There was a person
> Could not get rid of his mother
> As if he were her topmost twig.
> So he pounded and hacked at her
> With numbers and equations and laws
> Which he invented and called truth.
> He investigated, incriminated
> And penalized her, like Tolstoy,
> Forbidding, screaming and condemning,
> Going for her with a knife,
> Obliterating her with disgusts
> Bulldozers and detergents
> Requisitions and central heating
> Rifles and whisky and bored sleep.
>
> With all her babes in her arms, in ghostly weepings,
> She died.
>
> His head fell off like a leaf.

This poem is about the desecration of nature – 'the great civilised crime of intelligence that like the half-imbecile, omnipotent, spoiled brat Nero has turned on its mother' (*The Art of Sylvia Plath*, 190).

In 'Crow and Mama' also Hughes sees all our frenzied intellectual and technological activity as an attempt to get rid of the mother. The Rationalist pursues what he chooses to call 'truth' by means of his arbitrary systems. The idealist, the humanist, in his pursuit of improvements, turns his back on his own basic humanity, the bond of blood, the 'strandentwining cable of all flesh', as Stephen Dedalus calls it (*Ulysses*, 34), linking all back to Eden, back to that 'belly without blemish' which is also the 'womb of sin'. Crow can travel by car or plane or rocket, but he drives in a circle, arriving always at his point of origin, his consubstantiality with his mother, with his furthest ancestors, with 'all flesh'. This unbroken umbilical cord carries the doom of Oedipus or any man (nemesis in the chromosomes) but also 'the warrant of the gods'. It is the tap root, the source of vitality and creativeness as of sin and destruction. To cut it or repudiate it is suicidal.[3]

St George, in Crow's account of him, is just such a 'civilized man'. He is a mathematician, nuclear physicist, bio-chemist:

> He sees everything in the Universe
> Is a track of numbers racing towards an answer.
> With delirious joy, with nimble balance
> He rides those racing tracks. He makes a silence.
> He refrigerates an emptiness,
> Decreates all to outer space.

He is Einstein again

> Finding the core of the heart is a nest of numbers.

But

the centre of gravity is not within some postulate deep in space, or leaking away down the drill-shaft of mathematics, but inside man's sense of himself, inside his body and his essential human subjectivity, his refusal to surrender his individuality to any impersonal abstraction. (Introduction to Vasko Popa's *Selected Poetry*)

When a man does surrender his individuality he turns his heart into a nest of monsters whose shapes he then projects onto those nearest to him. Believing himself to be the pure heroic St George he kills these dragons of his own creating. St George, not the dragon, is the Black Beast.

Hughes is here bringing up-to-date not only the story of St George but 'the whole repetitive history of the militant ethos... and the madness behind it – unacknowledged because it contains everything rejected and ignored'. The immediate source was a Japanese folk tale about a Samurai whose professional pride and militancy ossifies into a madness in which he kills his wife and children. The same thing happened to Hercules in that little-known part of his story Seneca deals with in *Hercules Furens*.

There are even older sources, for example the brutal slaughter of Tiamat, the mother (often represented as serpent or dragon), by Marduk: 'Tiamat was a personification of the sea and represented the feminine element which gave birth to the world. In the continuation of the story she represents the blind forces of primitive chaos against which the intelligent and organising gods struggle' (Larousse *Encyclopaedia of Mythology*, 50).

The violence of 'Crow's Account of St George' is comparable with that of the *Epic of the Creation*:

> He let fly an arrow, it pierced her belly.
> Her inner parts he clove, he split her heart.
> He rendered her powerless and destroyed her life.
> He felled her body and stood upright on it.

St George killing the dragon is the debased form in which this myth has come down to us. Hughes takes him to stand for the kind of madness, which, in the name of intelligence, seeks to destroy or at least dissociate itself from Nature on the grounds that Nature eats her own offspring (in other words includes death).

> Hero by hero they go –
> Grimly get astride
> And their hair lifts.
>
> She laughs, smelling the battle – their cry comes back.
>
> Who can live her life?
> Every effort to hold her or turn her falls off her
> Like rotten harness.
>
> Their smashed faces come back, the wallets and the watches.

This is 'Bones', the crazy pony on which they ride out, the inevitable death within their own bodies. To seek out death itself, riding on death as we ride our own skeletons, hoping to kill death, would be madness.

The journey must be, as Lawrence says, 'into the everlasting hinterland of consciousness'. The dragon we must do something about is the terror, the fear of death and everything else in nature or space which we fear because we do not understand, or understanding, cannot be reconciled with. What would it mean to kill the dragon? Nature is indivisible. Kill the red dragon of destruction and you kill the green dragon of creation. Kill the powers of the non-human world and you kill the earth-mother, the tree upon which humanity is a leaf.

Numbers create bombs and monsters. Words, too, can kill. They have an existence quite apart from anything in the real world, especially those great abstractions like 'Freedom' to which many men have sacrificed themselves and others. We think in words, yet our vocabulary comes loaded with the assumptions of our culture:

Words are continually trying to displace our experience. And in so far as they are stronger than the raw life of our experience, and full of themselves and all the dictionaries they have digested, they do displace it. (*Poetry in the Making*, 120)

Words like 'civilization', 'science', 'progress' and 'productivity' displace an unspeakable reality

> ...burning whole lands
> To dusty char.

Such a word eats people and drains Nature until it puddles 'like a collapsing mushroom' for lack of any more to digest:

> Its era was over.
> All that remained of it a brittle desert
> Dazzling with the bones of earth's people
>
> Where Crow walked and mused.
>
> ('A Disaster')

In 'The Battle of Osfrontalis' words lay claim to determine Crow's life, responsibilities, aspirations, indulgences. But Crow, unlike man, is word-resistant. He is too firmly grounded for them in the reality of a pie, pickled onions, and a glass of water.

> Words retreated, suddenly afraid
> Into the skull of a dead jester
> Taking the whole world with them –
>
> But the world did not notice.
>
> And Crow yawned – long ago
> He had picked that skull empty.

A world given over to the pseudo-life of words might as well be inside the skull of a dead jester where ghostly words reverberate without meaning. Crow long ago learned what Hamlet so belatedly learns, the absurdity of words.

Nevertheless, in 'Crow Goes Hunting', Crow decides to try words. Surely you can catch things by simply naming them. But his words, clear-eyed, resounding and well-trained as they are, cannot pluck out the heart of the mystery of a hare:

> Crow was Crow without fail, but what is a hare?
>
> It converted itself to a concrete bunker.
> The words circled protesting, resounding.
>
> Crow turned the words into bombs – they blasted the bunker.
> The bits of bunker flew up – a flock of starlings.
>
> Crow turned the words into shotguns, they shot down the starlings.
> The falling starlings turned to a cloudburst.
>
> Crow turned the words into a reservoir, collecting the water.
> The water turned into an earthquake, swallowing the reservoir.
>
> The earthquake turned into a hare and leaped for the hill
> Having eaten Crow's words.

The elusiveness of real experience and real creatures when we try to capture them with words is cleverly conveyed here by refashioning an ancient magical formula found at its purest, perhaps, in the *Romance of Taliesin*:

And she went forth after him, running. And he saw her, and changed himself into a hare and fled. But she changed herself into a greyhound and turned him. And he ran towards a river, and became a fish. And she in the form of an otter-bitch chased him under the water, until he was fain to turn himself into a bird of the air. She, as a hawk, followed him and gave him no rest in the sky. And just as she was about to stoop upon him, and he was in fear of death, he espied a heap of winnowed wheat on the floor of a barn, and he dropped among the wheat, and turned himself into one of the grains. Then she transformed herself into a high-crested black hen, and went to the wheat and scratched it with her feet, and found him out and swallowed him. (Trans. Lady Charlotte Guest)

Thus Crow learns what Hughes tells us in *Poetry in the Making*:

The meaning of our experience is finally unfathomable, it reaches into our toes and back to before we were born and into the atom, with vague shadows and changing features, and elements that no expression of any kind can take hold of.

Crow is left at the end 'speechless with admiration'.

Proteus, the Old Man of the Sea, had the gift of prophecy, but was loth to reveal his secrets. He also had the ability to change shape at will. But if his questioner could keep a grip on him through all his changes, he would at last resume his natural shape and tell all. In 'Truth Kills Everybody' Crow finds Proteus, embodiment of all those exploding truths the sea contains ('the gulfing of the crab's last prayer'). Again the ancient formula of shape-changing offers Hughes a splendid model. Here, since the challenge is to hold on, not to change faster, and the contest is not between magicians, but between mere human tenacity and all the occult forces of the world, the appropriate model is 'Tam Lin', where Janet can only rescue her lover Tam Lin from the Queen o'Fairies by gripping him through all the changes he will undergo:

> They shaped him in her arms twa
>   An aske but and a snake;
> But aye she grips and hau'ds him fast,
>   To be her warldis make.
>
> They shaped him in her arms twa
>   A hot iron at the fire;
> But aye she grips and hau'ds him fast
>   To be her hearts desire.

Janet wins her lover. The ancient Greek who held Proteus won his secrets. But Crow's tenacity is rewarded with the truth to end all truths – universal disintegration:

> The ankle of a rising, fiery angel – he held it
>
> Christ's hot pounding heart – he held it
>
> The earth, shrunk to the size of a hand grenade
>
> And he held it he held it and held it and
>
> BANG!
>
> He was blasted to nothing.

It is the same truth Crow sees, when, in 'Crow's Vanity', he looks in 'the evil mirror'

> For a glimpse of the usual grinning face

but sees, with every breath, a new aeon of accomplishment or debacle appear, mist over, disappear. His allegiance to the illusory satisfaction of the temporal, physical world, is shaken again in 'Magical Dangers', where power, speed, freedom, wealth, sex, intelligence, all betray him. Finally

> Crow thought of nature's stupor –
> And an oak tree grew out of his ear.
> A row of his black children sat in the top.
> They flew off.
> Crow
> Never again moved.

Nature is no still life. The immense powers at work in, say, the growth of an oak, are not lessened because, by an arbitrary human time-scale, they work slowly. Time gives a little jolt and suddenly the oak-tree is fully grown with his own children perched aloft, superseding Crow.

Alan Watts could be summing up these poems when he writes: 'But the conduct and regulation of the whole human organism, not to mention the whole universe, is manifestly an affair so swift and so complex that no lumbering string of words can account for it.' He goes on to speak of those who believe in 'nature's stupor':

The academic materialist who is, perhaps, a scientific empiricist or a logical positivist or a 'sound' statistical psychologist, whose real aim is to demonstrate that all nature is perfectly banal and dull. The trouble with this fellow is that no one ever mixed raven's blood with his mother's milk. He is marvelously and uncannily bereft of any sense that existence is odd. (*Beyond Theology*)

It is the mistake of Einstein who believed that the miracle of the universe was its comprehensibility.

Owl in 'Owl's Song' does not make that mistake:

> He sang
> How the swan blanched forever
> How the wolf threw away its telltale heart
> And the stars dropped their pretence
> The air gave up appearances
> Water went deliberately numb
> The rock surrendered its last hope
> And cold died beyond knowledge
>
> He sang
> How everything had nothing more to lose
>
> Then sat still with fear
>
> Seeing the clawtrack of star
> Hearing the wingbeat of rock
>
> And his own singing.

The wolf is dead, but the star now leaves its clawtrack. The swan is dead, but the rock flies with its wingbeat. Magical transformations indeed, testifying to the power of life to renew itself. But though the roles may change, the pattern – clawtrack and wingbeat – is the same, horribly magnified to a cosmic scale. There is no reconciling predator and prey even among the stars. What frightens Owl as much as clawtrack of star or wing-beat of rock is the sound of his own singing. His singing seems no part of him. It is much more than the expression of his fear or despair which would express themselves in screaming or silence. You cannot *sing* that you have nothing more to lose; your song is something more. His singing does seem part of the total order, as though the universe were an infinite owl whose song was also his song.

What amazes Hughes is that so bleak a vision as his should issue in song, a song as unmelodious as Owl's or Crow's, but still a cry, an assertion of self-hood and consciousness against everything, or, it may even be, in harmony with everything.

'Crow's Undersong' is about an unspecified 'she', who is presumably the essential female, the eternal Eve, who guarantees the continuity of life through love, of suffering and death also, and of the hope which persists as long as there is life:

> She has come amorous it is all she has come for
>
> If there had been no hope she would not have come

And there would have been no crying in the city

(There would have been no city)

Perhaps Hughes was thinking of that other first woman, Pandora. Before she came to men Pandora was adorned with wreaths of flowers and in the wreath on her head many animals were portrayed. Her name means 'the all-giving', a name of the Earth itself. She gave to men all evils, including death, but she also brought hope, and, in her own person, a guarantee of the continuing of life, the means of replenishing the earth. Is she to be reviled for the one gift or worshipped for the other? For all her deficiencies and vulnerability, she seems able to bring human life into a living relationship with the richness of the natural world:

> She comes dumb she cannot manage words
> She brings petals in their nectar fruits in their plush
> She brings a cloak of feathers an animal rainbow
> She brings her favourite furs and these are her speeches

These rich lines suggest all the bounty of earth, an earth freely yielding far more than man needs. The phrase 'animal rainbow' suggests not only the amazing variety of creatures but also a harmonious and fruitful interrelationship, a reconciling of opposites (sun and rain, heaven and earth), and, together with the paradisal imagery of the context, the bow which the Creator sets in the cloud as the token of his covenant with the creatures of all flesh. Perhaps 'she' is the Creator, or Creatress, of all this, Nature. At all events she is the opposite of the St George figure, the man who comes so much further with his words and numbers and machines that he has utterly lost touch with nature.

Every fertility goddess is enigmatic, has her underworld or destructive form, as Hecate is the underground form of Aphrodite/Venus, and Persephone/Proserpina of Ceres/Demeter. Compare with Hughes' poem this prayer of Lucius:

Queen of Heaven, whether thou art the genial Ceres, the prime parent of fruits; – or whether thou art celestial Venus; – or whether thou art Proserpina, terrific with midnight howlings – with that feminine brightness of thine illuminating the walls of every city. (Apuleius, *The Golden Ass*)

Almost all mythologies have recognized the need for a female principle to balance and complete the male godhead. The Egyptians had Isis, the Assyro–Babylonians Ishtar (with her holy city Erech), the Greeks Astarte or Aphrodite, the Indians Shakti...In

Proverbs and Ecclesiasticus and the Song of Solomon we meet the figure of Sophia:

> The Lord possessed me in the beginning of his way,
>   before his works of old.
> I was set up from everlasting, from the beginning,
>   or ever the earth was.
> When there were no depths, I was brought forth:
>   when there were no fountains abounding with water.

She claims to have been with God during the creation, helping, delighting him and rejoicing:

> Rejoicing in the habitable part of his earth;
>   and my delights were with the sons of men.
>   (Proverbs, 8:22–4, 31)

> He created me from the beginning before the world,
>   and I shall never fail.
> In the holy tabernacle I served before him;
>   and so was I established in Sion.
> Likewise in the beloved city he gave me rest,
>   and in Jerusalem was my power.

She compares herself to many trees – cedar, cypress, palm-tree, rose, olive, terebinth – all from ancient times symbols of the Semitic love and mother goddess.

> As the vine brought I forth pleasant savour,
>   and my flowers are the fruit of honour and riches.
> I am the mother of fair love,
>   and fear, and knowledge, and holy hope:
> I therefore, being eternal, am given to all my children
>   which are named of him.
>   (Ecclesiasticus, 24: 9–11, 17–18)

Jung describes her as the

hypostatized pneuma of feminine nature that existed before the Creation... the feminine numen of the 'metropolis' par excellence, of Jerusalem the mother city. She is the mother-beloved, a reflection of Ishtar, the pagan city-goddess...She realizes God's thoughts by clothing them in material form, which is the prerogative of all feminine beings. (*Answer to Job*, ch. III)

I don't want to suggest that the 'she' of 'Crow's Undersong' *is* Sophia or Ishtar, or any other mythological figure. These myths testify to deep and permanent truths which the imaginative writer may rediscover quite independently. For a man to try to understand a mother, a wife, or a daughter is to try to understand his own underself, the repressed feminine nature in all men.[4] An undersong is a subordinate song or strain, figuratively, an underlying meaning. Perhaps under all the Crow songs with their bleakness runs this undersong, this counter-song of love, hope, bounty and all the varied colours and relationships of the created world.

Given the terrifying world of *Crow*, what human orientation towards it is remotely adequate? Hughes explores several possibilities (perhaps all the possibilities). To give a sense of the range of his explorations, I must refer to several poems not yet included in any edition of *Crow* – 'Crow's Song About God', 'Existential Song', 'Song of Woe', 'Crow Wakes' and 'The New World', and two poems which were added to the English text in the second edition – 'The Contender' and 'Crow's Elephant Totem Song'.

Kafka once said that there is no way from man to God, only a way from God to man. *The Castle* can be interpreted as an illustration of this. If this is true, it might seem at first that there is nothing to be done but wait, passively, for God (or Godot) to come. In *The Trial* a man waits all his life outside the doorway of the Law, forbidden by the fearsome doorkeeper to enter. He waits until he dies.

In 'Crow's Song About God'

> Somebody is sitting
> Under the gatepost of heaven
> Under the lintel
> On which are written the words:
> 'Forbidden To the Living'.

The next forty-six lines are a description of this person, deformed and mutilated to a degree no real person could ever be. It would be easy to discuss the poem as yet another Hughes caricature of mutilation if we did not register that this 'person' is no real individual man, but an image of what a single man might be like on whom had been perpetrated all the violations men perpetrate not only upon themselves and one another but upon the body of the earth:

> the life shape
> A rooty old oak-stump, aground in the ooze
> Of some putrid estuary
>   ...

His blood filtering between
In the coils of his body, like the leech life
In a slime and ochre pond
Under the smouldering collapse of a town dump

. . .

His solar plexus crimped in his gut, hard,
A plastic carnation
In a gutter puddle
Outside the registry office

. . .

Face gutted with shadow, like a village gutted with bombs

The man becomes the metaphor for a sick and polluted life which can neither cure itself nor die,

Clinging to the tick of his watch
Under a dream muddled as vomit
That he cannot vomit, he cannot wake up to vomit

The muddled dream is perhaps his hope that keeps him alive, his hope of being saved, admitted to heaven by God.

But God sees nothing of this person
His eyes occupied with His own terror
As he mutters
My Saviour is coming,
He is coming, who does not fear death,
He shares his skin with it,
He gives it his cigarettes,
He cuts up its food, he feeds it like a baby,
He keeps it warm he cherishes it
In the desolations of space,
He dresses it up in his best, he calls it his life –
He is coming.

God is also lost in a muddled dream, a nightmare terror of death, from which he cherishes the crazy hope that man will deliver him (the same man who lolls against his gatepost), since man, with death in his sperm, his body, his every act, must have come to terms with it. A God's-eye view of the havoc below confirms his assumption that man is in league with death. Meanwhile man waits at his last gasp for God to recognize his utter helplessness.

What else is open to man in this situation but to wait and hope? He can, if he thinks he has the strength, resist. 'The Contender' stiffens himself in absolute resistance:

He lay crucified with all his strength
On the earth
Grinning towards the sun
Through the tiny holes of his eyes
And towards the moon
And towards the whole paraphernalia of the heavens
Through the seams of his face
With the strings of his lips
Grinning through his atoms and decay
Grinning into the black
Into the ringing nothing
Through the bones of his teeth

Sometimes with eyes closed

In his senseless trial of strength.

His resistance is senseless because he makes no attempt to understand his position. He is without all knowledge of his enemy, until it seems to be life itself he is contending against. He is the prisoner of his own rigidity.

Yet rebellion, in a bid for freedom, is also doomed:

Once upon a time
There was a person
Running for his life.
This was his fate.
It was a hard fate.
But Fate is Fate.
He had to keep running.

He began to wonder about Fate
And running for dear life.
Who? Why?
And was he nothing
But some dummy hare on a racetrack?

At last he made up his mind,
He was nobody's fool.
It would take guts
But yes he could do it.
Yes yes he could stop.
Agony! Agony
Was the wrenching
Of himself from his running.
Vast! And sudden
The stillness
In the empty middle of the desert.

There he stood – stopped.
And since he couldn't see anybody

To North or to West or to East or to South
He raised his fists
Laughing in awful joy
And shook them at the Universe

And his fists fell off
And his hands fell off
He staggered and his legs fell off

It was too late for him to realize
That this was the dogs tearing him to pieces
That he was, in fact, nothing
But a dummy hare on a racetrack

And life was being lived only by the dogs.
('Existential Song')

The most fundamental tenet of Existentialism is that existence precedes essence. Therefore a man is what he freely chooses to become, and there is no such thing as fate. We have already seen Oedipus Crow trying to assert such freedom. 'Spontaneity', said Samuel Butler, 'is only a term for man's ignorance of the gods.' The dogs are merely the gods in their destructive aspect, the hounds of heaven.

The man in 'Criminal Ballad' is a man who suffers from a kind of double vision. Everything he looks at or experiences automatically tunes him to its opposite, which in normal experience is always at some other time, or happening only to someone else.

And when he walked in his garden and saw his children
Bouncing among the dogs and balls
He could not hear their silly songs and the barking
For machine guns
And a screaming and laughing in the cell
Which had got tangled in the air with his hearing
And he could not turn towards the house
Because the woman of complete pain rolling in flame
Was calling to him all the time
From the empty goldfish pond

He is like the god John Wain imagines in 'Poem', who is at every moment aware of 'the worst grief in the world':

To perceive that spirit of suffering in its raging purity
is to a god the burden of his divinity.

O then, if he exists, have pity on this god.
He is clamped to that wounded crust with its slime of blood.

He has no ignorance to hold him separate.
Everything is known to a god. The gods are desperate.

To perceive that spirit of suffering in its raging purity, to comprehend sympathetically the suffering of the universe as his own, is also the burden of the tragic artist. How is he to bear such a burden? Both poems are extraordinarily close to the feelings experienced by Jessie Watkins during a psychotic episode and recorded by Laing in *The Politics of Experience*:

'I had feelings of – er – of gods, not only God but gods as it were, of beings which are far above us capable of – er – dealing with the situation that I was incapable of dealing with, that were in charge and were running things and – um – at the end of it, everybody had to take on the job at the top. And it was this business that made it such a devastating thing to contemplate, that at some period in the existence of – er – of oneself one had to take on this job, even for only a momentary period, because you had arrived then at awareness of everything. What was beyond that I don't know. At the time I felt that – um – that God himself was a madman...because he's got this enormous load of having to be aware and governing and running things – um – and that all of us had to come up and finally get to the point where we had to experience that ourselves. (129)

It is the feeling that God himself is a madman which makes laughter a more ultimate response than tears to the absurd situation:

> And now he ran from the children and ran through the house
> Holding his bloody hands clear of everything
> And ran along the road and into the wood
> And under the leaves he sat weeping
>
> And under the leaves he sat weeping
>
> Till he began to laugh

'Excess of sorrow laughs' wrote Blake.[5] Hilarity and anguish become indistinguishable:

> Remembering the painted masks and the looming of the balloons
> Of the pinpricked dead
> He rolls on the ground helpless.
>
> ('Crow's Battle Fury')

Death is too like pricking balloons. 'Crow's Battle Fury' offers yet another way of responding to the agony. Crow's helpless unbearable laughter finally drives him mad. He explodes with Cuchulain's battle fury (lines 13–18 are from *The Tain*). Cuchulain's madness was his belief that he could impose his will upon the world by sheer strength and energy such as cannot be in this world. Crow's fury, denied an object, destroys himself. Not as

134

militant egotistical hero, but as reconstituted hair's-breadth survivor learning to walk again, he totters forward:

> (With his glared off face glued back into position
> A dead man's eyes plugged back into his sockets
>
> A dead man's heart screwed in under his ribs
> His tattered guts stitched back into position
> His shattered brains covered with a steel cowl)
>
> He comes forward a step,
>   and a step,
>   and a step –

The quotation from Jessie Watkins continues:

'The journey is there and every single one of us has got to go through it, and – um – everything – you can't dodge it...the purpose of everything and the whole of existence is – er – to equip you to take another step, and so on...'

'...it's an experience that – um – we have at some stage to go through, but that was only one – and that – many more – a fantastic number of – um – things have got to impinge upon us until we gradually build ourselves up into an acceptance of reality, and a greater and greater acceptance of reality and what really exists.' (129–30)

The horrors encountered by the schizophrenic on his psychic journey are often identical with the archetypes of world mythology, the visions of the mystic and the images of the poet. Mythology, mysticism (or the religious tradition in general) and art are all means of understanding and controlling forces which the schizophrenic cannot cope with, alienated as he is in our culture from the universe they inhabit. Tragic art is a sort of intentional schizophrenia, giving an intelligible context to experiences otherwise chaotic and terrifying, objectifying them in images and myths, distancing, creating a space for contemplation, transforming chaos into clarity or harmony. 'Getting clear' is thus both a psychic or spiritual journey, and a stylistic discipline.

In his introduction to Popa's *Selected Poetry*, Hughes claims that, though the world of those East European poets of whom Popa is representative is as horrible as Beckett's, it is not absurd:

It is the only precious thing, and designed in accord with the whole universe....Like men come back from the dead they have an improved perception, an unerring sense of what really counts in being alive. This helplessness in the circumstances has purged them of rhetoric. With delicate manoeuvring, they precipitate out of a world of malicious negatives a happy positive. And they have created a small ironic space, a work of lyrical art, in which their humanity can respect itself. (10–11)

The style of *Crow* is very much such a purged style, distilling at times an amazing clarity. 'My idea was to reduce my style to the simplest clear cell – then regrow a wholeness and richness organically from that point.' *Crow* was abandoned with Hughes scarcely beyond the first phase of this process.

In 'How Water Began to Play', water, having tried and failed both to live and to die, weeps itself clear of both life and death:

> It lay at the bottom of all things
> Utterly worn out utterly clear

The poem's title indicates a stage beyond its ending. Only after suffering the attempt to live and the desire to die is it possible to come through into a clarity of being in which innocence is regained and play is possible. The same journey is charted by Popa in 'Before Play'. Having jumped high to the top of oneself

> Thence one drops by one's own weight
> For days one drops deep deep deep
> To the bottom of one's abyss
>
> He who is not smashed to smithereens
> He who remains whole and gets up whole
> He plays

The theme of 'coming clear' is taken up again in 'Song of Woe':

> Once upon a time
> There was a person
> Wretched in every vein –
> His heart pumped woe.
> Trying to run it clear
> His heart pumped only more muddy woe.
> He looked at his hands, and they were woe.
> His legs there, long, bony and remote
> Like the legs of a stag in wet brambles,
> They also were woe.
> His shirt over the chair at night
> Was like a curtain over the finale
> Of all things.
>
> He walked out onto a field
> And the trees were grief –
> Cemetery non-beings.
> The clouds bore their burdens of grief
> Into non-being.

The flowers
The birds, the spiders
Staring into space like sacrifices
Clung with madman's grip
To the great wheel of woe.

So he flung them out among the stars –
Trees, toppling clouds, birds and insects,
He was rid of them.
He flung away the field and its grass,
The whole grievous funeral,
His clothes and their house,
And sat naked on the naked earth
And his mouth filled his eye filled
With the same muddy woe.

So he abandoned himself, his body, his blood –
He left it all lying on the earth
And held himself resolute
As the earth rolled slowly away
Smaller and smaller away
Into non-being.

And there at last he had it
As his woe struggled out of him
With a terrific cry
Staring after the earth
And stood out there in front of him,
His howling transfigured double.

And he was rid of it.
And he wept with relief,
With joy, laughing, he wept –

And at last, tear by tear,
Something came clear.

Again the poem describes a process of ego-destruction.

Reviewing a book on the Sufis Hughes described their disciplines as 'a highly refined course of moral self-development, annihilating themselves without heaven or hell or religious paraphernalia of any kind, and without leaving life in the world, into the living substance of Allah, the power of Creation' (*Listener*, 29 October 1964). In the same review Hughes claimed that 'Ash Wednesday' would qualify Eliot for the Shaman's magic drum. Hughes' 'Ash Wednesday' is 'Crow Wakes'. Here the speaker has exploded and entered a psychic landscape inside an atom. He sleeps in a stream of cleansing snow-water, but wakes to hear the voices of his bones chattering together. In Eliot there is no life in

the bones, they 'atone to forgetfulness'. But in Hughes each bone
takes on a life of its own. They glory in their vivid, but incompatible memories of life:

> And the breastbone was crying:
> 'I begot a million and murdered a million:
> I was a leopard.' And 'No, no, no, no,
> We were a fine woman,' a rib cried.
> 'No, we were swine, we had devils, and the axe halved us,'
> The pelvis was shouting. And the bones of the feet
> And the bones of the hands fought: 'We were alligators,
> We dragged some beauties under, we did not let go.'
> And, 'We were suffering oxen,' and 'I was a surgeon,'
> And 'We were a stinking clot of ectoplasm that suffocated a nun'

When they see him they pursue him, apparently intent on being
reassembled, binding him once again to a world of killing and
madness and obscenity.

> They came howling after me and I ran.
> A freezing hand caught hold of me by the hair
> And lifted me off my feet and set me high
> Over the whole earth on a blazing star
> Called

The poem ends there. Perhaps that is the moment Crow wakes
from his nightmare – or wakes to the nightmare of incarnation
from which, in his dream, he had been miraculously rescued.

The fate of the elephant in 'Crow's Elephant Totem Song' is
not dissimilar. This poem is a sort of Just So Story – How the
Elephant got his Invulnerability. The elephant, originally, was
delicate and small and beautiful, with 'aged eyes of innocence and
kindliness'. He knew 'the Land of Peaceful', being a vegetarian
who could afford to be kindly and bask in his own ease. But he
was vulnerable and he lived among hyenas, each locked in the
hell of his own carnivorous nature. They envied the elephant his
grace and prayed to him:

> Lift us from the furnaces
> And furies of our blackened faces
> Within these hells we writhe
> Shut in behind the bars of our teeth
> In hourly battle with a death
> The size of the earth
> Having the strength of the earth.

138

He could not 'correct' the hyenas, but they could force him to get himself corrected, to accommodate himself to their world, the world of the five senses.

> In rage in madness then they lit their mouths
> They tore out his entrails
> They divided him among their several hells
> To cry all his separate pieces
> Swallowed and inflamed
> Amidst paradings of infernal laughter.
>
> At the Resurrection
> The Elephant got himself together with correction
> Deadfall feet and toothproof body and bulldozing bones
> And completely altered brains
> Behind aged eyes, that were wicked and wise.
>
> So through the orange blaze and blue shadow
> Of the afterlife, effortless and immense,
> The Elephant goes his own way, a walking sixth sense,
> And opposite and parallel
> The sleepless Hyenas go
> Along a leafless skyline trembling like an oven roof
> With a whipped run
> Their shame-flags tucked hard down
> Over the gutsacks
> Crammed with putrefying laughter
> Soaked black with the leakage and seepings
> And they sing: 'Ours is the land
> Of loveliness and beautiful
> Is the putrid mouth of the leopard
> And the graves of fever
> Because it is all we have – '
> And they vomit their laughter.
>
> And the Elephant sings deep in the forest-maze
> About a star of deathless and painless peace
> But no astronomer can find where it is.

The elephant is resurrected massive and toothproof, his innocence now, on the far side of experience, become wisdom. He has come clear of the frenzied fevered life of the five senses, by becoming sufficiently thick-skinned, insulated, against the pressures of the outside world to be able to create and live in terms of an inner world which death and pain cannot penetrate. No astronomer can find the star the elephant sings of because it exists only in inner space.

These 'coming clear' poems seem not only to be enacting a

psychic death and resurrection, but also to be expressing a Manichean world-denying. If this world is 'the great wheel of woe', 'a grievous funeral', where the soul can find its peace only by creating a separate and opposite world within, and if this process involves jettisoning your own body and five senses, what is there left to be within? Once you have shed everything, said goodbye to the earth and your own body, where are you? Can there really be blazing stars and new worlds in a physical vacuum, in nothingness?

These are the questions Hughes asks in 'The New World', a sequence of six beautiful and eerie little lyrics written in 1968 to be set to music by Gordon Crosse. The six poems rock in a perfectly balanced tension between two impulses, the impulse to take off, to fling the world away and rush towards a distant star where all is light, and the impulse, once out there in emptiness and utter loneliness, unable to land on any star, to want desperately to get back.

The fourth poem is the most powerful of the set:

> I said goodbye to earth.
> I stepped into the wind.
> Which entered the tunnel of fire
> Beneath the mountain of water.
>
> I arrived at light
> Where I was shadowless.
> I saw the snowflake crucified
> On the nails of nothing.
>
> I heard the atoms praying
> To enter his kingdom,
> To be broken like bread
> On a warm sill, and to weep.

Here the desolation is invaded by an earthly, almost homely, image, the breaking of bread on a warm sill. The suggestion is of an open window and sunshine and birds to feed. Simultaneously, there is of course the imagery of crucifixion and holy communion. 'His kingdom' is equally the kingdom of pain and death and of joy and beauty. The atoms still pray to enter it, and God would rather be a man on a cross than not be man at all.

Hughes' introduction to his *A Choice of Shakespeare's Verse* is a valuable commentary on two important recent poems, 'Crow's

Song About Prospero and Sycorax', and 'Crow's Song About England'. In it he describes the symbolic fable Shakespeare found as a metaphor for his own nature. The fable is told in a fragmentary or oblique way in almost every play, but in the two long poems 'Venus and Adonis' and 'The Rape of Lucrece' we find 'the whole fable, beautifully intact and very precisely analysed'. The fable, which gives us Shakespeare's response to the permanent conflict between reason, control and morality on the one hand and Nature on the other, between Apollo (or Pentheus) and Dionysus, Adonis and Venus, Prospero and Sycorax, is also a metaphor for the crisis of sensibility through which England passed in Shakespeare's time. The dragon or savage bear is now the wild boar which killed Adonis:

The boar that demolished Adonis was, in other words, his own repressed lust – crazed and bestialized by being separated from his intelligence and denied. The Venus which he refused became a demon and supplanted his consciousness. The frigid puritan, with a single terrible click, becomes a sexual maniac – a destroyer of innocence and virtue, a violator of the heavenly soul, of the very thing he formerly served and adored. (192)

In *Measure for Measure* we see Adonis, now called Angelo, become Tarquin. And Hamlet is another product of the same crisis. The time is out of joint and his own split psyche mirrors the time:

And this is where Shakespeare's hero comes staggering in. Mother-wet, weak-legged, horrified at the task, boggling – Hamlet.

The young puritanical idealist from Wittenberg can cope neither with ghosts nor sexuality. Once disenchanted, he falls first into a suicidal cynicism, then into random cruelty and murderous madness. In giving him his task the ghost had warned Hamlet 'Taint not thy mind.' Only a balanced, untainted mind could possibly cope. But Hamlet, as Lawrence put it

is overpowered by horrible revulsion from his physical connection with his mother, which makes him recoil in similar revulsion from Ophelia and almost from his father, even as a ghost. He is horrified at the merest suggestion of physical connection, as if it were an unspeakable taint. This, no doubt, is all in the course of the growth of the 'spiritual-mental' consciousness, at the expense of the instinctive-intuitive consciousness. Man came to have his own body in horror, especially in its sexual implications and so he began to suppress with all his might his instinctive-intuitive consciousness, which is so radical, so physical, so sexual. (*Introduction to These Paintings*, 188)

In the terms of Hughes' analysis

Hamlet is Adonis, half-possessed by Venus (his black suit), refusing to become Tarquin complete. His madness is the first fear of the rip in his mind – through which the boar will enter. When Ophelia dies her flower-death, we know it has happened: Hamlet must now act out his Tarquin destiny – but in full consciousness, and resisting all the way, and never quite ceasing to be Adonis. It is the death of Adonis in very slow motion. (195)

Here is 'Crow's Song About Prospero and Sycorax':

> She knows, like Ophelia,
> The task has swallowed him.
> She knows, like George's dragon,
> Her screams have closed his helmet.
>
> She knows, like Jocasta,
> It is over.
> He prefers
> Blindness.
>
> She knows, like Cordelia,
> He is not himself now
> And what he speaks must be discounted
> Though it will be the end of them both.
>
> She knows, like God,
> He has found
> Something
> Easier to live with...
>
> His death and her death.

The 'she' is Sycorax, the 'he' Prospero. Prospero's task was to create for his daughter a world without monsters, without passion or conflict or tragedy – a Brave New World indeed. To stop the screams merely close your helmet. To see no evil, put your own eyes out. Oedipus says to his mother:

> You are spoiling my comfortable darkness
> forcing me to see again   go away
> (Seneca, *Oedipus*, 53)

King Lear repeats the pattern of *Hamlet*:

Hamlet, looking at Ophelia, sees his mother in bed with his uncle and goes mad...Lear, looking at Cordelia, sees Goneril and Regan and goes mad. (*Shakespeare's Verse*, 192)

His madness is the total repudiation of Nature, a repudiation more uncompromising even than Edmund's. What should have been a particular blessing becomes a general curse. To redeem Nature from that curse costs Cordelia her life.

Sycorax, the triple-Hecate, the life-bringing Venus, is Prospero's mother wife and daughter. She is the life of the senses which in his austere morality he tries to banish from his, or rather Caliban's, island.

In *The White Goddess* Graves claims that Shakespeare 'knew and feared' her:

Her last appearance in the plays is as the 'damned witch Sycorax' in *The Tempest*. Shakespeare in the person of Prospero claims to have dominated her by his magic books, broken her power and enslaved her monstrous son Caliban – though not before extracting his secrets from him under colour of kindness. Yet he cannot disguise Caliban's title to the island nor the original blueness of Sycorax's eyes. (426)

Hughes goes further:

Shakespeare's persistence has to be admired. After all his experience of the odds against the likelihood, he did finally succeed in salvaging Lucrece from the holocaust and Adonis from the boar. He rescued the puritan abstraction from the gulf of Nature. He banished Venus, as Sycorax, the blue-eyed hag. He humbled Tarquin as Caliban, the poetry crammed half-beast. And within an impenetrable crucible of magic prohibitions, he married Lucrece (Miranda) to Adonis (Ferdinand). But what a wooden wedding! What proper little Puritan puppets! And what a ghastly expression on Prospero's cynical face. We know why he wants to drown his book in the sea (where Venus was born – the lap of Creation) – it contains the tragedies, with their evidence. (198)

It is a commonplace in hostile criticism of Hughes that his poems, in Colin Falck's words, 'tell us nothing about the urban and civilised human world'. On the contrary, having found his bearings and standards in his earlier work Hughes has come more and more to concern himself in his poems with the failure of English intelligence and sensibility in the modern world, the causes and results of that alienation from the sources of life which characterizes our civilization, and the mass neurosis of our urban society. In his Introduction to *A Choice of Shakespeare's Verse* Hughes gives his version of how England lost her soul:

A historical development that worked itself out in theology as a war over metaphysical symbols, worked itself out in the imagination and nervous systems of individuals as a war over 'the dark and vicious place', a struggle over the fallen body, and a final loss of the creative soul. When the physical presence of love has been degraded to lust, and forbidden lust has combined with every other forbidden thing to become a murderous devil, life itself has become a horror, the maiden has become a whore and a witch, and the

miraculous source of creation has become the empty hole through into
Nothing. (199)

That development did not end with the Civil War. Industrialism
gave it a new impetus towards what Huxley, in 'To the Puritan
All Things Are Impure', called the religion of Fordism:

> Fordism demands that we should sacrifice the animal man (and along with
> the animal, large sections of the thinking, spiritual man) not indeed to God,
> but to the machine. There is no place in the factory, or in that larger factory
> which is the modern industrialised world, for animals on the one hand, or for
> artists, mystics, or even finally, individuals on the other. Of all the ascetic
> religions Fordism is that which demands the cruellest mutilations of the
> human psyche – demands the cruellest mutilations and offers the smallest
> spiritual returns. Rigorously practised for a few generations, this dreadful
> religion of the machine will end by destroying the human race.

Several poems show Crow moving in this world. The cruel
mutilations by which the maiden is turned into whore are shown
in 'Crow's Song About England', where Adonis, 'desensitized,
stupefied and brutalized by his rational scepticism', not only
denies Venus but savagely desecrates her.

> Once upon a time there was a girl
> Who tried to give her mouth
> It was snatched from her and her face slapped
> She tried to give her eyes
> They were knocked to the floor the furniture crushed them
> She tried to give her breasts
> They were cut from her and canned
> She tried to give her cunt
> It was produced in open court she was sentenced
>
> She stole everything back
>
> She was mad with pain she humped into a beast
> She changed sex he came back
>
> Where he saw her mouth he stabbed with a knife
> Where he saw her eyes he stabbed likewise
> Where he saw her breasts her cunt he stabbed
>
> He was sentenced
>
> He escaped lobotomised he changed sex
> Shrunk to a little girl she came back
>
> She tried to keep her mouth
> It was snatched from her and her face slapped
> She tried to keep her eyes
> They were knocked to the floor the furniture crushed them
> She tried to keep her breasts

They were cut from her and canned
She tried to keep her cunt
It was produced in open court she was sentenced
She did life

What is here done to the girl is exactly the process of desecration and profanation of personal worlds of experience which Laing and others have described from the point of view of those who have to try to put the pieces together again: 'When our personal worlds are rediscovered and allowed to reconstitute themselves, we first discover a shambles. Bodies half-dead; genitals dissociated from heart; heart severed from head; heads dissociated from genitals' (*Politics of Experience*, 46).

The poem is about England in that it describes, among other things, what Englishmen have done and are doing to their richest inheritance, their mother-land.

Most of the criticisms which have been levelled against Hughes are, up to a point, true. That is, they are true (with reservations) of his worst poems and passages. Every poet has his characteristic faults (often closely associated with his characteristic strengths, especially in a poet who takes such risks). In any collection of sixty poems there are bound to be a few bad patches. But it is critical dishonesty of the worst kind to review a book (as Ian Hamilton did in the *The Times Literary Supplement*) entirely in terms of those passages, as though there were nothing else. There are many poems in *Crow* which are not open to any of Hamilton's criticisms; but he never mentions them, nor the strengths they exemplify. And he must be the only reader of *Crow* who found the experience 'a cosy unperplexing wallow'.

The critic whose outlook is based on a rational scepticism...cannot distinguish between fears for his own mental security and the actions of the Universe...What he can do is judge works and deeds of rational scepticism within a closed society that agrees on the terms used. He can tell you why a poem is bad as a work of rational scepticism, but he cannot tell you why it is good as a poem. (*London Magazine*, January 1971)

Such critics want to safeguard their fragile values by dictating that all art which denies or even questions them is *ipso facto* bad art. For Hughes nothing is assumed in advance, no territory is out of bounds.

Crow was acclaimed by the great majority of reviewers. C. B.

Cox called it 'a most extraordinary work of genius'. Alan Brown-john wrote: 'It is not possible any longer to begrudge him major status among English poets of our time.' One would have thought not. Certainly there are faults. Crude, bludgeoning, portentous, fashionable, secondhand, facile, glib, self-indulgent – quotations could be found (and were found) to justify all these adjectives. I am sure that J. M. Newton is as aware of these faults as any other critic, but he generously saw that the only important job for the critic at this moment in response to a talent of this magnitude is to select the best poems and passages and try to account for the power and truth of them. As Jeremy Robson concluded: 'Although one may point to particular flaws and indulgences, they fall away within the context of the overall, heroic, tragic, achievement.'

PROMETHEUS ON HIS CRAG

From the point of view of a man alienated from his source creation arises from despair and ends in failure. But such a man has not trodden the path to the end of time, the end of space, the end of darkness, and the end of light. He does not know that where it all ends, there it all begins.

We are not able even to *think* adequately about the behaviour that is at the annihilating edge. But what we think is less than what we know: what we know is less than what we love: what we love is so much less than what there is. And to that precise extent we are so much less than what we are.

Yet if nothing else, each time a new baby is born there is a possibility of reprieve. Each child is a new being, a potential prophet, a new spiritual prince, a new spark of light, precipitated into the outer darkness. Who are we to decide that it is hopeless? (R. D. Laing, *The Politics of Experience*)

In 1971 Hughes accompanied Peter Brook and his International Centre for Theatre Research to Persia for the Fifth Shiraz Festival. There he wrote *Orghast* which is the name both of the play and of the invented language in which it is written. *Orghast* was based on several myths and folk tales, but at the centre was the story of Prometheus. At the same time Hughes wrote a number of little poems about Prometheus, twenty-one of which are collected in *Prometheus on His Crag*. The poems assume a knowledge of the basic myth.

Prometheus, a Titan (that is, an immortal, a primitive pre-Olympian god), created man according to some versions of the myth. According to all he became the self-elected champion of mankind against the injustice of Zeus, stealing fire from heaven that men might warm themselves and cook their meat and forge metal:

> And fire has proved
> For men a teacher in every art, their grand resource.
> (Aeschylus, *Prometheus Bound*)

His punishment was to be crucified upon a rock where a vulture gorged itself daily upon his liver, which grew again during the night. His name means Foresight, and his one weapon against Zeus was his foreknowledge that Zeus would be overthrown by his own son if he did not ultimately free Prometheus.

Zeus also punished mankind through Prometheus' brother Epimetheus (Hindsight) with the gift of the first woman, Pandora, beautiful, but bringing with her all the evils which have ever since beset mankind. She also brought Hope, lest man should seek to avoid these evils by suicide. Or in one version it is Prometheus who puts Hope into Pandora's jar. In Aeschylus Prometheus claims

> I caused men no longer to foresee their death.
> I planted firmly in their hearts blind hopefulness.

The poems are short, most of them of 11, 14 or 17 lines made up of single first and last lines with the rest in triplets. Many are internal monologues of Prometheus as he contemplates his own situation, the god who has condemned him to it, the vulture, and such fellow-sufferers as Io, a maiden turned by Zeus into a heifer perpetually pursued by a hornet, 'bucking the bee of the Creator'. They are poems stripped of everything but their meanings, of all rhetoric and imagery. They are the forged links of a chain, as hard as blue steel. The world is shrunk to the size of an icon, a water-bead, a grain of sand, an atom. Language is an instrument for probing relentlessly towards the centre. It is speech appropriate to one who says, in Aeschylus,

> Under such suffering, speech and silence are alike
> Beyond me.

When Hughes' Prometheus tries to speak

> the mouth shuts
> Savagely on a mouthful
> Of space-fright which makes the ears ring.

Ted Hughes has described *Prometheus on His Crag* as 'a limbo. . .a numb poem about numbness', but it is much more than that. It is the culmination of 'the search for liberation through knowledge' which has constituted Hughes' main creative effort for so long. In 'The Rock' Hughes wrote of the freedom of the moors and the constriction of the dark valley, his childhood home: 'That was where the division of body and soul, for me, began.' Its location is now the world's edge, the Caucasus, the needle of Elbruz, with Prometheus, a blue wedge through his breastbone into the rock, an immortal god nailed to the human world of injustice and agony.

Prometheus' first sensation when he recovers consciousness is that he has been changed into an eagle. He feels released rather than imprisoned.[1] All doubts and distractions fall from him as his 'lungs gulp huge clarity', the clarity of existence seen for the first time as it is:

> Unadjusted by vision or prayer–so.

He is utterly helpless, simplified to a wide eye taking all in.

> Nevertheless, now he exults – like an eagle
> In the broadening vastness, the reddening dawn
> Of the fact
> That cannot be otherwise
> And could not have been otherwise,
> And never can be otherwise.
> And now, for the first time
>   relaxing
>   helpless
> The Titan feels his strength.
>
>   (poem 2)

It is the strength which comes from knowing the worst, and knowing that he can survive it. But worse is yet to come. His shout announcing the end of the 'world of holy, happy notions' (the freezing clarity kills it) also wakes the vulture whose every feather says

> 'Today is a fresh start
> Torn up by its roots
> As I tear the liver from your body.'
>   (poem 4)

That too he must learn to live with. He has not foreseen the vulture. He has associated the 'reddening dawn' with his new awareness and power, but not his own blood suffusing heaven.

Poems 5 to 8 record the agony, and not just the agony of Prometheus:

>   So all that day
> The shuddering chestnut tree tore slowly open
> With its arms full,
> And under it – the woman again[2]
> With her brimming jar
> Calling to him.

The association of Prometheus with a chestnut tree (Yeats' 'great-rooted blossomer'), the tree with Pandora, and its arms full of chestnuts with her jar full of evils, suggests that the agony of Prometheus is comparable to all the birth-agonies of the world. Prometheus 'knew what was coming' only insofar as he knew now of the coming of the vulture and the pain. He did not know what was coming to birth. He did not foresee, blinded by pain, his own rebirth, with the splitting open of fig and mountain, the tearing of the shell by the vulture. The rough outer shell or husk of the chestnut must split open to release the gleaming kernel within.

In poem 6 Prometheus (who also gave men words, numbers, and the art of forecasting) bites his prophetic tongue off in his agony. Instead of a clearly articulated vision of the future, dead thoughts issue in senseless chatter, a heap of broken images, ancient proverbs mixed with fortune-telling and a dabbling in the occult, in a fragmented wasteland vision which is, if he only knew it, a true vision of our time:

> Below, among car-bumpers and shopping baskets,
> A monkey of voice, shuffling Tarot
> For corpses and embryos, quotes Ecclesiastes
> To the clock that talks backward.

In poem 8 Prometheus begins to recover his lucidity. He knows that the vulture holds the secret of his fate.

Eventually Prometheus begins to admire the vulture. Poem 9 is like a recapitulation of Hughes' career, with Prometheus envying the simply-mindedness and poised centrality of the vulture as Hughes had once of the hawk:

> It knew what it was doing
>
> It went on doing it
> Swallowing not only his liver
> But managing also to digest its guilt
>
> And hang itself again just under the sun
> Like a heavenly weighing scales
> Balancing the gift of life
>
> And the cost of the gift
> Without a tremor –
> As if both were nothing.

The gift is Prometheus' own gift of life and fire to men and the gods' balancing gift of Pandora ('All gifts'). The cost is her jar brimming with all the evils and pain and death. The gift and the cost together are everything, yet they balance as perfectly as if the scales were empty. Prometheus also hangs weighing the cost. In his case it seems there is the weight of the world in one pan and nothing in the other more substantial than the trembling swallow-tail butterfly which, in his dream, replaces the hammer-splayed head of the spike.

Poem 11 stands at the centre of the sequence. Here, for the first time, Prometheus is no longer screaming or incoherent. He is able to sing a song to his wounds even as the vulture reopens them.

> The sun signalled him red through his closed eyelids
> The vulture rustled
> And the smoulder of man rose from the cities.
>
> But he went on singing –
> A pure
> Unfaltering morphine
> Drugging the whole earth with bliss.

The body of Prometheus is the body of humanity, his wounds its smouldering cities. And it is no incomprehensible external evil which has caused the ruin of cities. It is the misuse of the gift of fire because the gift of knowledge was not accompanied by the gift of understanding. Prometheus has yet to win understanding from his wounds, but at least his pure unfaltering song brings to suffering mankind a blissful numbness.

Prometheus' first attempt to explain the vulture is as 'the revenge of the wombs/To show him what it was like' since

> He had invented them.
> Then stolen the holy fire, and hidden it in them.
>
> It seemed to him
> The wombs drummed like furnaces
> And that men were being fed to the wombs.
>
> And it seemed
> Babies were being dragged crying pitifully
> Out of the wombs.
>
> (poem 13)

The holy fire is the creative energy of the sun. But the sun derives its energy from nuclear processes which consume mass and convert it into energy. Various natural processes (wombs) convert the energy back into mass. But the system is circular. The scales are always balanced between creation and destruction. The whole process is speeded up in Prometheus' own body. What he grows in the night the sun takes back in the day.

In another attempt to understand the frenzy of life Prometheus sees everything whipping everything else with invisible whips. Men and women

> whip their animals and their engines
> To get them from under the whips
> . . .
>
> as if being were a whipping
>
> Even the earth leaping
>
> Like a great ungainly top
>
> (poem 14)

All life is a frantic effort to escape the lashes, the invisible tongues. But if being is a whipping there can be no escape in life. Escape, Freedom, is only 'his soul's sleepwalking'. Prometheus always wakes

> In a new aeon
> to the old chains
> and the old agony.

He is no exception. Rather he is the very prototype of the human condition. His body is at the centre of every aeon, like the grit at the centre of every pearl. Without the grit, which is suffering, there would be no pearl – the priceless recognition which can be won only from suffering.

Poem 18 is the first to suggest that the pearl is worth it. The whole scene with all the characters is presented as an icon. It is a scene of permanent religious significance, the characters fixed in their roles and relationships. But there is one tiny figure easily overlooked, not only because it is tiny, but because it does not seem to belong to the fixed tableau of torment, but seems quite free to come and go and quite insignificant:

> The figure overlooked in this fable
> Is the tiny trickle of lizard
>
> Listening near the ear of Prometheus,
> Whispering – at his each in-rip of breath,
> Even as the vulture buried its head –
>
> 'Lucky, you are so lucky to be human!'

The word 'trickle' has all the opposite associations from the word 'icon'. The lizard is part of the flux of life, an emanation of the earth itself. There is a Lawrence poem where being a lizard is contrasted with being human. It ends:

> If men were as much men as lizards are lizards
> they'd be worth looking it.
>
> ('Lizard')

All lizards are all lizard. And all are alike. A lizard has no under-standing of its condition, or, if it suffers, of its suffering. It has no imagination and therefore no hope. It seems to be free but is in fact eternally imprisoned within its own predestined lizardness. Even as the vulture buries its head Prometheus asserts his humanity in continuing to defy Zeus and in trying to convert the pain into THE PAYMENT, redeeming his people by teaching them precisely how lucky they are, not simply in spite of pain and death but in a mysterious way *because* of them, to be human.

By poem 20 Prometheus has accumulated so many alternative hypotheses for the vulture's mystery that his mind circles like the vulture, seems to be bound on a wheel or confronted by an in-finite recession of horrors. Or perhaps the vulture is all these things, the total, hardly conceivable cost, the dragon with a hundred mouths:

> Prometheus on his crag
> Pondered the vulture. Was this bird
> His unborn half-self, some hyena
> Afterbirth, some lump of his mother?
>
> Or was it his condemned human ballast –
> His dying and his death, torn daily
> From his immortality?
>
> Or his blowtorch godhead
> Puncturing those horrendous holes
> In his human limits?
>
> Was it his prophetic familiar?
> The Knowledge, pebble-eyed,
> Of the fates to be suffered in his image?
>
> Was it the flapping, tattered hole –
> The nothing door
> Of his entry, draughting through him?
>
> Or was it atomic law –
> Was Life his transgression?
> Was he the punished criminal aberration?
>
> Was it the fire he had stolen?
> Nowhere to go and now his pet,
> And only him to feed on?

Or the supernatural spirit itself
That he had stolen from,
Now stealing from him the natural flesh?
Or was it the earth's enlightenment –
Was he an uninitiated infant
Mutilated towards alignment?
Or was it his anti-self –
The him-shaped vacuum
In unbeing, pulling to empty him?
Or was it, after all, the Helper
Coming again to pick at the crucial knot
Of all his bonds...?
Image after image. Image after image. The vulture
Circled
Circled
Circled.

Prometheus is the locus of torment, the cross. He is a living oxy-moron, a fractured unity. As his brother Atlas stands for ever at the Western extremity of the world holding heaven and earth apart, so Prometheus hangs for ever at the Eastern edge 'nailing heaven and earth together'. He has the worst of both worlds. He cannot be a god because, having elected to share man's condition, his 'condemned human ballast' drags him down. Half of him is now tied to mere matter, undifferentiated, unborn, incapable of ever coming into being, coming clear of the earth and its processes, pain, change and death. He cannot be a man because his godhead gives him not only immortality but a knowledge of light, har-mony, ecstasy, which his human limits fall so short of.

But perhaps it is only by puncturing holes in human limits that they can be extended. Prometheus did not foresee the vulture; there may yet be other fates he has not foreseen. If 'a return to his earliest' is his only hope of freedom (poem 17) the door of his entry may be needed again. If his 'dissolution' is required, the fire must feed on him, his natural flesh be stolen. Mutilation may be the only way to achieve an enlightenment other than by alignment with the earth's laws, or perhaps the earth's laws may be seen very differently after enlightenment. Perhaps he needs to be emptied in order to make room for something new. The final image subsumes all these possibilities. The vulture may be the Helper after all.[3] Of the 'crucial knot' Joseph Campbell says:

In every system of theology there is an umbilical point, an Achilles tendon which the finger of mother life has touched, and where the possibility of perfect knowledge has been impaired. The problem of the hero is to pierce himself (and therewith his world) precisely through that point; to shatter and annihilate that key knot of his limited existence. (*The Hero With a Thousand Faces*, 147)

The tyrant Zeus, the 'supernatural spirit that he had stolen from', is the father. The 'filthy–gleeful' face of the vulture is the gloating face of that god.

The problem of the hero going to meet the father is to open his soul beyond terror to such a degree that he will be ripe to understand how the sickening and insane tragedies of this vast and ruthless cosmos are completely validated in the majesty of Being. The hero transcends life with its peculiar blind spot and for a moment rises to a glimpse of the source. He beholds the face of the father, understands – and the two are atoned. (*Ibid.*, p. 147)

Campbell defines atonement thus:

Atonement (at-one-ment) consists in no more than the abandonment of that self-generated double monster – the dragon thought to be God (superego) and the dragon thought to be Sin (repressed id). But this requires an abandonment of the attachment to ego itself, and that is what is difficult. One must have a faith that the father is merciful, and then a reliance on that mercy. Therewith, the centre of belief is transferred outside of the bedeviling god's tight scaly ring, and the dreadful ogres dissolve.

It is in this ordeal that the hero may derive hope and assurance from the helpful female figure, by whose magic (pollen charms or power of intercession) he is protected through all the frightening experiences of the father's ego-shattering initiation. For if it is impossible to trust the terrifying father-face, then one's faith must be centred elsewhere (Spider Woman, Blessed Mother); and with that reliance for support, one endures the crisis – only to find, in the end, that the father and mother reflect each other, and are in essence the same. (*Ibid.*, 130)

We are taken from the mother, chewed into fragments and assimilated to the world-annihilating body of the ogre for whom all the precious forms and beings are only the courses of a feast; but then, miraculously reborn, we are more than we were. (*Ibid.*, 162)

Prometheus' quest, like that of all heroes of myth, is, ultimately to find himself, that is, to recreate himself and the world:

> His mother covers her eyes.
> The mountain splits its sweetness.
> The blue fig splits its magma.
>
> Birth-hacked flesh-ripeness.
> The cry bulging, a slow mire
> Bubbles scalded.

The mountain utters
Blood and again blood.
Puddled, blotched newsprint.

Crocus evangels.
A mountain is flowering
A gleaming man.

Cloud-bird
Midwifes the upglare naphtha,
Opening the shell.

As Prometheus eases free
And sways to his stature
And balances, and treads

On the dusty peacock film where the world floats.
(*Prometheus on His Crag*, poem 21)

Prometheus' mother is the mountain, the whole earth, and the
fruit of the earth. The earth itself, the chestnut, the fig, all are
covered with a shell or skin within which is the magma (any crude
mixture of mineral or organic matters in their pasty state; a
stratum of fluid matter lying beneath the earth's crust). This
'slow mire' of unrealized life at the same time imprisons and
cradles, entombs and enwombs that which is always waiting to be
born. The crocus breaking through the lifeless winter earth is like
a herald angel announcing the coming of the new man. For him
what has to be broken through is the 'wordy earth' (poem 19), the
hard shell of the ego and the whole pseudo-reality built up by a
conspiracy of egos with their dependence on words to hold the
world together, like a paste of blood-sodden newsprint. When the
'crucial knot' is unpicked the ego-shell splits open.

Prometheus sheds his human ballast. He is neither nailed to the
world nor flying free of it. Prometheus gleams with newness, but
the world itself is also renewed. Prometheus 'balances' the gift and
the cost, humanity and godhead, heaven and earth:

The universe flows through its full circuit, materialized spirit and spiritualized
matter, undivided and reconciled to itself. (A. G. H. Smith, *Orghast at
Persepolis*, 96)

The transfigured world is beautifully evoked in the last line with
its delicate evanescence and weightless splendour. These last
lines of his latest volume come clear of that sense of down-
dragging, earth-bound mortality which the first lines of his first
volume so powerfully conveyed:

I drown in the drumming ploughland, I drag up
Heel after heel from the swallowing of the earth's mouth.

The earth was then a dragon. Now it is resplendent as a peacock.[4]

Campbell describes the psychic journey of the mythological hero
in terms extraordinarily appropriate to *Prometheus on his Crag*:

Fundamentally it is inward – into depths where obscure resistances are overcome, and long lost, forgotten powers are revivified, to be made available for
the transfiguration of the world. This deed accomplished, life no longer suffers
hopelessly under the terrible mutilations of ubiquitous disaster, battered by
time, hideous throughout space; but with its horror visible still, its cries of
anguish still tumultuous, it becomes penetrated by an all-suffusing, all-
sustaining love, and a knowledge of its own unconquered power. Something
of the light that blazes invisible within the abysses of its normally opaque
materiality breaks forth, with an increasing uproar. The dreadful mutilations
are then seen as shadows, only, of an immanent, imperishable eternity; time
yields to glory; and the world sings with the prodigious, angelic, but perhaps
finally monotonous, siren music of the spheres. (*The Hero With a Thousand
Faces*, 29–30)

There is no sense, in *Prometheus on his Crag*, of any system being
worked out. The poems are the stages of the psychic journey sub-
jectively experienced, objectified as myth. The ending, however,
is abrupt and elusive, since, up to that point, we have had no more
than hints – butterfly, pearl, lizard, Helper – of the possibility of
rebirth. For a more systematic, objective account of the process
we must turn to *Orghast* itself, or rather, since *Orghast* is unpublished, to Hughes' own commentary on it in Smith's *Orghast at
Persepolis*.

In the beginning was the Sun, Light, the creative fire (orghast
itself), the Father, and Moa, incarnation, the womb of all things,
the Mother. Their son in time is Krogon who is both Kronos and
Zeus (the syllable Kr in Orghast means 'devour'). Krogon fractures the Divine Harmony of the universe, 'the bliss of making
and unmaking', by trying to stop time, natural processes, replacement, in order to retain his own power for ever. He fears the
energies of the universe, so he imprisons (represses) them. Krogon
has thrown his shadow across the sun, so that his sickness is
within all created beings. It is within Prometheus (here called
Pramanath). But Prometheus has the vision to see beyond
Krogon's world to the eternal harmonies:

Conscious in eternity, he has to live in time. And he cannot solve his dilemma.

He hangs between heaven and earth, almost torn apart, an open wound, immortal.

Something prevents him from solving his dilemma – Krogon. Krogon is in the soul of Pramanath like a demon, who regards his own arrangement as the only one truly suited to this impossible situation.

If Pramanath could abjure his mortal Moa nature, he would no longer be the victim of Krogon. But he remains loyal to his mortal human self. And if he foreswore his immortal nature, he would become one of Krogon's enslaved prisoners.

To solve this demon of disunity within himself, Pramanath descends into the warfare within himself, repeatedly. (94–5)

The vulture is the holy fire, the energies, but seen only through Krogon's sickness, seen as wholly destructive, dragonish, obscene, perhaps even become these things because denied. The only possible resolution of this conflict is to 'unriddle the Vulture', not as Oedipus had tried to unriddle the Sphinx, with an axe, nor as Crow had responded to the serpent (his mother), 'the sphinx of the final fact':

> But Crow only peered.
> > Then took a step or two forward,
> Grabbed this creature by the slackskin nape,
>
> Beat the hell out of it, and ate it
> > > ('A Horrible Religious Error')

nor as Hercules in the original myth simply shot the Vulture with a poisoned arrow. Hercules is a demented St George killing whatever he does not understand and does not like the look of. For every dragon he kills, many more appear. He ends in madness slaughtering his own wife and children whom he mistakes for monsters, as did St George in Crow's account of him.

And Agoluz (Hercules), the hero, will have to misunderstand and die in suffering as often as he is created... The cure, for Man, will be to understand this bird and come to some final reconciliation, not to heroify the sickness, as Agoluz does. (*Orghast at Persepolis*, 96–7)

Hughes sums up *Orghast* in these words:

Part 1
is the story of the crime against material nature, the Creatress, source of life and light, by the Violater, the mental tyrant Holdfast, and her revenge. The first plan of her revenge is on the animal level, and it fails, because on the animal level the situation is unalterable, or rather inevitably reproduces itself; the second plan is on the truly human level, and it succeeds, transcending the conflict by creating a being which, like Prometheus (this is the story

of how he survives), includes the elemental opposites, and in whom the collision and pain become illumination, because it is the true account.

Part II
is the story of the tyrant Holdfast in the Underworld, the decomposition of the fallen ego among the voices of its crimes, oversights and victims. Hercules, his son, descends to raise him up, back into the world, but death gives instead the vulture (the mystery of Prometheus's physical/spiritual dilemma), transformed into a woman. (*Orghast at Peresepolis*, 132–3)

Thus Crow, the serpent, the dragon, the vulture, the fallen god, anathema, is restored as Anath, the supreme goddess who preceded Jehovah in Jerusalem, the goddess responsible for perpetuating the life of the gods and of the crops, for sacrifices and for the dew. The transformation is a direct result of the 'final reconciliation' of man and his suffering to which the 'negotiations with whatever happened to be out there', opened in *The Hawk in the Rain*, have brought Hughes.[5]

NOTES

1. In May 1957 Hughes had published in *Granta* a splendid short story called 'O'Kelly's Angel'. O'Kelly captures an Angel and puts it on show on Salisbury Plain. Inevitably, a Protestant mob marches from the north to liberate the Angel, and the Catholics mass to take it to Rome. O'Kelly finds there is more money in instant religion and founds the O'Kellians who soon number ten million fanatics. The army is powerless to prevent the ensuing massacre.

Meanwhile the Angel hangs in its cage:

'a flung tense uprightness, as though it were holding itself by pure intensity in the very tiptop of heaven. Its great eyes stared fixedly beyond the world . . . Its huge unfocussed eyes stared into nothing.'

The Angel shows no awareness of the battle raging around it. In a desperate effort to remove the cause of the chaos the army shells the stadium. The third shell hits the cage, killing O'Kelly and bringing sudden peace to the plain.

'From the little grisly pyre the Angel was rising. Its head flung back, as ever, its wings were folded motionless, and its great eyes gazed out beyond the battlefield, beyond the world, beyond the end of the end.'

A ring of angels descends to meet it.

'Then, as slowly, all the Angels rose together.
All those thousands of bloody eyes stared up.
The Angels rose.

Smaller and smaller grew the bright ring. At last it was only a star. For five long minutes it was a star.
Then the star went out.

Life came back to the Plain terribly. The wounded and the dead lay like the furrows of ploughland. The living stood and looked at their hands, and their arms bloody to the armpits. Then they looked out across the reeking stilled plain. Then they looked at the twisted remains of the cage, and the whitening ashes of O'Kelly's pulpit. Then they looked at the blue zenith of heaven, which was darker now, and where the ordinary stars were beginning.
Then, finally, they looked at each other.'

The Hawk has much in common with this Angel.

2. Emily Brontë described Heathcliff's eyes as 'the clouded windows of hell'. The house described in 'Wind' is at Heptonstall, not far from the Brontë

moors. In *Wuthering Heights* the window does come in. Its breaking is associated with violent emotions, bloodshed, violation and the supernatural. What has there been shut out is not only the stormy elements, but a child from her rightful physical and spiritual home and her inheritance. You cannot shut out death and danger without also shutting out life and love. Yet the body cannot bear total exposure. Heathcliff and Cathy reject book, thought, and (in the sense that they never recognize each other as *separate* people) each other. They dare to be struck dead and are struck dead, finding, in death, that heaven which is forbidden to the living.

3. Between *The Hawk in the Rain* and *Lupercal* there slipped through a magnificent prophetic poem 'Quest', published in an obscure periodical in February 1958 and never reprinted. It is quite unlike anything else of the period in its visionary intensity.

> I know clearly, as at a shout, when the time
> Comes I am to ride out into the darkened air
> Down the deserted streets. Eyes, terrified and hidden,
> Are a weight of watching on me that I must ignore
> And a charge in the air, tingling and crackling bluely
> From the points and edges of my weapons, and in my hair.
> I shall never see the monster that I go to kill.
>
> And how it is ever to be killed, or where it is,
> No one knows, though men have ridden a thousand times
> Against it as I now with my terror standing in my hair,
> Hardly daring risk into my lungs this air the same
> As carried the fire-belch and boistering of the thing's breath
> Whose mere eye unlidded anywhere were a flame
> To stir the marrow deep under most ignorant sleep.
>
> I ride, with staring senses, but in
> Complete blackness, knowing none of these faithful five
> Clear to its coming till out of the blind-spot
> Of the fitful sixth – crash on me the bellowing heaving
> Tangle of a dragon all heads all jaws all fangs,
> And though my weapons were lightning I am no longer alive.
> My victory to raise this monster's shadow from my people
>
> Shall be its trumpeting and clangorous flight
> Over the moon's face to its white-hot icy crevasse
> With fragments of my body dangling from its hundred mouths.

'Quest' may well have grown out of 'Bayonet Charge'. There too the man responds to some incomprehensible but inescapable cosmic imperative:

> In what cold clockwork of the stars and the nations
> Was he the hand pointing that second?

He runs, apparently alone (at least in his own consciousness) towards an enemy he cannot see, nor, with his single bayonet, hope to kill. His terror is like a charge of electricity in 'that blue crackling air'. The relationship with

'Bayonet Charge' might suggest an interpretation of 'Quest' as a war poem. A volunteer soldier goes to raise the shadow of war from his people. Thousands will die and their deaths will buy a brief period of peace. Then thousands more must march to feed the insatiable monster.

Such an interpretation is, by itself, much too small for the poem, though the poem certainly includes it. Too much would be left unaccounted for, or explicable only as exaggeration or posturing – an explanation which the sweep, power and coherence of the poem rules out. 'Quest' is terrifying in the hero's quiet acceptance of the inevitable horror. And the terror is not in the description of the dragon, of which there is only a line, but in that complete blackness in which it must be faced, with all five senses straining but sealed, relying on the unreliable sixth sense to give a moment's warning which would, in any case, be quite useless against such an antagonist, with any weapons. This is some metaphysical horror.

'Quest' could also be an image of the necessary self-surrender of the artist. The artist is a hero who seeks to open negotiations with whatever happens to be out there, who dares to be struck dead, exposing himself to 'manslaughtering shocks', and, far from peeping through his fingers, or watching it on television, rides into the blackness 'with staring senses'. His people on whose behalf he goes would rather he stayed at home with a nice cigarette and a nice view of the park and wrote poems about waiting for the bus. We have become expert at living (or partly living) as though there were no dragon.

But the hero of 'Quest' is obviously not going to negotiate. Nor is he going naked. He is going as fully armed as he can, in darkness possibly because he dare not open his helmet. He is going theoretically to kill, actually to be killed. To what end?

There are several sequels to 'Quest' notably 'Gog', 'A Horrible Religious Error', 'Crow's Account of St George' and 'Bones'.

WODWO

1.   Several of Hughes' works, especially those for children, are remakings of that 'suspect' legend of St George and the Dragon.

The Iron Man, for example, offers an alternative to ruthless cruelty. A terrible space-dragon lands on the earth. Mankind tries to destroy it:

> 'They want to bring the whole world back to the status quo of no space monsters, no intrusion from the unknown. They want the whole world to be settled back to its worldly affairs and to be able to ignore the terrible energies of space.' ('Myth and Education', 65)

In a traditional story, the Iron Man, St George, would kill the dragon. In a more realistic story he would be killed by it. Neither story does anything to resolve the problem, to cure the sickness. The St George story simply advocates 'the complete suppression of the terror':

> 'In other words it is the symbolic story of Christianity, it's the key to the neurotic-making dynamics of Christianity. Christianity in suppressing the

devil, in fact suppresses imagination and suppresses vital natural life. (*Ibid*, 66)

The little boy and the Iron Man make friends with the dragon. They 'Invite space to take part in the life of the world'. His story, Hughes claims, connects you 'with the deepest and most alien seeming powers in your own mind, which are the correspondents of the outermost demon powers of space'.

If Hughes regards the fable of St George as 'suspect', he wholeheartedly approves of Beauty and the Beast. In his own version of this story, the Beast is again a bear. Floreat, the rich man's daughter, is sick in her mind. She dreams she is visited at night by a horrible beast. But when her father and the doctor hide in her bedroom they too see it. They shoot and wound it. It escapes, leaving its blood on mirror and powder-compact. To entertain Floreat they hire a bearkeeper with his dancing bear. (It is the same bear the brother killed 'with claws like garden-forks'.) The bear is bandaged, but dances. Floreat dances with the bear. When her father goes for his camera the bear picks up Floreat and runs off with her. It keeps her in its cave and seems gentle. She comes to love the bear and is happy, cured. But the father comes and shoots the bear again. When he goes into the cave to finish him off, he finds a young man:

> I am the bear. I am the monster in the night.
> Give your belief time. For fifteen years
> I have been a bear in the sight of men and women.
> And at all other times, a flying dragon.
> I would have been a bear and a flying dragon
> To the end of my days
> If Floreat had never said she loved me.
> Those were the words I needed to break the spell.

Of course the words 'befriend' and 'love' are appropriate only within a fantasy, a children's tale. You cannot really befriend or love an angel or a dragon. The dragon, however, is not an actual space being, but the shape given within the psyche to powers which are terrifying and felt to be hostile. Some of them really are hostile, possibly even evil, in which case it is perhaps even more important to recognize them in their true nature. To abolish Satan puts him 'beyond control – gives him complete freedom. As if we should deny an enemy, rather than pin him down in everlasting negotiations' (*Ibid.*, 69).

2. The source is, in fact, *The Golden Bough* (p. 869) where Frazer writes of the brotherhood of the Green Wolf:

'Thus it has been shown that the leading incidents of the Balder myth have their counterparts in those fire-festivals of our European peasantry which undoubtedly date from a time long prior to the introduction of Christianity. The pretence of throwing the victim chosen by lot into the Beltane fire, and the similar treatment of the man, the future Green Wolf, at the midsummer bonfire in Normandy, may naturally be interpreted as traces of an older custom of actually burning human beings on these occa-

sions; and the green dress of the Green Wolf, coupled with the leafy en-
velope of the young fellow who trod out the midsummer fire at Moosheim,
seems to hint that the persons who perished at these festivals did so in the
character of tree-spirits or deities of vegetation. From all this we may
reasonably infer that in the Balder myth on the one hand, and the fire-
festivals and custom of gathering mistletoe on the other hand, we have, as
it were, the two broken and dissevered halves of an original whole. In other
words, we may assume with some degree of probability that the myth of
Balder's death was not merely a myth, that is, a description of physical
phenomena in imagery borrowed from human life, but that it was the same
time the story which people told to explain why they annually burned a
human representative of the god and cut the mistletoe with solemn ceremony. If I am right, the story of Balder's tragic end formed, so to say, the
text of the sacred drama which was acted year by year as a magical rite to
cause the sun to shine, trees to grow, crops to thrive, and to guard man and
beast from the baleful arts of fairies and trolls, of witches and warlocks.
The tale belonged, in short, to that class of nature myths which are meant
to be supplemented by ritual; here, as so often, myth stood to magic in the
relation of theory to practice.'

3.   Lawrence tried to restore the older pagan meanings of the dragon symbolism in Revelation:

'The dragon and serpent symbol goes so deep in every human consciousness, that a rustle in the grass can startle the toughest "modern" to depths
he has no control over . . .

From earliest times, man has been aware of a "power" or potency within
him – and also outside him – which he has no ultimate control over. It is a
fluid, rippling potency which can lie quite dormant, sleeping, and yet be
ready to leap out unexpectedly...

It is swift and surprising as a serpent, and overmastering as a dragon. It
leaps up from somewhere inside him, and has the better of him...

A hero was a hero, in the great past, when he had conquered the hostile
dragon, when he had the power of the dragon *with him* in his limbs and
breast...

The usual vision of the dragon is, however, not personal but cosmic. It is
in the vast cosmos of the stars that the dragon writhes and lashes. We see
him in his maleficent aspect, red. But don't let us forget that when he stirs
green and flashing on a pure dark night of stars it is he who makes the
wonder of the night, it is the full rich coiling of his folds which makes the
heavens sumptuously serene, as he glides around and guards the immunity,
the precious strength of the planets, and gives lustre and new strength to
the fixed stars, and still more serene beauty to the moon. His coils within
the sun make the sun glad, till the sun dances in radiance. For in his good
aspect, the dragon is the great vivifier, the great enhancer of the whole
universe.' (*Apocalypse*, ch. XVI)

4. Hughes read *The Rainbow* when he was about eighteen. He read it in a tent in a field which held horses. During the night a heavy rainstorm came on, and the horses spent the whole night charging from one corner of the field to the other around his tent. But there were several other sources for 'The Rain Horse' including a recurrent dream when he was a boy.

5. 'A man has a persistent fear-dream about horses. He suddenly finds himself among great, physical horses, which may suddenly go wild. Their great bodies surge madly round him, they rear above him, threatening to destroy him. At any minute he may be trampled down...

Examining the emotional reference we find that the feeling is sensual, there is a great impression of the powerful, almost beautiful physical bodies of the horses, the nearness, the rounded haunches, the rearing. Is the dynamic passion in a horse the danger-passion? It is a great sensual reaction at the sacral ganglion, a reaction of intense, sensual, dominant volition. The horse which rears and kicks and neighs madly acts from the intensely powerful sacral ganglion. But this intense activity from the sacral ganglion is male: the sacral ganglion is at its highest intensity in the male. So that the horse-dream refers to some arrest in the deepest sensual activity of the male. The horse is presented as an object of terror, which means that to the man's automatic dream-soul, which loves automatism, the great sensual male activity is the greatest menace. The automatic pseudo-soul, which has got the sensual nature repressed, would like to keep it repressed. Whereas the greatest desire of the living spontaneous soul is that this very male sensual nature, represented as a menace, shall be actually accomplished in life. The spontaneous self is secretly yearning for the liberation and fulfilment of the deepest and most powerful sensual nature.' (D. H. Lawrence, *Fantasia of the Unconscious*, 167–8)

6. Hughes wrote 'The Suitor' on the day after the birth of his son Nicholas. When he read it to Sylvia she said 'That is your best story. But the girl is me, and the flute player is death.'

7. 'The Wound' is what Hughes managed to retain and put into shape of a dream. The dream was of a film, complete, very long, with many episodes. Along with the action, in which he was Ripley, he dreamed a very full written text which was both dramatic and descriptive at the same time, by John Arden. (He had just read *Sergeant Musgrave's Dance*.) He woke up feeling very disappointed that Arden had written something Hughes felt to be absolutely his own. Then he realized that it was his own. He drifted back to sleep and dreamed the whole thing again, in exact detail, perfectly repeated. He woke up and wrote down all he could remember. It faded rapidly, but he managed to get the main thread and most of the episodes. At the time Hughes was working on the Bardo Thodol and that too was in the dream. His first interpretation was that this was his parallel Gothic–Celtic version. When he came later to write up 'The Wound' for radio he changed a great deal and lost much of the original dream which was too cinematic to convert.

8. Of his male tortoise Lawrence wrote:

> Poor little earthy house-inhabiting Osiris,
> The mysterious bull tore him at adolescence into pieces,
> And he must struggle after reconstruction, ignominiously.

The cross on which the tortoise is broken is sexuality. The bull is Dionysus, the torn adolescent Pentheus, or his cousin Acteon, or Adonis.

9. One of Lawrences's finest poems 'Tortoise Shout' comes very close here. The cry of the tortoise *in extremis* is also interpreted as 'incomprehensively both ways':

> A scream,
> A yell,
> A shout,
> A paean,
> A death-agony,
> A birth-cry,
> A submission
> All tiny, tiny, far away, reptile under the first dawn.
> War-cry, triumph, acute-delight, death-scream reptilian,
> Why was the veil torn?
> The silken shriek of the soul's torn membrane?
> The male soul's membrane
> Torn with a shriek half music, half horror.

Lawrence goes on to list cries, including 'the nightingale's piercing cries and gurgles' which have startled the depths of his soul. They are the cries of both joy and pain. What they have in common is that they are torn from us

> Torn, to become whole again, after long seeking for what is lost,
> The same cry from the tortoise as from Christ, the Osiris-cry of
>   abandonment,
> That which is whole, torn asunder,
> That which is in part, finding its whole again through the universe.

The secret Lawrence learns from the tortoise is that giving up the ghost is also receiving the ghost. The spear through the side of the tortoise is sexuality, the command to 'seek his consummation beyond himself'. Lawrence, like Hughes, sees sexuality as a tragic condition. But the last words of self-abandonment 'Consummatum Est' mean not only 'it is finished' but also 'it is accomplished', and Yeats knew that Hamlet and Lear, even in the moment when heaven blazed into their heads, were gay.

10. In Yeats' play *The Death of Cuchulain*, Cuchulain is butchered by a blind old man for twelve pennies and says bitterly: 'Twelve pennies! What better reason for killing a man?' Yeats gives him these last words:

> There floats out there
> The shape that I shall take when I am dead,
> My soul's first shape, a soft feathery shape,

And is not that a strange shape for the soul
Of a great fighting-man?
I say it is about to sing.

In 'Cuchulain Comforted' Yeats follows him beyond the grave where he sews his shroud and joins a chorus of birds who are all the ghosts of 'convicted cowards'.

CROW

1.   Nevertheless, it is a pity that readers are obliged to come to terms with Crow through only a selection of the poems about him and without the folktale context. This makes more likely the mistaken assumption that Crow is merely a mouthpiece for Hughes. Sometimes Hughes admires Crow, sometimes is horrified by him, sometimes both at once. Often we can have no idea where Hughes stands, since he withdraws from the poems. Crow is a technique for total objectivity, like the hypothetical Martian who observes this world and its denizens without preconceptions or habituation. Crow's attitudes are frequently mistaken, confused, or wildly contradictory. For example, the folktale context would make it impossible to assume, as David Holbrook does, that 'Lovesong' gives us Hughes' fixed personal attitude towards sexual love.

   Crow comes to a river. Beside it sits a gigantic horrible female who gets him to carry her across. As they cross, she gets heavier and heavier, driving Crow into the riverbed until the water is up to his mouth. Then she asks him a question which he must answer correctly if her weight is to decrease again. This happens seven times. All the questions concern various mistaken encounters he has had with her in various forms before. His answers recapitulate his progress from his earliest desolation to his ultimate marriage in the Happy Land across the river. 'Lovesong' is one of his earlier answers, to the question 'Who paid most, him or her?' The later question 'Who gives most, him or her?' elicits a very different answer:

Bride and groom lie hidden for three days

She gives him his eyes, she found them
Among some rubble, among some beetles

He gives her her skin
He just seemed to pull it down out of the air and lay it over her
She weeps with fearfulness and astonishment

She has found his hands for him, and fitted them freshly at the wrists
They are amazed at themselves, they go feeling all over her

He has assembled her spine, he cleaned each piece carefully
And sets them in perfect order
A superhuman puzzle but he is inspired
She leans back twisting this way and that, using it and laughing
                                                    incredulously

167

Now she has brought his feet, she is connecting them
So that his whole body lights up

And he has fashioned her new hips
With all fittings complete and with newly wound coils, all shiningly oiled
He is polishing every part, he himself can hardly believe it

They keep taking each other to the sun, they find they can easily
To test each new thing at each new step

And now she smooths over him the plates of his skull
So that the joints are invisible

And now he connects her throat, her breasts and the pit of her stomach
With a single wire

She gives him his teeth, tying their roots to the centrepin of his body

He sets the little circlets on her fingertips

She stitches his body here and there with steely purple silk

He oils the delicate cogs of her mouth

She inlays with deeply-cut scrolls the nape of his neck

He sinks into place the inside of her thighs

So, gasping with joy, with cries of wonderment
Like two gods of mud
Sprawling in the dirt, but with infinite care

They bring each other to perfection.

(Cave Birds, Poem 28)*

2.   The tablet of which this is a fragment is probably the Smaragdine or
Emerald Tablet on which were engraved the thirteen precepts of Hermes
Trismegistus. These precepts formed the basis of both Alchemy and Gnosticism. Any reader well grounded in Alchemy, Gnosticism and Manichaeism
(as I am not) will find many new insights and connections in *Crow*.

3.   J. M. Newton adduces two highly relevant passages from Alan Watts:

'Every individual is an expression of the whole realm of nature, a unique
action of the total universe. This fact is rarely, if ever, experienced by most
individuals. Even those who know it to be true in theory do not sense or
feel it, but continue to be aware of themselves as isolated "egos" inside
bags of skin.
    The first result of this illusion is that our attitude to the world outside
us is largely hostile. We are forever "conquering" nature, space, mountains,
deserts, bacteria, and insects instead of learning to co-operate with them
in a harmonious order. In America the great symbols of this conquest are
the bulldozer and the rocket...' (*The Book : On the Taboo Against Knowing
Who you Are*)

168

'Obviously, I exist only in relation to everything else, but I did not come into that relation from somewhere outside – in such a way that "everything else" would be foreign to or other than myself. I did not alight in this universe like a bird arriving upon a branch from some alien limbo. I grew upon that branch like a leaf. For I am something which everything is doing: I am the whole process waving a flag named me, and calling out "Yoo-hoo!" ' (*Beyond Theology*)

4. One underlying meaning is suggested by Jung:

'*Perfection* is a masculine desideratum, while woman inclines by nature to *completeness*. If a woman strives for perfection she forgets the complementary role of completeness, which, though imperfect by itself, forms the necessary counterpart to perfection. For just as completeness is always imperfect, so perfection is always incomplete, and therefore represents a final state which is hopelessly sterile.' (*Answer to Job*)

In the Kundalini yoga system there are six bodily centres corresponding to six psychological states, and the object of the system is to activate these centres one by one, by awakening the sleeping power called Kundalini, the serpent. This serpent is 'the feminine, form-building, life-giving and -supporting force by which the universe and all its beings are rendered animate' (Campbell, *Myths to Live By*, 108). The first centre is torpid and of the earth. The second, situated in the genitals, is sexuality

(She has come amorous it is all she has come for).

Its name, Svadhishthana, means 'her favourite resort', and its element is water

(She comes as far as water no further).

The first two centres are not specifically human, as distinct from animal, and if further centres are not activated, there is no power (3) or enlightenment (4), no coming clear of this world and exposure to 'the terrifying, devastating aspects of the cosmic powers in their ego-shattering roles' (5), no perception of them in 'their bliss-bestowing, fear-dispelling, wondrous, peaceful, and heroic forms' (6), and no ultimate reconciliation (7). (Campbell, *op. cit.*, 114)

5. There are several poems in *Crow* in which laughter, or a grin, or a smile, seems to have a life of its own. A grin is, of course, the permanent expression of a skull, and takes over the living face at moments other than those of amusement, the face of a woman in labour or a man in a crashing car, a murderer's face or 'the face in the electric chair' ('A Grin'). Such grins are not laughter. But even laughter is perhaps, as Shaw puts it, 'the natural recognition of destruction, confusion, and ruin'. And Beckett defines the 'mirthless laugh' (the 'risus purus', 'the laugh laughing at the laugh') as the laugh at that which is unhappy.

'The Smile' has a different dimension. Like the grin it ranges the earth

Looking for its occasion.

And its occasion is also death. But to die grinning is surely different from to die smiling. At one extreme there is the sordid, vulgar, derisive rictus of Crystalman in David Lindsay's *Voyage to Arcturus*, signifying that there is nothing beyond physical death, and that physical death is obscene. At the other extreme is the expression on the face of the dying Lear, whose heart, like Gloucester's, bursts 'smilingly', signifying a momentary vision of eternity. If Hughes' Grin is nearer the former, his Smile is nearer the latter:

> And the crowd, shoving to get a glimpse of a man's soul
> Stripped to its last shame,
> Met this smile
> That rose through his torn roots
> Touching his lips, altering his eyes
> And for a moment
> Mending everything
>
> Before it swept out and away across the earth.

If creation fails every time in its attempt to adjust man to the universe, at least it ultimately mends everything by returning him to the kind darkness of nothingness.

PROMETHEUS ON HIS CRAG

1. As part of their research into the Manichean themes of the myths and of Calderon's *La Vida Es Sueno*, Peter Brook's company studied a book by Victor Serge called *Men in Prison*. In prison Serge had gradually learned to separate his inner world, which nothing could touch, from the outer world in which he was helpless: 'My lucidity, my freedom are irrevocably mine... Among those who succeed in resisting madness, their intense inner life brings them to a higher conception of life, to a deeper consciousness of the *self*, its values, its strength. At certain moments you feel astonishingly *free*.' Hughes never read the book.

2. My quotations from *Prometheus on His Crag* differ in three places from the Rainbow Press text. These are Hughes' revisions. Poem 5 should read ' – the woman again' not ' – that woman'. Poem 20 should end as quoted on p. 154, and poem 21 is now as quoted on p. 156.

3. In *Orghast* the vulture reaches into the womb saying:

> come from darkness
>   come through nothingness
>   come into peace
> I am the god from beyond division
>
>   · · ·
>
> it is your fate
>   your fear your truth is your terror

> this is your nothingness
> come into light
> and be devoured by truth
> give yourself to god
> surrender to me your god of truth
> of light your god of light your light
> come and lose your darkness

Hughes found that the Prometheus myth fused with, almost subsumed, Crow, St George, Beauty and the Beast, The New World. It also comes close to the Manichean vision of one of the neglected masterpieces of this century, David Lindsay's *A Voyage to Arcturus* (1920). There the protagonist, an Everyman figure called Maskull, goes to the planet Tormance in the system of Arcturus in search of the source of Muspel, a pure white radiance which is God. As he crosses the continents of Tormance he meets with life in an amazing variety of forms. He meets with beauty and love and kindness in purer forms than they are ever known on earth, but he has to learn to reject them all, since they are all deceiving manifestations of Crystalman, whose obscene rictus disfigures even the most beautiful face at the moment of death. (The grin has a similarly independent existence in several Hughes poems.) The Crystalman principle is precisely the attachment to self and to the created world, whose varied colours and forms have been produced by Crystalman (also called Shaping) casting his shadow across the face of Muspel so that the white radiance is split and stained as by a prism, broken down into colours, shapes, phenomena, the whole material universe. Maskull is accompanied on his quest by Krag, who is pain, and who puts him through many ordeals.

Lindsay himself had seen the relevance of the Prometheus myth. Panawe, the first man Maskull meets on Tormance, identifies him with Prometheus. At the half-way stage of his journey Dreamsinter says to him: 'You came to steal Muspel-fire, to give a deeper life to men.' And Maskull's last vision before he dies and is reborn as Nightspore is so close to the image of Prometheus on his Crag as to suggest that Krag's name derives from it:

'He floated towards an immense perpendicular cliff of black rock, without top or bottom. Half-way up it Krag, suspended in mid-air, was dealing blows at a blood-red spot with a huge hammer. The rhythmical, clanging sounds were hideous . . .

'What are you doing, Krag?' he asked. Krag suspended his work and turned round.

'Beating on your heart, Maskull,' was his grinning response.' (239)

Krag's other name, Surtur, suggests both vulture and wounds. Surtur, in Teutonic myth was a fire-giant. Krag's name on earth is Pain. Maskull had thought Krag (the midwife at the birth of Nightspore) to be his enemy and persecutor until the eleventh hour.

He comes ultimately to realize that it is only with Krag's aid, only through the most complete renunciation and self-exposure to redemptive pain that Muspel can be reached.

4. Joseph Campbell, speaking of regression and rebirth experienced in a therapeutic session using L.S.D., uses similar images, including the peacock:

'...a regression to this level may be carried to culmination in an utterly terrifying crisis of actual ego-death, complete annihilation on all levels, followed by a grandiose, expansive sense of release, rebirth, and redemption, with enormous feelings and experiences of decompression, expansion of space, and blinding, radiant light: visions of heavenly blue and gold, columned gigantic halls with crystal chandeliers, peacock-feather fantasies, rainbow spectrums, and the like. The subjects, feeling cleansed and purged, are moved now by an overwhelming love for all mankind, a new appreciation of the arts and of natural beauties, great zest for life, and a forgiving, wonderfully reconciled and expansive sense of God in his heaven and all right with the world.' (*Myths to Live By*, 262)

Laing, in recording a very similar experience, found the image of a Bird of Paradise:

'Garden. Cat at bird. Shoo off nasty cat, and catch bird. How elusive she is, and I am turning into a cat myself. Stop. Cat is a cat is a bird is a non-bird of ineffably frail space suddenly spreading in parabolic grace of authority. How foolish to worry, to try to save her, or grasp her. Perhaps the cat was trying to save her. Let be. Cat and bird. Begriff. The truth I am trying to grasp is the grasp that is trying to grasp it.
    I have seen the Bird of Paradise, she has spread herself before me, and I shall never be the same again.
    There is nothing to be afraid of. Nothing.
    Exactly.
    The Life I am trying to grasp is the me that is trying to grasp it.'
(*The Bird of Paradise*, 156)

'Perhaps the cat was trying to save her.' In a recent Hughes poem, 'Crow's Table Talk', we find a complete revaluation of the relationship between predator and prey:

The tiger
Kills like the fall of a cliff, one-sinewed with the earth,
Himalayas under eyelid, Ganges under fur –
Does not kill.

Does not kill. The tiger blesses with a fang.
The tiger does not kill but opens a path
Neither of life nor of death:
The tiger within the tiger:
The tiger of the earth.
                    O tiger!
O brother of the viper! O beast in blossom!

5.   The only respite ever granted Prometheus was when the vulture stopped, like the rest of creation, to listen to the strains of Orpheus as he charmed Pluto in the Underworld. If we feel that the reconciliation, the ultimate harmony desiderated in *Orghast* is merely theoretical, and that evoked in *Prometheus* 21 a declaration of faith and hope rather than fully substantiated experience, perhaps 'Orpheus', certainly the most beautiful expression of this mystery, is also the most accessible. We can understand and imaginatively share the experience of Orpheus at every stage. The myth, especially in the fresh and moving way Hughes handles it, relates much more easily than the lofty Prometheus myth to common human experience and to familiar tragic art. This treatment, simplified for children, is of course very different from the treatment Hughes would have given the same material had he been writing for adults.

Orpheus plays music so magic that it makes not only the animals but even the trees and stones dance. The secret of his music is happiness, and the secret of his happiness is his wife Eurydice. But a voice (a bird? a spider? a serpent?) keeps coming to Orpheus telling him that every song must be paid for. Orpheus believes that the world is a gift and plays on. Suddenly his hand goes numb and a terrible cry announces that his wife has been bitten by a snake and is dead. Orpheus mourns for a month in silence, then decides to go down to the underworld to find Eurydice. Using his guitar like the drum of a shaman (Orpheus was the first shaman) he beats a path through space:

It carries him
Through the storm of cries,
The last cries of all who have died on earth,
The jealous, screaming laments
Of all who have died on earth and cannot come back.

He lays his road of sound across the heavens.
His guitar carries him.
Into the storm of blood,
The electrical storm of all the blood of all who have died on earth.
He is whirled into the summit of the storm.
Lightnings strike through him, he falls –

He falls into the mouth of the earth.
He falls through the throat of the earth, he recovers.
He rides his serpent of sound through the belly of the earth.
He drives his spear of sound through the bowels of the earth.
Mountains under the earth fall on him, he dodges.
He flies through walls of burning rock and ashes.
His guitar carries him.
He hurtles towards the centremost atom of the earth.
He aims his beam of sound at the last atom.

He smashes through the wall of the last atom.
He falls
He falls
At the feet of Pluto, King of the kingdom of the dead.

Beside Pluto sits Persephone, her face, made of white ivory, 'the pointed, eyeless face of a maggot'. Persephone is also Hecate, the snake goddess, or Agriope ('savage face'), the underground form of Demeter or Aphrodite or Semele. Orpheus was a priest of Dionysus and repeats the journey to the underworld made by Dionysus himself to recover from Persephone his mother Semele. Eurydice is a name for the underground form of the triple goddess, therefore she *is* Persephone, and Orpheus' task is to transform Persephone who has never spoken in the underworld, whose face, a flower on earth, Pluto has never seen open. Orpheus plays, a new solemn music, and gradually her face, 'the white beak of the first sprout of a flower', begins to open. Orpheus offers Pluto a wife for a wife. Pluto can give him only the soul of Eurydice. She returns to earth with him and once again he plays for her, but not as he once played. His new music is tragic art, the opposite of that art which exists only to deceive grief. It creates a context within which experiences otherwise intolerable can be confronted and accommodated. It enables humanity to be reconciled to its losses in the knowledge that they are the price of its joys, of living itself. The roots of life and beauty and joy are in death and corruption and horror (the underworld). It is the music of nature itself:

The trees did not dance. But the trees listened.
The music was not the music of dancing
But of growing and withering,
Of the root in the earth and the leaf in the light,
The music of birth and of death.
And the stones did not dance. But the stones listened.
The music was not the music of happiness
But of everlasting, and the wearing away of the hills,
The music of the stillness of stones,
Of stones under frost, and stones under rain, and stones in the sun,
The music of the seabed drinking at the stones of the hills.
The music of the floating weight of the earth.
And the bears in their forest holes
Heard the music of bears in their forest holes,
The music of bones in the starlight,
The music of many a valley trodden by bears,
The music of bears listening on the earth for bears.
And the deer on the high hills heard the crying of the wolves,
And the salmon in the deep pools heard the whisper of the snows,
And the traveller on the road
Heard the music of love coming and love going
And love lost forever,
The music of birth and of death.
The music of the earth, swaddled in heaven,
    kissed by its cloud and watched by its ray.
And the ears that heard it were also of leaf and of stone.
The faces that listened were flesh of cliff and of river.
The hands that played it were fingers of snakes and a tangle of flowers.

BIBLIOGRAPHY

A. WORKS BY TED HUGHES

(Publication London unless otherwise stated)

The Hawk in the Rain, Faber and Faber, 13 September 1957. First American edition, Harper, 18 September 1957. First paperback edition, Faber and Faber, 1968.

REVIEWS: *Birmingham Post*, 26 Nov. 1957 (Sir Ifor Evans); *Books and Bookmen*, Nov. 1957 (J. C. Hall); *Church Times*, 28 Mar. 1958; *Daily Telegraph*, 4 Oct. 1957 (Kenneth Young); *Delta*, Spring 1958 (W. I. Carr); *Encounter*, Nov. 1957 (Graham Hough); *Halifax Courier*, 6 Dec. 1957; *Irish Times*, 14 Sept. 1957 (Austin Clarke); *Isis*, 23 Oct. 1957 (Judith Spink); *Library Journal*, 1 Dec. 1957; *Listen*, Spring 1958 (Alan Brownjohn); *Listener*, 23 Jan. 1958; *Manchester Guardian*, 4 Oct. 1957 (Robin Skelton); *New Statesman*, 28 Sept. 1957 (Edwin Muir); *New York Times*, 6 Oct. 1957 (W. S. Merwin); *Observer*, 6 Oct. 1957 (A. Alvarez); *Oxford Magazine*, 22 May 1958 (G. J. Warnock); *Oxford Times*, 20 Sept. 1957 (E.E.); *Saturday Review*, 9 Nov. 1957 (Philip Booth); *Spectator*, 11 Oct. 1957 (Robert Conquest), *Sunday Times*, 3 Nov. 1957 (John Press); *Time and Tide*, 19 Oct. 1957 (John Heath-Stubbs); *Times*, 23 Jan. 1958; *Times Literary Supplement*, 18 Oct. 1957; *Voices 165*, Jan.–Apr. 1958; *Yorkshire Post*, 30 Apr. 1959 (Leonard Clark).

Pike. A broadside poem, woodcut illustration by Robert Bermelin; Gehenna Press, Northampton, Mass., 1959. Limited edition, 200.

Lupercal, Faber and Faber, 18 March 1960. First American edition, Harper, 3 August 1960. First paperback edition, Faber and Faber, 1970.

REVIEWS: *Atlantic*, Nov. 1961 (Peter Davison); *Audience*, Summer 1960; *Christian Science Monitor*, 25 Aug. 1960 (John Holmes); *Critical Quarterly*, Summer 1960 (Alun Jones); *Daily Telegraph*, 14 Apr. 1960 (Kenneth Young); *Delta*, Winter 1961 (J. M. Newton); *Essence*, Winter 1960; *Granta*, 30 Apr. 1960; *Guardian*, 18 Mar. 1960 (Robin Skelton); *Halifax Courier*, 8 Mar. 1960; *Irish Times*, 9 Apr. 1960 (Austin Clarke); *Isis*, 11 May 1960 (Greysteil Ruthven); *Library Journal*, Aug. 1960 (B. A. Robie); *Listener*, 28 July 1960 (Graham Hough); *New Statesman*, 9 Apr. 1960 (Donald Hall); *New York Herald Tribune*, 22 Jan. 1961 (Paul Engel); *New York Times*, 14 Aug. 1960 (Philip Booth); *Observer*, 27 Mar. 1960 (A. Alvarez); *Oxford Times*, 15 Apr. 1960 (E.E.); *Poetry*, Jan. 1961 (Thom Gunn); *Poetry Dial*, Winter 1961; *Poetry Review*, July 1960 (Robert Armstrong); *Prairie Schooner*, Fall 1962; *Spectator*, 22 Apr. 1960 (Norman MacCaig); *Sunday Times*, 3 Apr. 1960 (John Press); *Time and Tide*, 14 May 1960; *Times*, 25 Aug. 1960; *Times Literary Supplement*, 15 Apr. 1960; *Virginia Quarterly*, Winter 1962 (E. Lucas Myers); *Voices 174*, Jan.–Apr. 1961; *Yorkshire Post*, 24 Mar. 1960 (Leonard Clark).

175

Meet My Folks! Illustrated by George Adamson; Faber and Faber, 7 April 1961. First American edition, illustrated by Mila Lazarevich, Bobbs-Merrill, 1973. This edition omits 'My Grandpa' and 'Grandma' and adds four new poems 'My Uncle Mick', 'My Aunt Flo', 'My Granny' and 'My Own True Family'.
REVIEWS: *Christian Science Monitor*, 7 Nov. 1973; *Kirkus*, 1 Aug. 1973; *Library Journal*, 15 Sept. 1973; *Times Literary Supplement*, 19 May 1961.

Selected Poems, Thom Gunn and Ted Hughes; Faber and Faber, 1962.

How the Whale Became, with drawings by George Adamson: Faber and Faber, 8 November 1963. First American edition, with drawings by Rick Schreiter, Atheneum, 1964. First paperback edition, illustrated by George Adamson, Penguin, 1971.
REVIEWS: *Birmingham Post*, 26 Nov. 1963; *Book Week*, 22 Nov. 1964 (M. S. Libby); *Guardian*, 6 Dec. 1963 (Robert Nye); *Horn Book*, Oct. 1964 (E.L.H.); *Irish Times*, 7 Dec. 1963; *Library Journal*, 15 October 1964 (W. M. Crossley); *Listener*, 21 Nov. 1963 (Elizabeth Brewer); *New Statesman*, 8 Nov. 1963 (Christopher Ricks); *New York Review of Books*, 3 Dec. 1964 (J. A. Smith); *New York Times Book Review*, 8 Nov. 1964 (Gloria Vanderbilt); *School Librarian*, March 1964 (Laurence Adkins); *Sunday Telegraph*, 24 Nov. 1963; *Sunday Times*, 24 Nov. 1963 (Oscar Turnhill).

The Earth-Owl and Other Moon People, with drawings by R. A. Brandt; Faber and Faber, 22 November 1963.
REVIEWS: *Agenda*, Dec.–Jan. 1963-4 (Anita Auden); *Birmingham Post*, 26 Nov. 1963 (Pauline Smith); *English*, Summer 1964 (Howard Sergeant); *Guardian*, 22 Nov. 1963 (Richard Keel); *Hudson Review*, Autumn 1964 (Ian Hamilton); *Irish Times*, 4 April 1964; *New Statesman*, 6 Dec. 1963 (Christopher Ricks); *Observer*, 22 Dec. 1963 (A. Alvarez); *Outposts*, Spring 1964 (Philip Hobsbaum); *Review*, Jan. 1964 (P. Marsh); *Scotsman*, 4 Jan. 1964 (Martin Seymour-Smith); *Spectator*, 27 March 1964 (Elizabeth Jennings); *Teacher*, 24 Jan. 1964 (Ray Sparkes); *Times*, 5 Dec. 1963; *Times Literary Supplement*, 27 Feb. 1964; *Tribune*, 7 Feb. 1964 (Jeremy Robson); *Western Daily Press*, 18 Nov. 1963 (Keith Turner).

Nessie the Mannerless Monster, with pictures by Gerald Rose; Faber and Faber, 24 April 1964. First American edition illustrated by Jan Pyk. Bobbs-Merrill, 1974 (as *Nessie the Monster*).
REVIEWS: *Coventry Evening Telegraph*, 30 Apr. 1964 (Susan Hill); *Guardian*, 10 July 1964 (Robert Nye); *Listener*, 28 May 1964 (Anthony Thwaite); *New Statesman*, 15 May 1964 (Mary Scrutton); *Sunday Telegraph*, 29 November 1964 (Ian Serraillier); *Teacher*, July 1964; *Times Literary Supplement*, 9 July 1964.

Recklings, Turret Books, 1966. Limited edition, 150, signed.

The Burning of the Brothel, Turret Books, October 1966. Limited edition, 300 (75 signed).

Scapegoats and Rabies, Poet and Printer, March 1967. Limited edition, 400.

Wodwo, Faber and Faber, 18 May 1967. Contains one poem, 'Logos', not in the American edition. First American edition, Harper, 22 Nov. 1967; contains two poems 'Root, Stem, Leaf' and 'Scapegoats and Rabies' not in the English edition. First paperback edition, Faber and Faber, 1971. REVIEWS: *Books and Bookmen*, Nov. 1967 (Michael Baldwin); *Book World*, 24 Dec. 1967 (Chad Walsh); *Birmingham Post*, 17 June 1967 (Barbara Lloyd-Evans); *Cambridge Evening News*, 8 July 1967; *Cambridge Quarterly*, Autumn 1967 (J. M. Newton); *Carleton Miscellany*, Summer 1968 (D. Galler); *Church Times*, 15 Sept. 1967 (Norman Nicholson); *Delta 42*, Feb. 1968 (Sydney Bolt); *English Studies*, June 1968 (M. Thorpe); *Glasgow Herald*, 17 June 1967 (Charles Senior); *Guardian*, 19 May 1967 (Donald Davie); *Hudson Review*, Spring 1968 (A. Hecht); *Irish Times*, 20 May 1967 (Eavan Boland); *Kentish Gazette*, 18 July 1967 (R.A.F.); *Library Journal*, 1 Nov. 1967 (Jerome Cushman); *Listener*, 6 July 1967 (Graham Martin); *New Statesman*, 16 June 1967 (Julian Symonds); *New Yorker*, 30 May 1968 (Louise Bogan); *New York Review of Books*, 1 Aug. 1968 (John Thompson); *Northwest Review*, Summer 1968 (R. Mariels); *Observer*, 21 May 1967 (A. Alvarez); *Poetry*, September 1968 (Hayden Carruth); *Poetry Review*, Autumn 1967 (L. Clark); *Scotsman*, 24 June 1967 (Martin Seymour-Smith); *Sheffield Star*, 1 July 1967 (Byron Rogers); *Spectator*, 28 July 1967 (C. B. Cox); *Sunday Times*, 28 May 1967 (Jeremy Rundale); *Tablet*, 8 July 1967 (John Juniper); *Times*, 13 July 1967 (Derwent May); *Times Literary Supplement*, 6 July 1967; *Tribune*, 30 June 1967 (Jeremy Robson); *Virginia Quarterly*, Summer 1968 (S. F. Morse); *Yorkshire Post*, 6 July 1967 (Leonard Clark).

Gravestones. A series of 6 poster poems (all from *Wodwo*) designed by Gavin Robbins; Turret Books, 1967. Limited edition, 40, signed.

Animal Poems, Richard Gilbertson, Bow, Crediton, Devon, 1967. Limited edition, 100, signed.

Poetry in the Making. An Anthology of Poems and Programmes from 'Listening and Writing', Faber and Faber, 6 December 1967. First American edition as *Poetry Is*, Doubleday, 1970. REVIEWS: *Horn Book*, Feb. 1971; *Kentish Gazette*, 23 Jan. 1970 (C.R.E.P.); *Library Journal*, 15 Dec. 1970 (M. A. Dorsey); *New Statesman*, 9 Feb. 1968; *New York Times Book Review*, 8 November 1970 (Thomas Lash); *Saturday Review*, 14 Nov. 1970 (Zena Sutherland); *Times Literary Supplement*, 14 March 1968; *Tribune*, 12 Sept. 1969 (Robert Nye).

The Iron Man, with drawings by George Adamson; Faber and Faber, 26 February 1968. First American edition as *The Iron Giant* with drawings by Robert Nadler, Harper, 23 Oct. 1968. First paperback edition, Faber and

THE ART OF TED HUGHES

Faber, 1971. Adaptation for children learning to read, with illustrations by Colin Smithson; Penguin, 1973.
REVIEWS: *Book World*, 23 Feb. 1969; *Guardian*, 29 March 1968 (J.R.T.); *Horn Book*, Dec. 1968 (V.H.); *Library Journal*, 15 Dec. 1968 (Elva Harmon); *Listener*, 16 May 1968 (Naomi Lewis); *New York Times Book Review*, 3 Nov. 1968 (Robert Nye); *Spectator*, 14 June 1968 (Colin MacInnes); *Tablet*, 27 April 1968 (Janet Bruce); *Teacher*, 13 Sept. 1968 (Margery Fisher); *Teachers' World*, 19 April 1968; *Times*, 13 April 1968 (Robert Nye); *Times Educational Supplement*, 8 March 1968; *Times Literary Supplement*, 14 March 1968.

Poems: Ted Hughes, Linocuts: Gavin Robbins; Bartholomew Books, Exeter College of Art, 1968. Limited edition, 300, signed.

Five Autumn Songs for Children's Voices, Richard Gilbertson, Bow, Crediton, Devon, December 1968. Limited edition, 500 (188 signed).

The Demon of Adachigahara. Music by Gordon Crosse, words by Ted Hughes; Oxford University Press, 1969. First performed 27 March 1968.

I Said Goodbye to Earth. A poster poem designed by Gavin Robbins; Turret Books, 1969. Limited edition, 75, signed.

Seneca's 'Oedipus' adapted by Ted Hughes; Faber and Faber, 8 December 1969. First American edition, illustrated by Reginald Pollack, Doubleday, 1972. First performance by the National Theatre Co. at the Old Vic, 19 March 1968, produced by Peter Brook.

The Martyrdom of Bishop Farrar, Richard Gilbertson, Bow, Crediton, Devon, 4 March 1970. Limited edition, 100, signed.

The Coming of the Kings and other plays, Faber and Faber, 1 September 1970. First American edition (as *The Tiger's Bones*) illustrated by Alan E. Cober, Viking, 1974. Also contains 'Orpheus'.
REVIEWS: *Teachers' World*, 19 Feb. 1971 (Sidney Robbins); *Times Literary Supplement*, 30 Oct. 1970; *Use of English*, Spring 1971 (David A. Male).
'Sean, the Fool, the Devil and Cats' and 'Beauty and the Beast' were given their first productions at the Arts Theatre, London in September 1971.
An acting text of 'The Coming of the Kings' alone was published by the Dramatic Publishing Company, Chicago, in 1972.
REVIEWS: *Jewish Chronicle*, 1 Oct. 1971 (A.F.); *Sunday Times*, 10 Oct. 1971 (Harold Hobson).
'The Coming of the Kings' was first produced also at the Arts Theatre on 4 November 1972.
REVIEW: *Stage and Television Today*, 9 Nov. 1972 (H.G.M.).

Crow, Faber and Faber, 12 October 1970. First American edition, Harper, 3 March 1971; contains 7 poems not in the first English edition: 'Crow Hears Fate Knock on the Door', 'Crow's Fall', 'The Contender', 'Crow

178

Tries the Media', 'Crow's Elephant Totem Song', 'Crow Paints Himself into a Chinese Mural' and 'The Lovepet'. Second English edition, Faber, 1972; contains all the poems in the American edition with the exception of 'The Lovepet' and with the addition of 'Crowcolour'. Limited edition, with drawings by Leonard Baskin, Faber, December 1973, 400, signed; contains three further poems: 'Crow Rambles', 'Crow's Courtship' and 'Crow's Song about Prospero and Sycorax'.

REVIEWS: *Agenda*, Spring–Summer 1971 (Peter Dale); *Ambit 46*, 1971 (Martin Bax); *Birmingham Post*, 17 Oct. 1970 (Barbara Lloyd Evans); *Book World*, 2 Jan. 1972; *Books and Bookmen*, Dec. 1970 (Derek Stanford); *Cambridge Quarterly*, Autumn 1971 (J. M. Newton); *Church Times*, 27 Nov. 1970 (Norman Nicholson); *Christian Science Monitor*, 29 April 1971 (Victor Howes); *Commonweal*, 17 Sept. 1971 (B. Wallenstein); *Contemporary Literature*, Winter 1973 (Marjorie G. Perloff); *Critical Quarterly*, Spring 1971 (David Lodge); *Delta*, Spring 1972 (N. Roberts); *Encounter*, March 1971 (Douglas Dunn); *Guardian*, 15 Oct. 1970 (Peter Porter); *Hudson Review*, Summer 1971 (H. Carruth); *Human World*, Nov. 1972 (I. Robinson and D. Sims); *Irish Times*, 31 Oct. 1970 (Eavan Boland); *Library Journal*, July 1971 (Sanford Dorbin); *Listener*, 29 Oct. 1970 (Derwent May); *London Magazine*, Jan. 1971 (Tony Harrison); *Malahat Review*, April 1971 (R.S.); *Mediterranean Review*, Fall 1971 (Dabney Stuart); *New Statesman*, 16 Oct. 1970 (Alan Brownjohn); *Newsweek*, April 1971 (J. Kroll); *New York Review of Books*, 22 July 1971 (Stephen Spender); *New York Times Book Review*, 18 April 1971 (Daniel Hoffman); *Observer*, 11 Oct. 1970 (A. Alvarez); *Platform*, Summer 1971 (Luke Spencer); *Partisan Review*, Winter 1971/2 (G. S. Fraser); *Poetry*, Feb. 1972 (C. Kizer); *Prairie Schooner*, Fall 1972 (Mordecai Marcus); *The Review*, Dec. 1970 (John Fuller); *Saturday Review*, 2 Oct. 1971 (J. Kessler); *Scotsman*, 31 Oct. 1970 (Martin Seymour-Smith); *Shenandoah*, Winter 1972 (Peter Cooley); *Southern Arts*, Jan. 1971 (John Fairfax); *Stand*, Vol. 12, No. 2, 1971 (Anne Cluysenaar); *Sunday Telegraph*, 11 Oct. 1970 (Brian Cox); *Sunday Times*, 25 Oct. 1970 (Lyman Andrews); *Sydney Morning Herald*, 5 June 1971 (Philip Roberts); *Tablet*, 21 Nov. 1970 (Damian Grant); *Time*, 5 April 1971 (Christopher Porterfield); *Times*, 17 Dec. 1970 (Richard Holmes); *Times Literary Supplement*, 8 Jan. 1971 (Ian Hamilton); *Tribune*, 11 Dec. 1970 (Jeremy Robson); *Use of English*, Vol. 22, No. 3, 1971 (Sandy Cunningham).

A Few Crows, illustrated by Reiner Burger: Rougemont Press, Exeter, Oct. 1970. Limited edition, 75, signed.

Four Crow Poems ('Crow and the Birds', 'King of Carrion', 'That Moment', 'Crow's Last Stand'). Silkscreen prints by R. J. Lloyd, 1970. Limited edition, 20.

A Crow Hymn, Sceptre Press, Frensham, Surrey, 1970. Limited edition, 100 (26 signed).

Fighting for Jerusalem. Graphics by Ron Brown. Mid NAG poetry poster, No. 7, 1970.

Shakespeare's Poem, Lexham Press, March 1971. Limited edition, 150 (75 signed).

Crow Wakes, Poet and Printer, April 1971. Limited edition, 200.

Poems – Ruth Fainlight, Ted Hughes, Alan Sillitoe, Rainbow Press, April 1971. Limited edition, 300, signed.

Eat Crow, Rainbow Press, 1971. Limited edition, 150, signed. (Out of print.)

Autumn Song, a poster poem by Nina Carroll, Kettering, 1971.

Selected Poems 1957–1967, Faber, 1972. First American edition, with drawings by Leonard Baskin, Harper, 1974 (omits 'Kafka').
REVIEWS: *Kirkus,* 1 Aug. 1973; *New Republic,* 16 Feb. 1974; *New York Times Book Review,* 13 Jan. 1974 (Calvin Bedient); *New York Review of Books,* 7 March 1974 (Karl Miller); *Saturday Review World,* 20 Nov. 1973.

In the Little Girl's Angel Gaze. A broadsheet designed by Ralph Steadman, Steam Press 1972. Limited edition, 50, signed.

Prometheus on His Crag, Rainbow Press, November 1973. Limited edition, 160, signed.

The Story of Vasco, Libretto by Ted Hughes from the play by Shehadé, Oxford University Press, March 1974. The opera by Gordon Crosse first produced by Sadler's Wells at the London Coliseum, 13 March 1974.

Spring, Summer, Autumn, Winter, Rainbow Press, June 1974. Limited edition, 140, signed.

Most Hughes limited editions henceforth are likely to be published by the Rainbow Press, 100 Chetwynd Road, London NW5 1BH.

B. HUGHES IN TRANSLATION

Selected poems by Ted Hughes are available in parallel texts in German, Spanish and Italian.

Ted Hughes, Gedanken-Fuchs Gedichte, ed. Faas, Literarisches Colloquium, Berlin, 1971.

Ted Hughes, Antologia Poetica, ed. Pardo, Plaza and Janes, S.A., 1971.

Ted Hughes, Pensiero-Volpe e Altre Poesie, ed. Pennati, Arnoldo Mondadori, 1973.

C. WORKS EDITED BY TED HUGHES
(Publication London unless otherwise stated.)

New Poems, Hutchinson, 1962. Edited Ted Hughes, Patricia Beer and Vernon Scannell.
REVIEWS: *Times Literary Supplement,* 23 Nov. 1962.

Five American Poets, Faber and Faber, 1963. Edited by Thom Gunn and Ted Hughes; contains foreword by the editors.
REVIEWS: *Encounter,* Jan. 1964 (John Hollander); *Critical Quarterly,* Autumn 1963 (John Stallworthy); *Times Literary Supplement,* 1 Nov. 1963.

Selected Poems, Keith Douglas, Faber and Faber, 1964. Contains introduction and biographical note by Ted Hughes. First American edition, Chilmark Press, 1964.
REVIEWS: *English,* Summer 1964 (Howard Sergeant); *Saturday Review,* 2 Jan. 1965 (Chad Walsh); *Stand,* Vol. 6, no. 4 (Geoffrey Hill); *Times Literary Supplement,* 19 March 1964.

A Choice of Emily Dickinson's Verse, Faber and Faber, 1968. Selected with an introduction by Ted Hughes.
REVIEWS: *Listener,* 1 Aug. 1968 (Margaret Drabble); *New Statesman,* 16 Aug. 1968 (Elizabeth Jennings); *Times Literary Supplement,* 25 July 1968.

Crossing the Water, Sylvia Plath, Faber and Faber, 1971. Contains note by Ted Hughes.

A Choice of Shakespeare's Verse, Faber and Faber, 1971. Selected with an introduction by Ted Hughes. First American edition as *With Fairest Flowers While Summer Lasts,* Doubleday, 1971.
REVIEWS: *Books and Bookmen,* April 1972 (Marie Peel); *Guardian,* 25 Nov. 1971 (Martin Dodsworth); *Irish Times,* 20 Nov. 1971 (Elgy Gillespie); *Sunday Times,* 16 Jan. 1972 (Christopher Ricks), and Ted Hughes replied to this review the following Sunday.

D. CONTRIBUTIONS BY TED HUGHES TO BOOKS AND PERIODICALS
(excluding the reprinting of already collected pieces)

I. POEMS

Poems not published separately are also included so that this section constitutes a complete check-list of Hughes' poems for adults.

'Wild West': *Don and Dearne*, Mexborough Secondary School, 1946; *Scotsman*, 14 Sept. 1968; *Young Winter's Tales*, Macmillan, 1970.

'The Little Boys and the Seasons': *Granta*, 8 June 1954; *Accent*, Spring 1957; *Poetry from Cambridge 1952-4*, ed. Karl Miller, Fantasy Press, 1955.

'The Jaguar' (*The Hawk in the Rain; Selected Poems*): *Chequer 7*, Nov. 1954; *Poetry from Cambridge 1952-4*; *Poetry XC*, 5, August 1957.

'The Casualty' (*The Hawk in the Rain*): *Chequer 7*, Nov. 1954; *Poetry XC*, 5, August 1957.

'The Court Tumbler and Satirist': *Poetry from Cambridge 1952-4*.

'The Woman With Such High Heels She Looked Dangerous': *Delta 5*, Spring 1955.

'Fallgrief's Girl-friends' (*The Hawk in the Rain; Selected Poems*): *St Botolph's Review*, 1956.

'Law in the Country of Cats' (*The Hawk in the Rain*): *St Botolph's Review*, 1956.

'Soliloquy of a Misanthrope' (*The Hawk in the Rain; Selected Poems* as 'Soliloquy'): *St Botolph's Review*, 1956.

'Secretary' (*The Hawk in the Rain*): *St Botolph's Review*, 1956; *Spectator*, 30 Aug. 1957.

'Scene Without an Act': *Granta*, 12 May 1956.

'The Hag' (*The Hawk in the Rain*): *Nation*, 18 Aug. 1956; *Times Literary Supplement*, 16 Aug. 1957.

'Bawdry Embraced' (*Recklings*): *Poetry LXXXVIII*, 5, August 1956; *Gemini 5*, Spring 1958.

'Wind' (*The Hawk in the Rain; Selected Poems*): *Nation*, 10 Nov. 1956; *Gemini 2*, Summer 1957.

'Roarers in a Ring' (*The Hawk in the Rain*): *Nation*, 22 Dec. 1956.

'The Hawk in the Rain' (*The Hawk in the Rain*): *Atlantic Monthly*, Feb. 1957.

'The Drowned Woman': *Poetry LXXXIX*, 5, Feb, 1957.

'Billet-Doux' (*The Hawk in the Rain*): *Accent*, Spring 1957.

'The Martyrdom of Bishop Farrar' (*The Hawk in the Rain; Selected Poems*): Broadcast 14 April 1957; *Granta*, 18 May 1957; *Poetry XC*, 5, Aug. 1967.

'The Dove Breeder' (*The Hawk in the Rain*): *Granta*, 18 May 1957; *Harper's*, Aug. 1957.

'Famous Poet' (*The Hawk in the Rain; Selected Poems*): *Gemini 2*, Summer 1957; *London Magazine*, Sept. 1957.

'Macaw and Little Miss' (*The Hawk in the Rain*): *Gemini 2*, Summer 1957.

'Six Young Men' (*The Hawk in the Rain; Selected Poems*): *Delta 12*, Summer 1957.

'Meeting' (*The Hawk in the Rain; Selected Poems*): *Spectator*, 19 July 1957.

'Incompatibilities' (*The Hawk in the Rain*): *Nation*, 20 July 1957.

'September' (*The Hawk in the Rain*): *Spectator*, 2 Aug. 1957 (as 'Parting').

'The Ancient Heroes and the Bomber Pilot' (*The Hawk in the Rain*): *Poetry XC*, 5, Aug, 1957 (as 'The Ancient Heroes and the Pilot').

'The Thought-Fox' (*The Hawk in the Rain; Selected Poems*): *New Yorker*, 31 Aug. 1957.
'Two Wise Generals' (*The Hawk in the Rain*): *Spectator*, 6 Sept. 1957.
'The Horses' (*The Hawk in the Rain; Selected Poems*).
'Song' (*The Hawk in the Rain; Selected Poems*).
'Parlour Piece' (*The Hawk in the Rain*).
'A Modest Proposal' (*The Hawk in the Rain*).
'Two Phases' (*The Hawk in the Rain*).
'The Decay of Vanity' (*The Hawk in the Rain*).
'Fair Choice' (*The Hawk in the Rain*).
'The Conversion of the Reverend Skinner' (*The Hawk in the Rain*).
'Complaint' (*The Hawk in the Rain*).
'Phaetons' (*The Hawk in the Rain*).
'Egg-head' (*The Hawk in the Rain; Selected Poems*).
'The Man Seeking Experience Enquires His Way of a Drop of Water' (*The Hawk in the Rain; Selected Poems*).
'October Dawn' (*The Hawk in the Rain; Selected Poems*).
'Vampire' (*The Hawk in the Rain*).
'Childbirth' (*The Hawk in the Rain*).
'Invitation to the Dance' (*The Hawk in the Rain*).
'Bayonet Charge' (*The Hawk in the Rain; Selected Poems*).
'Griefs for Dead Soldiers' (*The Hawk in the Rain*).
'Letter': *New Statesman*, 28 Sept. 1957.
'Everyman's Odyssey' (*Lupercal*): *Landmarks and Voyages*, ed. Vernon Watkins, Poetry Book Society Supplement, Christmas 1957.
'Quest': *The Grapevine*, University of Durham Institute of Education, Feb. 1958.
'Crow Hill' (*Lupercal; Selected Poems*): *New Statesman*, 15 March 1958; *Poetry from Cambridge*, ed. Levenson, Fortune Press, 1958; *Paris Review* 21, Spring–Summer 1959.
'Thrushes' (*Lupercal; Selected Poems*): *Encounter*, March 1958; *Observer*, 23 Nov. 1958; *New Poems*, Hutchinson, 1958; *Poetry from Cambridge*, ed. Levenson, Fortune Press, 1958; *Audience*, Summer 1959; *Living Voices*, ed. Silkin, 1960; *The Golden Year*, Cane, Farrar, Nicholl eds., Fine Editions Press, 1960.
'The Good Life' (*Lupercal*): *Sewanee Review*, LXVI, 2, Spring 1958; *Spectator*, 4 July 1958; *Poetry from Cambridge*, ed. Levenson, Fortune Press, 1958.
'Witches' (*Lupercal; Selected Poems*): *Sewanee Review*, LXVI, 2, Spring 1958; *New Statesman*, 9 Aug. 1958; *The Golden Year*, Cane, Farrar, Nicholl eds., Fine Editions Press, 1960.
'Things Present' (*Lupercal*): *Sewanee Review*, LXVI, 2, Spring 1958; *Spectator*, 3 Oct. 1958.
'Of Cats' (*Lupercal*): *Harper's*, June 1958.
'Crag Jack's Apostasy' (*Lupercal*): *Spectator*, 4 July 1958.
'Historian' (*Lupercal*): *Poetry from Cambridge*, ed. Levenson, Fortune Press, 1958; *Nation*, 15 Nov. 1958; *Encounter*, July 1959.
'Dick Straightup' (*Lupercal*): *Poetry from Cambridge*, ed. Levenson, Fortune Press, 1958.

THE ART OF TED HUGHES

'Constancy': *London Magazine*, Aug. 1958.
'A Dream of Horses' (*Lupercal*): *London Magazine*, Aug. 1958; *Grecourt Review*, May 1959; *Guinness Book of Poetry* 3, 1960, all as 'Groom's Dream'.
'The Retired Colonel' (*Lupercal; Selected Poems*): *Spectator*, 22 Aug. 1958.
'Relic' (*Lupercal; Selected Poems*): *Harper's*, Nov. 1958; *Encounter*, Sept. 1959.
'Pennines in April' (*Lupercal*): *Spectator*, 26 Dec. 1958; *Mademoiselle*, Jan. 1959.
'Wilfred Owen's Photographs' (*Lupercal; Selected Poems*): *Spectator*, 2 Jan. 1959.
'The Bull Moses' (*Lupercal; Selected Poems*): *London Magazine*, April 1959; *Audience*, Summer 1959.
'The Voyage' (*Lupercal*): *London Magazine*, April 1959; *Audience*, Summer 1959.
'February' (*Lupercal*): *London Magazine*, April 1959.
'Hawk Roosting' (*Lupercal; Selected Poems*): *Grecourt Review*, May 1959; *Critical Quarterly*, Summer 1959; *Poetry*, 1960 (*Critical Quarterly Supplement*); *Partisan Review*, Spring 1960.
'Sunstroke' (*Lupercal; Selected Poems*): *Observer*, 17 May 1959.
'Pike' (*Lupercal; Selected Poems*): *Audience*, Summer 1959; *Encounter*, March 1960.
'November' (*Lupercal; Selected Poems*): *Critical Quarterly*, Summer 1959.
'Strawberry Hill' (*Lupercal; Selected Poems*): *Critical Quarterly*, Summer 1959.
'Nicholas Ferrer' (*Lupercal*): *Audience*, Summer 1959.
'Fourth of July' (*Lupercal; Selected Poems*): *Massachusetts Review*, Vol. 1, No. 2, 1959; *New Statesman*, 28 Nov. 1959; *Harper's*, July 1960.
'Snowdrop' (*Lupercal; Selected Poems*): *Massachusetts Review*, Vol. 1, No. 2, 1959; *Observer*, 29 Nov. 1959.
'Shells': *New Yorker*, 1 Aug. 1959; *London Magazine*, March 1961.
'View of a Pig' (*Lupercal; Selected Poems*): *Times Literary Supplement*, 7 Aug. 1959.
'Bullfrog' (*Lupercal*): *New Yorker*, 8 Aug. 1959.
'Lupercalia' (*Lupercal*): *Poetry*, Vol. XCV, 5, Aug. 1959.
'To Paint a Water-lily (*Lupercal*): *Poetry*, Vol. XCIV, 5, Aug. 1959.
'A Woman Unconscious' (*Lupercal; Selected Poems*): *Poetry*, Vol. XCIV, 5, Aug. 1959.
'Cat and Mouse' (*Lupercal; Selected Poems*): *Poetry*, Vol. XCIV, 5, Aug. 1959.
'Gulls Aloft': *Christian Science Monitor*, 15 Dec. 1959.
'Snails': *Christian Science Monitor*, 15 Dec. 1959.
'Cleopatra to the Asp' (*Lupercal; Selected Poems*): *New Statesman*, 19 Dec. 1959.
'Esther's Tomcat' (*Lupercal; Selected Poems*): *New Yorker*, 9 Jan. 1960 (as 'Tomcat').
'Mayday on Holderness' (*Lupercal; Selected Poems*): *Spectator*, 22 Jan. 1960.
'An Otter' (*Lupercal; Selected Poems*): *Encounter*, March 1960.
'The Perfect Forms' (*Lupercal*): *Sewanee Review*, LXVIII, 2, Spring 1960.
'Urn Burial' (*Lupercal*): *Sewanee Review*, LXVIII, 2, Spring 1960.

184

'Fire-eater' (*Lupercal; Selected Poems*): *Sewanee Review*, LXVIII, 2, Spring 1960.

'Singers' (*Lupercal*).

'Acrobats' (*Lupercal*).

'Thistles' (*Wodwo; Selected Poems*): *Times Literary Supplement*, 9 Sept. 1960; *Mademoiselle*, March 1961; *New Poems*, Hutchinson, 1961.

'Fable': *Times Literary Supplement*, 9 Sept. 1960; *Mademoiselle*, March 1961.

'Poltergeist' (*Recklings*): *Spectator*, 25 Nov. 1960.

'Unknown Soldier' (*Recklings*): *Critical Quarterly*, 2, 4, Winter 1960; *New Poems*, Hutchinson, 1961; *Guinness Book of Poetry*, 5, 1962.

'Pibroch' (*Wodwo; Selected Poems*): *Critical Quarterly*, 2, 4, 1960; *New Poets of England and America*, 2, eds. Hall and Pack, World Pub. Co., 1961; *Poets Reading* 5, Jupiter, recorded Spring 1962; *The New Poetry*, Penguin, 1962; *Poet's Choice*, eds. Engle and Langland, Dial Press, 1962.

'Lines to a Newborn Baby': *Texas Quarterly*, 3, 4, Winter 1960.

'To F.R. at Six Months': *Western Daily Press*, 22 Feb. 1961 (as 'For Frieda in her First Months'); *Sewanee Review*, LXXI, i, January 1963.

'Dully Gumption's College Courses': 'Semantics'; 'Political Science'; 'Theology' (*Wodwo; Selected Poems*); 'Humanities' (*Recklings*); *London Magazine*, March 1961.

'Her Husband' (*Wodwo; Selected Poems*); *Spectator*, 24 March 1961; *Harper's*, Dec. 1961; *Listening and Writing*, 1963; *New Poems*, Hutchinson, 1963; *The Poet Speaks*, Argo, recorded 29 Aug. 1962.

'Flanders' (*Recklings*): *Observer*, 16 April 1961; *Spectator*, 26 May 1961; *Sewanee Review*, LXXI, i, January 1963.

'Gog I, II, III' (*Wodwo;* Part I *Selected Poems*): *Observer*, 16 April 1961 (Part I only); *Nation*, 22 April 1961 (Part I only); *The Poet Speaks*, Argo, recorded 29 Aug. 1962 (Part I only); *The New Poetry*, Penguin, 1962 (Part I only); Part III broadcast 17 Oct. 1965 as 'The Knight'; *Critical Quarterly*, 8, i, Spring 1966 (Part III only).

'Sugar Loaf' (*Wodwo*): *Observer*, 16 April 1961; *Atlantic Monthly*, May 1962.

'Wino' (*Wodwo; Selected Poems* as 'Boom' III): *Observer*, 16 April 1961.

'Last Lines' (*Recklings*): *Observer*, 16 April 1961; *Sewanee Review*, LXXI, i, January 1963.

'Toll' (*Recklings*): *Observer*, 16 April 1961.

'Fishing at Dawn' (*Recklings*): *New Statesman*, 26 May 1961.

'Memory' (*Recklings*): *Times Literary Supplement*, 14 July 1961; *Sewanee Review*, LXXI, i, January 1963.

'Still Life' (*Wodwo; Selected Poems*); *New Yorker*, 15 July 1961; *The Poet Speaks*, Argo, recorded 19 Aug. 1962; *London Magazine*, February 1962.

'My Uncle's Wound': broadcast 26 July 1961; *Poetry at the Mermaid*, 1961.

'Wodwo' (*Wodwo; Selected Poems*): *New Statesman*, 15 Sept. 1961; *The Poet Speaks*, Argo, recorded 29 Aug. 1962; *Listening and Writing*, 1963; *New Poems*, Hutchinson, 1963; *Of Books and Humankind*, ed. John Butt, Routledge and Kegan Paul, 1964; *Today's Poets*, ed. Chad Walsh, Scribner, 1964.

'The Lake' (*Recklings*): *New Yorker*, 21 Oct. 1961; *London Magazine*, July, 1963; *The Faber Book of Twentieth Century Verse*, 1965.

'Public Bar T.V.' (1) (*Wodwo; Selected Poems* as 'Boom' II): *New Statesman*, 27 Oct. 1961.

'The Rescue' (*Wodwo*): *Observer*, 29 Oct. 1961; *Atlantic Monthly*, March 1962.

'Dully Gumption's Addendum' (*Recklings*): *Poetry* C, 2, May 1962.

'Mountains' (*Wodwo; Selected Poems*): *Observer*, 5 Aug. 1962; *The Poet Speaks*, Argo, recorded 29 Aug, 1962; *Poetry in the Making*, Turret Books, 1967.

'Bowled Over' (*Wodwo; Selected Poems*): *The Poet Speaks*, Argo, recorded 29 Aug. 1962; *New Statesman*, 28 Sept. 1962; *Northern Review*, I, i, 1965 (as 'One').

'Full Moon and Little Frieda' (*Wodwo; Selected Poems*): *The Poet Speaks*, Argo, recorded 29 Aug. 1962 (as 'Full Moon'); *Observer*, 27 Jan. 1963; *Atlantic Monthly*, Dec. 1963 (as 'Full Moon'); *Today's Poets*, ed. Chad Walsh, Scribner, 1964 (as 'Encounter').

'Out' I, II and III (*Wodwo; Selected Poems*): *The Poet Speaks*, Argo, recorded 29 Aug. 1962; III, 'Remembrance Day', *Granta*, 19 Oct. 1963.

'The Warriors of the North' (*Wodwo; Selected Poems*); *The Poet Speaks*, Argo, recorded 29 Aug. 1962; *Observer*, 4 Nov. 1962.

'Tutorial' (*Recklings*): *New Statesman*, 2 Nov. 1962; *Northern Review*, I, i, 1965 (as 'Two').

'Vegetarian' (*Wodwo*): *Observer*, 4 Nov. 1962.

'The Road to Easington': broadcast 24 July 1962; *English Poetry Now*, *Critical Quarterly Supplement* 3, 1962; *New Lines 2*, ed. Robert Conquest, Macmillan 1963.

'The Green Wolf' (*Wodwo: Selected Poems*): *Observer*, 6 Jan. 1963 (as 'Dark Women'); *Today's Poets*, ed. Chad Walsh, Scribner, 1964.

'New Moon in January' (*Wodwo; Selected Poems*): *Observer*, 6 Jan. 1963; *Today's Poets*, ed. Chad Walsh, Scribner, 1964.

'Water' (*Recklings*): *Observer*, 4 Nov. 1962.

'Sunday Evening': *Atlantic Monthly*, May 1963.

'Kreutzer Sonata' (*Wodwo; Selected Poems*): *New Statesman*, 23 Aug. 1963.

'Era of Giant Lizards': *Poetry*, Vol. CIII, 3, Dec. 1963.

'On Westminster Bridge': *Poetry*, Vol. CIII, 3, Dec. 1963.

'After Lorca': *Poetry*, Vol. CIII, 3, Dec. 1963; *New Poetry 1964*, *Critical Quarterly Supplement*, 1964.

'Poem to Robert Graves Perhaps': *Poetry*, Vol. CIII, 3, Dec. 1963.

'Small Hours': *Poetry*, Vol. CIII, 3, Dec. 1963.

'Heatwave' (*Recklings*): *Poetry*, Vol. CIII, 3, Dec. 1963; *London Magazine*, September 1966.

'Bad News Good!': *Agenda*, Dec./Jan. 1963/4.

'Stealing Trout on a May Morning' (*Recklings*): *New Yorker*, 21 March 1964; *Books, Plays, Poems*, B.B.C., Summer 1965.

'Cadenza' (*Wodwo; Selected Poems*): *New Yorker*, 30 May 1964; *Agenda*, April–May 1965.

'Dice' including 'Guinness' (*Recklings*): *Critical Quarterly*, Vol. 6, No. 2, Summer 1964.

'O White Elite Lotus': *Critical Quarterly*, Vol. 6, No. 4, Winter 1964.
'The Howling of Wolves' (*Wodwo; Selected Poems*): *Observer*, 10 Jan. 1965.
'Heptonstall' (*Wodwo; Selected Poems*): *New Yorker*, 27 Feb. 1965 (as 'Hill Top').
'Fallen Eve' (*Recklings*): *Agenda*, Vol. 4, No. 1, April/May 1965.
'Trees' (*Recklings*): *New Yorker*, 17 July 1965.
'The Brother's Dream': broadcast 22 Nov. 1965; *Poetry 1900–1965*, ed. MacBeth, Longman with Faber and Faber, 1967.
'Christmas Carol': *Sunday Times Weekly Review*, 19 Dec. 1965.
'A Colonial' (*Recklings*): *New Statesman*, 8 April 1966.
'Gibraltar': *New Statesman*, 8 April 1966.
'A Match' (*Recklings*; American *Wodwo* and *Selected Poems* as 'Root Stem, Leaf' 1): *Critical Quarterly*, Vol. 8, i, Spring 1966.
'Folk-Lore': *Critical Quarterly*, Vol. 8, i, Spring 1966.
'Warm Moors': *Critical Quarterly*, Vol. 8, i, Spring 1966.
'Stations' (*Wodwo; Selected Poems*): *Critical Quarterly*, Vol. 8, no. i, Spring 1966.
'Wings I, II and III' (*Wodwo*; Part II *Selected Poems*): III, *London Magazine*, September 1966; I and II, *New York Review of Books*, 3 Nov. 1966.
'Kafka' (*Selected Poems; Wodwo* as 'Wings' II, 'Kafka Writes').
'Gnat-Psalm' (*Wodwo; Selected Poems*): *London Magazine*, Sept. 1966.
'Birdsong': *London Magazine*, Sept. 1966.
'Don Giovanni' (*Recklings*): *New Statesman*, 17 June 1966.
'Ludwig's Death Mask' (*Wodwo*): *New Statesman*, 17 June 1966.
'Ghost Crabs' (*Wodwo; Selected Poems*): broadcast 17 Oct. 1965 (as 'Nightfall'); *Listener*, 21 July 1966 (as 'Nightfall').
'Second Glance at a Jaguar' (*Wodwo; Selected Poems*): broadcast 31 July 1966; *New Yorker*, 25 March 1967.
'As Woman's Weeping' (*Recklings*): *Critical Quarterly*, Vol. 8, ii, Summer 1966.
'The Bear' (*Wodwo; Selected Poems*): *Critical Quarterly*, Vol. 8, ii, Summer 1966.
'Logos' (*Recklings; Wodwo*): *Critical Quarterly*, Vol. 8, ii, Summer 1966.
'On the Slope' (*Recklings*; American *Wodwo* and *Selected Poems* as 'Root, Stem, Leaf' II): *Poetry Review*, Autumn 1966; *New Yorker* (as 'A Pause for Breath'), 27 Aug. 1966.
'Skylarks' (*Wodwo: Selected Poems* – longer version): *Critical Quarterly*, Vol. 8, iii, 1966.
'Boom' (*Wodwo; Selected Poems*): *New Statesman*, 7 Oct. 1966.
'To be a Girl's Diary' (*Recklings*; American *Wodwo* and *Selected Poems* as 'Root, Stem, Leaf' III): *New Statesman*, 7 Oct. 1966.
'The Burning of the Brothel', Turret Books, Oct. 1966.
'Beech Tree' (*Recklings*): *A Tribute to Austin Clarke*, Dolman Press (O.U.P.), 1966; *Poetry Review*, Autumn 1966.
'Root, Stem, Leaf' (American *Wodwo; Selected Poems*; and in *Recklings* as 'A Match', 'On the Slope' and 'To be a Girl's Diary).
'Plum Blossom' (*Recklings*): Part I, *Transatlantic Review*, 22, Autumn 1966 (this version is three times as long as that in *Recklings*); Part II, *Moments of Truth*, Keepsake Press, 1965 (as 'More Theology').
'Keats' (*Recklings*).

'The Toughest' (*Recklings*): *Paris Review*, 40, Winter–Spring 1967.
'Public Bar TV' (2) (*Recklings*): *Paris Review*, 40, Winter–Spring 1967.
'Karma' (*Wodwo*): *Critical Quarterly*, Vol. 8, iv, Winter 1966 (as 'Public Speech').
'A Wind Flashes the Grass' (*Wodwo; Selected Poems*): *Critical Quarterly*, Vol. 8, iv, Winter 1966.
'Reveille' (*Wodwo*): *Critical Quarterly Supplement*, 7, 1966.
'The Last Migration': *The Animal Anthology*, ed. Diana Spearman, 1966.
'Scapegoats and Rabies' (American *Wodwo; Selected Poems*): *New Statesman*, 13 Jan. 1967; *Poet and Printer*, March 1967.
'To W. H. Auden': *Sunday Times*, 19 Feb. 1967.
'Small Events' (*Recklings*): *New Yorker*, 18 March 1967.
'Thaw' (*Recklings*): *New Yorker*, 18 March 1967.
'You Drive in a Circle' (*Wodwo*): *New Yorker*, 18 March 1967.
'Fern' (*Wodwo; Selected Poems*): *New Yorker*, 18 March 1967.
'Song of a Rat', I, II and III (*Wodwo*: Part I in *Selected Poems* as 'The Rat's Dance').
'Ballad from a Fairy Tale' (*Wodwo*).
'A Disaster' (*Crow*): *Scotsman*, 22 July 1967.
'Three Legends' (the first of these is the first of the 'Two Legends' in *Crow*): *Journal of Creative Behaviour*, 1, 3, July 1967.
'Lineage' (*Crow*): *Animal Poems*, Crediton, August 1967.
'TV On': *Listener*, 28 Sept. 1967.
'Crow's Account of the Battle' (*Crow*): *Outposts* 74 (as 'A Battle'), Autumn 1967.
'A Motorbike': *Listener*, 30 Nov. 1967.
'Lovesong' (*Crow*): *Northwest Review*, IX, 2, Fall–Winter 1967–8; and as 'Second Bedtime Story': *Critical Quarterly*, Vol. 10, Nos. 1, 2, 1968; *Word in the Desert*, Oxford 1968; *Poetry* 1969, *Critical Quarterly*.
'Anecdote' (*Crow Wakes*): *Northwest Review*, Fall–Winter 1967–8.
'Revenge Fable' (*Crow*): *Times Literary Supplement*, 11 Jan. 1968.
'Crow's Last Stand' (*Crow*): *Listener*, 25 Jan. 1968; *Quarterly Review of Literature*, XVI, i, 1969; *Michigan Quarterly Review*, Summer 1970.
'Crow's First Lesson' (*Crow*): *Listener*, 25 Jan. 1968; *Quarry* 18, 4, Fall 1968; *Quarterly Review of Literature*, XVI, i, 1969; *Michigan Quarterly Review*, Summer 1970.
'A Childish Prank' (*Crow*): *Listener*, 25 Jan. 1968; *Quarry* 18, 4, Fall 1968; *Quarterly Review of Literature*, XVI, i, 1969.
'The Battle of Osfrontalis' (*Crow*): *Listener*, 25 Jan. 1968; *Quarterly Review of Literature*, XVI, i, 1969.
'That Moment' (*Crow*): *Listener*, 25 Jan. 1968; *Quarterly Review of Literature*, XVI, i, 1969; *Michigan Quarterly Review*, Summer 1970.
'In Laughter' (*Crow*): *Times Literary Supplement*, 14 March 1968.
'Criminal Ballad' (*Crow*): *Listener*, 6 June 1968 (as 'Cautionary Tale').
'Dog Days on the Black Sea': *Critical Quarterly*, Vol. 10, Nos. 1, 2, 1968; *Word in the Desert*, Oxford, 1968.
'?': *Critical Quarterly*, Vol. 10, Nos. 1, 2, 1968; *Word in the Desert*, 1968.
'A Bedtime Story' (*Crow*): *Listener*, 18 July 1968 (as 'Fifth Bedtime Story'); *British Poetry Since 1945*, Penguin, 1970 (as 'Fifth Bedtime Story').

'King of Carrion' (*Crow*): *Listener*, 26 Sept. 1968.
'Two Legends' (*Crow*): the first in *Journal of Creative Behaviour*, 1, 3, July 1967 (cf. 'Three Legends'); the second in *The Listener*, 26 Sept. 1968.
'Crow and the Birds' (*Crow*): *Poetry Gala*, 1968.
'Crowquill': *Poetry Gala*, 1968.
'Examination at the Womb-door' (*Crow*): *Listener*, 2 Jan. 1969; *Michigan Quarterly Review*, Summer 1970.
'Crow Tyrannosaurus' (*Crow*): *Observer*, 12 Jan. 1969.
'A Grin' (*Crow*): *Observer*, 12 Jan. 1969.
'Notes for a Little Play' (*Crow*): *Observer*, 12 Jan. 1969; *Poetry* 1969, *Critical Quarterly Supplement*.
'A Kill' (*Crow*): *Observer*, 12 Jan. 1969.
'Littleblood' (*Crow*): *New Statesman*, 31 Jan. 1969.
'The New World' (Three Choirs Festival Programme, 1972) 1 'It is Not Long You'll be Straddling the Rocket'; 2 'When the Star was on Her Face'; 3 'A Star Stands on Her Forehead'; 4 'I said Goodbye to Earth' (Poster Poem, Gavin Robbins, 75 numbered and signed, 1969); 5 'The Street was Empty and Stone'; 6 'Where Did We Go?' These poems were set by Gordon Crosse in 1969.
'Two Eskimo Songs' (*Crow*): 'Fleeing from Eternity', 'How Water Began to Play': *Listener*, 20 March 1969; second in *New American Review* 8, Jan. 1970 (as 'Watersong').
'Truth Kills Everybody' (*Crow*): *Listener*, 24 July 1969.
'Crow Alights' (*Crow*): *Listener*, 24 July 1969; *Poetry* 1970, *Critical Quarterly Supplement*; *Michigan Quarterly Review*, Summer 1970.
'Song for a Phallus' (*Crow*): *Transatlantic Review*, 32, Summer 1969.
'Crow's Table Talk'. (*Crow Wakes*): *Sad Traffic*, Vol. 1, no. 1, Dec. 1969.
'Ballad of Bauble-Head': *New American Review* 8, Jan. 1970.
'Song of Woe': *Critical Quarterly*, Vol. 12, no. 2, Summer 1970.
'Conjuring in Heaven' (*Crow*): *Critical Quarterly*, Vol. 12, No. 2, Summer 1970.
'Crow and Stone' (*Crow*): *Critical Quarterly*, Vol. 12, No, 2, 1970.
'Crow Blacker Than Ever' (*Crow*): *Critical Quarterly*, Vol. 12, No. 2, 1970.
'Crow Sickened' (*Crow*): *Critical Quarterly*, Vol. 12, No. 2, 1970.
'Crow's Song of Himself' (*Crow*): *Critical Quarterly*, Vol. 12, No. 2, 1970; *Poetry* 1970, *Critical Quarterly Supplement*; *New Poems*, 1970–71, Hutchinson, 1971 (as 'The Space-Egg War Sailing').
'Dawn's Rose' (*Crow*): *Observer*, 15 Feb. 1970.
'Fragment of an Ancient Tablet' (*Crow*): *Observer*, 15 Feb. 1970.
'Owl's Song' (*Crow*): *Observer*, 15 Feb. 1970; *Poetry* 1970, *Critical Quarterly Supplement*.
'Snake Hymn' (*Crow*): *Sunday Times*, 24 May 1970 (as 'Crow Hymn').
'Robin Song' (*Crow*): *Sunday Times*, 24 May 1970.
'Crow's Theology' (*Crow*): *Spectator*, 30 May 1970.
'A Horrible Religious Error' (*Crow*): *Spectator*, 30 May 1970.
'Crowego' (*Crow*): *Transatlantic Review*, 36, Summer 1970.
'The Black Beast' (*Crow*): *Transatlantic Review*, 36, Summer 1970.
'Crow and Mama' (*Crow*): *New Yorker*, 18 July 1970.

'Crown Frowns' (*Crow*): *New Yorker*, 18 July 1970.
'Crow Tries the Media' (*American Crow*; *Crow*, second edition): *New Yorker*, 18 July 1970.
'Magical Dangers' (*Crow*): *New Yorker*, 18 July 1970.
'Crow's Undersong' (*Crow*): *New Yorker*, 18 July 1970.
'Crow Goes Hunting' (*Crow*): *New Statesman*, 24 July 1970.
'Crow's Nerve Fails' (*Crow*): *Listener*, 30 July 1970.
'Crow's Battle Fury' (*Crow*) (written 20 March 1969): *Listener*, 30 July 1970.
'Crow Communes' (*Crow*): *Listener*, 30 July 1970.
'Crow and the Sea' (*Crow*): *New Statesman*, 25 Sept. 1970.
'Oedipus Crow' (*Crow*): *Listener*, 1 Oct. 1970.
'Crow's Vanity' (*Crow*): *Listener*, 1 Oct. 1970.
'Apple Tragedy' (*Crow*): *Twelve to Twelve*, Poet's Trust, 1970.
'Glimpse' (*Crow*).
'The Door' (*Crow*).
'Crow's Playmates' (*Crow*).
'Crow's Account of St George' (*Crow*).
'Crow on the Beach' (*Crow*).
'Crow Improvises' (*Crow*).
'The Smile' (*Crow*).
'A Crow Hymn', Sceptre Press, 1970.
'Carnival': *A Few Crows*, Rougemont Press, Oct. 1970.
'Bones' (*Crow Wakes*): *Listener*, 1 Oct. 1970.
'Fighting for Jerusalem': *Mid-NAG* Poetry Poster No. 7; *Times Literary Supplement*, 9 Oct. 1970.
'A Lucky Folly': *Workshop* 10, 1970.
'Existential Song': *London Magazine*, July/August 1970; *Corgi Modern Poets in Focus 1*, 1971; *New Poems 1971–2*, Hutchinson, 1972.
'Song Against the White Owl' (*Crow Wakes*): *London Magazine*, July/August 1970; *Corgi Modern Poets in Focus 1*, 1971; *New Poems 1971–2*, Hutchinson, 1972.
'The Contender' (*Crow*, second edition; *American Crow*): *London Magazine*, July/August 1970; *Crow Wakes*, *Poet and Printer*, April 1971; *Corgi Modern Poets in Focus 1*, 1971.
'Crow Hears Fate Knock on the Door' (*Crow*, second edition; *American Crow*): *London Magazine*, July/August 1970; *Corgi Modern Poets in Focus 1*, 1971.
'Crow's Elephant Totem Song' (*Crow*, second edition; *American Crow*): *London Magazine*, July/August 1970; *Works in Progress 2*, Anchor 1971 (as 'Crow Totem').
'Crowcolour' (*Crow*, second edition): *New Yorker*, 14 Nov. 1970.
'Crow's Fall' (*Crow*, second edition; *American Crow*): *New Yorker*, 19 Dec. 1970.
'The Space-Egg was Sailing': *New Poems 1970–1*, Hutchinson, 1971.
'The Lovepet' (*American Crow*): *New Yorker*, 2 Jan. 1971.
'Crow Paints Himself into a Chinese Mural' (*Crow*, second edition; *American Crow*): *New Yorker*, 23 Jan. 1971.

'Crow's Song About Prospero and Sycorax' (*Crow*, limited edition): *Shakespeare's Poem*, Lexham Press, March 1971; *Vogue*, 15 April 1971; *New Poems 1971-2*, Hutchinson, 1972.

'Crow's Courtship' (*Crow*, limited edition): *Vogue*, 15 April 1971; *Poems: Fainlight, Hughes, Sillitoe*, Rainbow Press, April 1971; *Critical Quarterly*, Autumn 1971; *New Poems 1972-3*, Hutchinson, 1973.

'Crow Rambles' (*Crow*, limited edition): *Vogue*, 15 April 1971; *Poems: Fainlight, Hughes, Sillitoe*, Rainbow Press, April 1971.

'Genesis of Evil': *Vogue*, 15 April 1971; *Poems: Fainlight, Hughes, Sillitoe*, Rainbow Press, April 1971; *Critical Quarterly*, Autumn 1971; *Poetry 1972*, *Critical Quarterly Supplement*; *New Poems 1972-3*, Hutchinson, 1973.

'Crow's Song About England': *Poems: Fainlight, Hughes, Sillitoe*, Rainbow Press, April 1971.

'Crow the Just': *Poems: Fainlight, Hughes, Sillitoe*, Rainbow Press, April 1971.

'Crow's Song About God': *Poems: Fainlight, Hughes, Sillitoe*, Rainbow Press, April 1971.

'Crow Wakes' (*Crow Wakes*).

'Amulet' (*Crow Wakes*).

'In the Land of the Lion' (*Crow Wakes*).

'I See a Bear' (*Crow Wakes*).

'Snow Song' (*Crow Wakes*).

'The Ship' (*Crow Wakes*).

'Lullaby' (*Crow Wakes*).

'Prometheus on His Crag' (1-21), Rainbow Press, Nov. 1973; 4: *Workshop* 13, September 1971; 9, 10, 15: *Réalités*, March 1973; 20: *Oxford Poetry Magazine*, Summer 1973; 21: *New Poems 1973-4*, Hutchinson 1974 (revised version).

'In the Little Girl's Angel Gaze' (Steam Press, March 1972).

'An Alchemy': *Poems for Shakespeare 2*, ed. Graham Fawcett, The Globe Playhouse Trust Publications, 1973.

'The Stone': *New Statesman*, 6 Sept. 1974.

'The Summoner' (*Cave Birds*): *New Statesman*, 27 Sept. 1974.

'The Executioner' (*Cave Birds*): *New Statesman*, 27 Sept. 1974.

'The Sentenced' (*Cave Birds*): *New Statesman*, 27 Sept. 1974.

'That Girl': *New Statesman*, 18 Oct. 1974.

'Welcombe': *Bananas* 1, Jan.-Feb. 1975.

'Exits': *Bananas* 1, Jan.-Feb. 1975.

'Festival of Poets': *Bananas* 1, Jan.-Feb. 1975.

'Apple Dumps': *Bananas* 1, Jan.-Feb. 1975.

'The Oak': *Bananas* 1, Jan.-Feb. 1975.

Six Poems from *Lumb's Remains*: *Listener*, 20 March 1975.

'March Morning Unlike Others': *New Statesman*, 28 March 1975.

'A Primrose Petal's Edge' (*Lumb's Remains*): *Boston University Journal*, Winter 1975.

'Calves Harshly Parted' (*Lumb's Remains*): *Boston University Journal*, Winter 1975.

'The Dead Man' (*Lumb's Remains*): *Boston University Journal*, Winter 1975.

'The Night Wind' (*Lumb's Remains*): *Boston University Journal*, Winter 1975.

2. TRANSLATIONS

Poems by Janos Pilinszky, *Modern Poetry in Translation* 7, June 1970.
Selected Poems of Yehuda Amichai, Penguin, 1971.

3. STORIES

'Bartholomew Pygge Esq.': *Granta*, 4 May 1957.
'O'Kelly's Angel': *Granta*, 18 May 1957.
'The Rain Horse' (*Wodwo*): *Harper's*, Jan. 1960; *London Magazine*, Feb. 1960; *Introduction*, Faber, 1960; broadcast, 29 Aug. 1960; *Listening and Writing*, Autumn 1961.
'Snow' (*Wodwo*): *Introduction*, Faber, 1960; *Bazaar*, Oct. 1961; broadcast 8 Jan. 1963.
'Sunday' (*Wodwo*): *Introduction*, Faber, 1960.
'The Caning': *Texas Quarterly* III, 4, Winter 1960.
'The Harvesting' (*Wodwo*): broadcast 17 Dec. 1960; *London Magazine*, April 1961.
'Miss Mambrett and the Wet Cellar': *Texas Quarterly*, IV, 3, Autumn 1961.
'The Suitor' (*Wodwo*): *Encounter*, May 1964.

4. DRAMA
(including unpublished broadcast plays)

'The House of Aries': broadcast 16 Nov. 1960; *Audience* 8, 2, Spring 1961; *Two Cities*, Summer 1961 (3 excerpts).
'The Wound' (*Wodwo*): broadcast 1 Feb. 1962.
'Difficulties of a Bridegroom': broadcast 21 Jan. 1963.
'Dogs': broadcast 12 Feb. 1964.
'Eat Crow' (1971): written 1964; part published in *Encounter*, July 1965.
'Oedipus of Seneca': *Arion* 7, Autumn 1968.
'Orghast': performed by Peter Brook's Experimental Theatre Co. at the Shiraz Festival 1971; 'The Birth of Sogis' in *Performance*, Dec. 1971.

5. WRITINGS FOR CHILDREN

A. *Poems*

'My Grandpa', 'My Brother Bert', 'My Sister Jane' (*Meet My Folks*): *Sunday Times*, 26 March 1961.
'Foxgloves' (*The Earth Owl*): *New Yorker*, 27 July 1963.
'Music on the Moon' (*The Earth Owl*): *New Yorker*, 10 Aug. 1963.
'Horrible Song': *Winter's Tales for Children*, Macmillan, 1968.
'Stag Hunt' (*Five Autumn Songs for Children's Voices*): *Allsorts 4*, Macmillan, 1971.
'My Aunt Flo' (American *Meet My Folks*): *Young Winter's Tales 4*, Macmillan, 1973.

'New Year Song', 'A March Calf', 'The River in March' (*Spring, Summer, Autumn, Winter*): *Listener*, 16 Aug. 1973.
'The Warm and the Cold' (*Spring, Summer, Autumn, Winter*): *Listener*, 8 Nov. 1973.
'Spring Nature Notes' (*Spring, Summer, Autumn, Winter*): *Listener*, 10 Jan. 1974.
'Sheep': *Listener*, 4 April 1974.
'Swifts': *Listener*, 16 May 1974.
'December River'; *New Yorker*, 24 June 1974.
'Autumn Nature Notes': *Listener*, 26 Sept. 1974.
'The Harvest Moon' (*Spring, Summer, Autumn, Winter*): *Listener*, 7 Nov. 1974.

B. *Plays*
(including unpublished or part-published broadcast plays)

'The House of Donkeys': first broadcast 30 Sept. 1965; *Living Language*, Autumn 1970 (first half only).
'The Tiger's Bones' (*The Coming of the Kings*): first broadcast in two parts, 26 Nov. and 3 Dec. 1965; *Listening and Writing*, Autumn 1965.
'Beauty and the Beast' (*The Coming of the Kings*): first broadcast, 2 Dec. 1965; *Living Language*, Autumn 1968.
'The Price of a Bride': first broadcast, 22 Sept. 1966; *Living Language*, Autumn 1966 (opening only); *Here Now and Beyond*, Oxford University Press, 1968.
'The Head of Gold': first broadcast 21 Sept. 1967.
'The Coming of the Kings' (*The Coming of the Kings*): first broadcast 17 Nov. 1967; *Listening and Writing*, Autumn 1967.
'Sean, the Fool, the Devil and the Cats' (*The Coming of the Kings*): first broadcast 2 May 1968; *Living Language*, Summer 1968.
'Orpheus' (*The Tiger's Bones*): first broadcast 29 Jan. 1971; *Listening and Writing*, Spring 1971, Spring 1974.

C. *Talks*

'Capturing Animals' (*Poetry in the Making*).
'Writing a Novel' (*Poetry in the Making*): *Listening and Writing*, Autumn 1971.
'Wind and Weather' (*Poetry in the Making*): *Listening and Writing*, Autumn 1962.
'Learning to Think' (*Poetry in the Making*): *Listening and Writing*, Summer 1963.
'Writing About People' (*Poetry in the Making*): *Listening and Writing*, Autumn 1963.
'Water and Landscape' (*Poetry in the Making*): *Listening and Writing*, Summer 1967.

6. ESSAYS, INTRODUCTIONS, INTERVIEWS AND AUTOBIOGRAPHICAL PIECES

'Ted Hughes Writes', *Poetry Book Society Bulletin*, 15, 1957.
'Context', *London Magazine*, February 1962.
'The Poetry of Keith Douglas', *The Listener*, 21 June 1962.
Introduction to *Here Today*, Hutchinson, 1963.
'The Poet Speaks', XVI, British Council, 1963.
'The Rock', *Writers on Themselves*, B.B.C., 1964; *Worlds*, Penguin, 1974.
'Sylvia Plath', *Poetry Book Society Bulletin*, 44, 1965.
'Desk Poet', *Guardian*, 23 March 1965.
'The Genius of Isaac Bashevis Singer', *New York Review of Books*, 22 April 1965.
Biographical Notes, *Poetry International '67 Programme*.
Introduction to Vasko Popa's *Selected Poetry*, translated by A. Pennington, Penguin, 1969.
'The chronological order of Sylvia Plath's poems', *The Art of Sylvia Plath*, ed. Charles Newman, Faber 1970.
'Ted Hughes' Crow', *Listener*, 30 July 1970.
'Myth and Education', *Children's Literature in Education* I, 1970.
'Ted Hughes and Crow' an interview with Egbert Faas, *London Magazine*, January 1971.
'Sylvia Plath', *Critical Quarterly*, Summer 1971.
Introduction to *Fiesta Melons* by Sylvia Plath, Rougemont Press, 1971.
Note in *Winter Trees* by Sylvia Plath, Faber, 1971.
'Orghast', by Tom Stoppard, *Times Literary Supplement*, 1 Oct. 1971.
'Orghast: Talking Without Words', *Vogue*, Dec. 1971.
'The Persepolis Folies of 1971', Geoffrey Reeves, *Performance*, Dec. 1971, pp. 61–6.
Orghast at Persepolis by A. C. H. Smith, Eyre Methuen, 1972; pp. 91–8, 131–3.
'Playing with Words at Persepolis', Ossia Trilling, *Theatre Quarterly*, Jan.– Mar. 1972; p. 35.
Sleeve note for Shusha, *Song of Long-Time Lovers*, TGS 114, 1972.
Blurb for *On the Coast* by Wayne Brown, André Deutsch, 1972.
Blurb for *Noth* by Daniel Huws, Secker and Warburg, 1972.
Introductory note to *Stones* by Paul Merchant, Rougemont Press, January 1973.
Sleeve note for *The Battle of Aughrim* by Richard Murphy, Claddagh, CCT 7.
Sleeve note for *Crow*, Claddagh, CCT 9–10, 1973.

7. REVIEWS

Weekend in Dinlock by Clancy Segal, *Nation*, 2 July 1960.
The Wesker Trilogy, *Nation* 19 November 1960.
The Loch Ness Monster by Tim Dinsdale, *New Statesman*, 2 June 1961.
Nimrod Smith by Alan Wykes, *New Statesman*, 23 June 1961.
The Cat in the Hat Comes Back by Dr Seuss, *New Statesman*, 1 Nov. 1961.

BIBLIOGRAPHY

Barnaby and the Horses by Lydia Pender, *New Statesman*, 10 November 1961.
Timba and Gringolo by Lilli Keenig, *New Statesman*, 10 November 1961.
The Cricket in Times Square by George Selden, *New Statesman*, 10 Nov. 1961.
Born Free by Joy Adamson, *New Statesman*, 10 November 1961.
The Nerve of Some Animals by Robert Froman, *New Statesman*, 23 March 1962.
Man and Dolphin by Dr J. C. Lilly, *New Statesman*, 23 March 1962.
Primitive Song by C. M. Bowra, *Listener*, 3 May 1962.
One Fish Two Fish Red Fish Blue Fish by Dr Seuss, *New Statesman*, 18 May 1962.
The Cat's Opera by Eilis Dillon, *New Statesman*, 18 May 1962.
The Otter's Tale by Gavin Maxwell, *New Statesman*, 18 May 1962.
Everyman's Ark by Sally Patrick Johnson, *New Statesman*, 9 November 1962.
Here Come the Elephants by Alice Goudey, *New Statesman*, 9 November 1962.
Rule and Energy by John Press, *New Statesman*, 9 August 1963.
Vagrancy by Philip O'Connor, *New Statesman*, 6 September 1963.
Emily Dickinson's Poetry by Charles R. Anderson, *Listener*, 12 Sept. 1963.
Folk Tales of Japan, Folk Tales of Israel, *Listener*, 12 December 1963.
Voss by Patrick White, *Listener*, 6 February 1964; broadcast 23 Jan. 1964.
Myth and Religion of the North by E. O. G. Turville-Petre, *Listener*, 19 March 1964.
The Collected Poems of Wilfred Owen, *New York Times Book Review*, 16 April 1964.
A Selection of African Prose, ed. W. H. Whiteley, *Listener*, 28 May 1964.
The Heroic Recitation of the Bahima of Ankile, *Somali Poetry*, ed. B. W. Andrzejewski and I. M. Lewis, *Listener*, 28 May 1964.
The Three Christs of Ipsilanti by Milton Rokeach, *New Statesman*, 4 September 1964.
The Letters of Alexander Pushkin, ed. J. T. Shaw, *Listener*, 1 Oct. 1964.
Astrology by Louis MacNeice, *New Statesman*, 2 October 1964.
Ghost and Divining Rod by T. C. Lethbridge, *New Statesman*, 2 Oct. 1964.
Shamanism by Mircea Eliade, *Listener*, 29 October 1964.
The Sufis by Idries Shah, *Listener*, 29 October 1964.
Mysterious Senses by Vitus Dröscher, *New Statesman*, 27 November 1964.
Heimskringla by Snorri Sturluson, *The Prose Edda, Gods, Demons and Others* by R. K. Narayan, *New York Review of Books*, 31 December 1964.
The Faber Book of Ballads, *Guardian*, 14 May 1965.
Men Who March Away, ed. I. M. Parsons, *Listener*, 5 August 1965.
Literature Among the Primitives, The Primitive Reader by John Greenway, *New York Review of Books*, 9 December 1965.
Selected Letters of Dylan Thomas, *New Statesman*, 25 November 1966.
Folktales of Chile, Hindoo Fairy Legends, The Glass Man and The Golden Bird, The Black Monkey, *New Statesman*, 24 May 1968.
The Environmental Revolution by Max Nicholson, *Spectator*, 21 March 1970. (A longer version of this essay appeared in *Your Environment* No. 3, Summer 1970.)
Imaginary Beings by Borghese, *Guardian*, 26 November 1970.
A Separate Reality by Carlos Castaneda, *Observer*, 5 March 1972.

E. HUGHES ON RECORD

Listening and Writing, BBC Records, RESR 19M 1971. Two talks by Ted
Hughes, 'Capturing Animals', transmitted 6 October 1961, and 'Learning
to Think', transmitted 10 May 1963. In the course of these talks Hughes
reads 'The Thought Fox', 'Pike', 'View of a Pig' and 'Bare Almond Trees'
by D. H. Lawrence.

Poets Reading No. 5 Jupiter jep OC27. Recorded Spring 1962. Hughes reads
'The Thought Fox', 'Soliloquy of a Misanthrope', 'May Day on Holderness' and 'Pibroch'.

The Poet Speaks No. 5 Argo PLP 1085. Recorded 29 August 1962. Hughes
reads nine poems from *Wodwo*.

Here Today Part 1 Jupiter JUR OOA6. Recorded Autumn 1962–Spring 1963.
Hughes reads 'View of a Pig'.

Jupiter Anthology of 20th Century English Poetry Part III Jupiter JUR OOA8.
Recorded 1963. Hughes reads 'The Hawk in the Rain' and 'Hawk Roosting'.

Poetry 1900 to 1965 34155 (Longman) 1967. Hughes reads 'Hawk Roosting',
'Humming Bird' by D. H. Lawrence and 'Vergissmeinnicht' by Keith
Douglas.

The Battle of Aughrim by Richard Murphy. Claddagh CCT 7 read by
C. Day Lewis, Cyril Cusack, Niall Toibin, Ted Hughes and Margaret
Robertson.

Crow Claddagh CCT 9–10 1973. Hughes reads all but three of the poems in
the first English edition of *Crow*.

F. SETTINGS

Meet My Folks, Gordon Crosse, O.U.P., 1965. First performed, 1964.
Recorded HMV XLP 40001, 1965.

Three Choruses, Hugh Wood, Universal Edition, 1967. Includes setting of
'The Hawk in the Rain'.

The Horses, Hugh Wood. Settings of 'The Horses', 'Pennines in April' and
'September'. Broadcast 24 October 1971.

Water-Song (Crow), Stanley Myers. Recorded by Shusha, *Song of Long-Time
Lovers*, Tangent TGS 114 1972.

The New World, Gordon Crosse. First performed 30 August 1972.

G. CRITICISM
(see also the list of reviews in section A)

'Ted Hughes', by A. E. Dyson, *Critical Quarterly*, I, iii, 1959.

'The Violence of Ted Hughes', by C. B. Cox, *John O'London's Weekly*,
13 July 1961.

Rule and Energy, by J. Press (1963). Contains a chapter 'Metaphysics and
Mythologies' discussing Hughes' poetry.

'The Cult of Hughes and Gunn', by David Holbrook, *The Poetry Review*,
Summer 1963.

'Extremes in Poetry: R. S. Thomas and Ted Hughes', by J. D. Hainsworth, *English*, Autumn 1963.

'Ted Hughes: A Reappraisal', by C. J. Rawson, *Essays in Criticism*, January 1965.

'Ted Hughes and Violence', by J. D. Hainsworth, *Essays in Criticism*, July 1965.

A Vision of Reality, by F. Grubb (1965). Contains a chapter 'Thinking Animal: Ted Hughes'.

'The New Pedantry and "Hawk Roosting" ', by P. E. Lewis, *Stand*, VIII, i, 1966.

'Ted Hughes: Poet at the Master-Fulcrum of Violence', by B. John, *Arizona Quarterly*, XXIII, Spring 1967.

The New Poets, by M. L. Rosenthal, New York, 1967. Contains an essay 'Ted Hughes'.

'The Animal Poems of Ted Hughes: A Devaluation', by G. Ingli James, *Southern Review*, II, 1967.

'Talking Beasts: The "Single Adventure" in the Poems of Ted Hughes', by D. Hoffman, *Shenandoah*, Summer 1968.

Criticism in Action, ed. M. Hussey, 1969. Contains 'Ted Hughes', by A. Grant.

The Survival of Poetry, ed. M. Dodsworth, 1970. Contains 'Ted Hughes' by D. May.

'Black Rainbow', by Marie Peel, *Books and Bookmen*, February 1971.

'Mythical Elements in the Poetry of Ted Hughes', by A. Mollema, *Dutch Quarterly Review*, i, 1972.

'Plucking Bark: an Interpretation of Ted Hughes's "Wodwo"', by Afra Sinnige-Bread, *Dutch Quarterly Review*, i, 1972.

'On Ted Hughes', by Calvin Bedient, *Critical Quarterly*, XIV, Summer 1972; reprinted in *Eight Contemporary Poets* (Oxford, 1974).

Ted Hughes by Keith Sagar, Writers and Their Work, Longman for the British Council, 1972.

'The Poetry of Ted Hughes', by P. E. Strauss, *Theoria* 38.

'Fire and Light, Four Poets to the End and Beyond', by Anthony Libby, *Iowa Review*, Spring 1973.

'Ted Hughes' Crow', by Ian Hamilton, in *A Poetry Chronicle*, Faber, 1973.

Contemporary Literary Criticism, Vol. 2, ed. Riley and Harte, Gale Research Company, Detroit, 1974.

'God's Lioness and the Priest of Sycorax: Plath and Hughes', by Anthony Libby, *Contemporary Literature*, Summer 1974.

The Ironic Harvest, by Geoffrey Thurley (1974). Contains 'Beyond Positive Values: Ted Hughes'.

'Beasts/Shamans/Baskin: The Contemporary Aesthetics of Ted Hughes', by David Porter, *Boston University Journal*, Winter 1975.

'Ted Hughes's' Crow and the Longing for Non-Being', by David Holbrook, in *The Black Rainbow*, ed. Peter Abbs, Heinemann, 1975.

H. OTHER BOOKS USED
(excluding the pre-twentieth-century English classics)

Aeschylus, *Prometheus Bound*, trans. Vellacott, Penguin, 1961.

Alvarez, A., *The Savage God*, Weidenfeld and Nicolson, 1971.
Beckett, Samuel, *Waiting for Godot*, Faber, 1956.
Endgame, Faber, 1958.
Beer, John, *Blake's Visionary Universe*, Manchester U.P., 1969.
Campbell, Joseph, *The Hero with a Thousand Faces*, Pantheon, 1949.
Myths to Live By, Souvenir Press, 1973.
Castaneda, Carlos, *The Teachings of Don Juan*, Penguin, 1970.
A Separate Reality, Bodley Head, 1971.
Journey to Ixtlan, Bodley Head, 1973.
Conquest, Robert (ed.), *New Lines*, Macmillan, 1956.
Eliade, Mircea, *Shamanism*, Routledge, 1964.
Eliot, T. S., *Collected Poems*, Faber, 1936.
Euripides, *The Bacchae*, trans. Vellacott, Penguin, 1954.
Frazer, J. G., *The Golden Bough*, Macmillan, 1957.
Golding, William, *Lord of the Flies*, Penguin, 1960.
Graves, Robert, *The White Goddess*, Faber, 1961.
The Greek Myths, Penguin, 1960.
Ionesco, Eugene, *The Killer*, Plays Vol. 3, Calder, 1960.
The Chairs, Plays Vol. 1, Calder, 1958.
Jung, Carl, *Answer to Job*, Routledge, 1954.
Psychology of the Unconscious, Kegan Paul, 1921.
Psychological Types, Routledge, 1964.
Kafka, Franz, *The Trial*, Penguin, 1953.
The Castle, Penguin, 1957.
The Diaries, Penguin, 1964.
Kerenyi, C., *The Gods of the Greeks*, Thames and Hudson, 1951.
Prometheus, Pantheon, 1963.
Eleusis, Routledge, 1967.
Laing, R. D., *The Politics of Experience* and *The Bird of Paradise*, Penguin, 1967.
Larousse *Encyclopaedia of Mythology*, Batchworth, 1959.
Lawrence, D. H., *The Rainbow*, Penguin, 1950.
Women In Love, Penguin, 1950.
St Mawr, Penguin, 1950.
Selected Poems, Penguin, 1972.
Fantasia of the Unconscious, Penguin, 1971.
Apocalypse, Heinemann, 1972.
Phoenix, Heinemann, 1936.
Collected Letters, Heinemann, 1962.
Leavis, F. R., *Revaluation*, Chatto and Windus, 1956.
Lindsay, David, *A Voyage to Arcturus*, Gollancz, 1963.
Mabinogion, ed. Lady Charlotte Guest, 1848.
Nietzsche, Friedrich, *The Birth of Tragedy*, Doubleday Anchor, 1956.
Owen, Wilfred, *Collected Poems*, Chatto and Windus, 1963.
Plath, Sylvia, *Ariel*, Faber, 1965.
The Bell Jar, Faber, 1966.
The Colossus, Faber, 1967.
Radin, Paul, *The Trickster*, Bell, 1956.

Richards, I. A., *Beyond*, Harcourt Brace Jovanovich, 1974.
Seneca, *Oedipus*, Penguin, 1966.
 Hercules Furens, in Tragedies I, Heinemann, 1960.
Sophocles, *The Theban Plays*, trans. Watling, Penguin, 1947.
Tain, trans. Kinsella, Oxford, 1970.
Thomas, Dylan, *Collected Poems*, Dent, 1952.
Tibetan Book of the Dead, ed. W. Y. Evans-Wentz, Oxford, 1960.
Watts, Alan, *The Way of Zen*, Penguin, 1962.
 Beyond Theology, Wildwood House, 1974.
Whitman, Walt, *Complete Poetry*, Nonesuch, 1938.
Yeats, W. B., *Selected Plays*, Macmillan, 1966.
 Collected Poems, Macmillan, 1955.

INDEXES

'Snake Hymn', 189
'Snow', 83–5, 192
'Snowdrop', **36–7**, 103, 184
'Snow Song', 191
'Soliloquy of a Misanthrope', 10, 182, 196
'Song', 8, 183
'Song Against the White Owl', 190
'Song for a Phallus', **119**, 158, 189
'Song of a Rat', 61, **85–7**, 188
'Song of Woe', 130, **136–7**, 189
'Space-Egg Was Sailing, The', 189, 190
'Spring Nature Notes', 193
Spring, Summer, Autumn, Winter, 180, 192
'Stag Hunt', 192
'Stations', 102, 187
'Stealing Trout on a May Morning', 186
'Still Life', 63, **68–9**, 185
'Stone, The', 191
Story of Vasco, The, 180
'Strawberry Hill', **57–8**, 184
'Sugar Loaf', 185
'Suitor, The', **80–1**, 85, 165, 192
'Summoner, The', 191
'Sunday', **79–80**, 85, 192
'Sunday Evening', 186
'Sunstroke', 184
'Swifts', 193
'Sylvia Plath', 194

'That Girl', 191
'That Moment', 112, 179, 188
'Thaw', 62, 188
'Theology', 64, **73–4**, 102, 185
'Things Present', 52, 183
'Thistles', **62–3**, 185
'Thought-Fox, The', 16, 17, 19, 183, 196
'Three Legends', 188–9
'Thrushes', **46**, 89, 183
Tiger's Bones, The, 178
'Tiger's Bones, The', 193
'To Be a Girl's Diary', 62, 187
'To F.R. at Six Months', 185
'Toll', 185
'Tomcat', 184
'To Paint a Water Lily', 42, 45, 184

'Toughest, The', 54, 188
'To W. H. Auden', 188
'Trees', 187
'Truth Kills Everybody', **125–6**, 189
'Tutorial', 186
'TV On', 188
'Two', 186
'Two Eskimo Songs', 189
'Two Legends', **108–9**, 188–9
'Two Phases', 183
'Two Wise Generals', 183

'Unknown Soldier', 62, 185
'Urn Burial', 57, 184

'Vampire', 183
'Vegetarian, A', 82, 87, 186
'View of a Pig', 11, 36, 184, 196
'Voyage, The', 70, 184

'Warm and the Cold, The', 193
'Warm Moors', 187
'Warriors of the North, The', 80, 186
'Water', 186
'Water and Landscape', 193
'Watersong', 136, 196
'Welcombe', 191
'Wild West', 7, 182
'Wilfred Owen's Photographs', 184
'Wind', **27–8**, 52, **160–1**, 182
'Wind and Weather', 193
'Wind Flashes the Grass, A', 188
'Wings', **94–7**, 187
'Wino', 185
'Witches', 183
With Fairest Flowers While Summer Lasts, 181
Wodwo, 1, 4, 11, 36, **61–100**, 102–3, 162–7, 177, 185–8, 192, 196
'Wodwo', 83, **97–9**, 102, 185, 197
'Woman Unconscious, A', 184
'Woman with Such High Heels She Looked Dangerous, The', 182
'Wound, The', 78, **81–3**, 85, **165–6**, 192
'Writing About People', 193
'Writing a Novel', 193

'You Drive in a Circle', 85, 188

GENERAL

GENERAL

Human World, The, 179
Hussey, M., *Criticism in Action,* 197
Huws, Daniel, *Noth,* 194
Huxley, Aldous, 'To the Puritan All Things Are Impure', 144

Icarus, 94
International Centre for Theatre Research, 147
Io, 148
Ionesco, Eugene, 2; *The Chairs,* 88; *The Killer,* 113
Iowa Review, 197
Irish Times, 175–7, 179, 181
Ishtar, 128–9
Isis, 48, 128
Isis, 175

jaguars, 9, 16–18, 37, 40, 81
James, G. Ingli, 197
Jehovah, 48–50, 78, 159
Jennings, Elizabeth, 176, 181
Jerusalem, 56, 129, 159
Jewish Chronicle, 178
Job, 48–50, 117
John, B., 197
John O'London's, 196
Johnson, Dr, 8
Jones, Alun, 175
Journal of Creative Behaviour, 188–9
Joyce, James, *Ulysses,* 43, 121
Jung, Carl, 'On the Psychology of the Trickster Figure', 113; *Answer to Job,* 113, 129, 169; *Psychology of the Unconscious,* 120
Juniper, John, 177
Jupiter Records, 185, 196

Kafka, Franz, 1, 94; 'Metamorphosis', 83; *Reflections,* 96; *Letters to Milena,* 96; *Diaries,* 96; *The Castle,* 96, 130; *The Trial,* 130
Keats, John, 'Epistle to John Hamilton Reynolds', 36; 'Ode to a Nightingale', 90–1
Keel, Richard, 176
Kentish Gazette, 177
Kessler, J., 179
Kipling, Rudyard, 7
Kirkus, 176, 180
Kizer, C., 179
Kroll, J., 179
Kundalini Yoga, 169

Laing, R. D., *The Politics of Experience,* 134–5, 145, 147; *The Bird of Paradise,* 172
Larkin, Philip, 'I Remember, I Remember', 14
Lash, Thomas, 177
Lawrence, D. H., 1, 5, 7, 12, 18, 38–45, 66, 123; 'Fish', 42; 'Reflections on the Death of a Porcupine', 43; 'The Crown', 44, 90; 'A Living', 45; *Apocalypse,* 63, 77, 164; *The Rainbow,* 78, 165; 'Introduction to These Paintings', 141; 'Lizard', 153; *Fantasia of the Unconscious,* 165; 'Tortoises', 166; 'Humming Bird', 196; 'Bare Almond Trees', 196
Lazarevitch, Mila, 176
Leavis, F. R., 1, 8, *Revaluation,* 1
leopards, 18, 44, 70, 81, 138–9
Levenson, Christopher, 183
Leviathan, 49
Lewis, Naomi, 178
Lewis, P. E., 197
Lexham Press, 180, 191
Libby, Anthony, 197
Libby, M. S., 176
Library Journal, 175–9
Lindsay, David, *Voyage to Arcturus,* 170, 171
Listen, 175
Listener, 175–9, 181, 187–90, 193–5
Listening and Writing, 177, 185, 193, 196
Living Language, 193
Lloyd, R. J., 179
Lloyd-Evans, Barbara, 62, 177, 179
Locke, John, 94
Lodge, David, 179
London Magazine, 14, 18, 32–3, 48, 81, 104–5, 115, 145, 179, 182, 184–7, 190, 192, 194
Lucifer, 76 (*see also* Satan and devil)
Lupercus, 58

MacBeth, George, 66, 187
MacCaig, Norman, 175
MacInnes, Colin, 178
Mademoiselle, 10, 184–5
Malahat Review, 179
Male, David, A., 178
Manchester Guardian, 175
Manicheeism, 107–8, 140, 168–71
Marcus, Mordecai, 179
Marduk, 122

vulture, 149–59, 170–1

Wain, John, 'Poem', 133
Wallenstein, B., 179
Walpole, Horace, 57
Walsh, Chad, 177, 181, 185–6
Warnock, J. G., 175
Watkins, Jesse, 134–5
Watts, Alan, *Beyond Theology*, 126, 169; *The Book*, 168
Wesker, Arnold, 194
Western Daily Press, 176, 185
war, 6, 14, 17, 28–31, 44, 70, 106, 143–4, 160–1, 166
water, 14, 24–7, 39, 42, 65, 81, 97–8, 124–5, 136–7, 140, 148
White Goddess, the, 11, 14, 23, 67, 72–3, 76, 81–2
Whitman, Walt, 'Song of Myself', 20, 46–8
Williams, Raymond, 108
winter, 26–7, 37, 53, 55, 61, 156
wolves, 11, 22, 54–8, 61, 67, 80, 127
wombs, 40, 75–6, 110, 118, 121, 151, 157, 167, 170

Wood, Hugh, 196
Woodthorpe, Peter, 8
words, 3–4, 8, 14, 19, 27, 33, 87, 105, 109, 120–6, 128, 130, 141, 156, 162–3, 166
Wordsworth, William, 'Resolution and Independence', 20–1
Works in Progress, 190
Workshop, 190–1

Yaddo, 36
Yeats, W. B., 1, 4, 17, 33, 72; 'Death', 16; *A Vision*, 16; 'The Second Coming', 74; 'Among School Children', 150; 'Lapis Lazuli', 166; *The Death of Cuchulain*, 166–7; 'Cuchulain Comforted', 167
yoga, 169
Yorkshire Post, 175, 177
Young, Kenneth, 175
Your Environment, 195

Zeno, 84
Zeus, 56, 147–8, 153, 155, 157